HERO OF FORT SUMTER

C&C

CAMPAIGNS & COMMANDERS

GREGORY J. W. URWIN, SERIES EDITOR

CAMPAIGNS AND COMMANDERS

HERO OF FORT SUMTER

The Extraordinary Life of Robert Anderson

BY WESLEY MOODY

UNIVERSITY OF OKLAHOMA PRESS : NORMAN

Library of Congress Cataloging-in-Publication Data

Names: Moody, Wesley, author.
Title: Hero of Fort Sumter : the extraordinary life of Robert Anderson / by Wesley Moody.
Other titles: Extraordinary life of Robert Anderson
Description: First edition. | Norman : University of Oklahoma Press, [2025] | Series: Campaigns
    and commanders ; volume 80 | Includes bibliographical references and index. | Summary:
    "The first biography of a military officer famous then and now for his role on the Union
    side at Fort Sumter, who also played an overlooked role in mentoring future general
    William T. Sherman"—Provided by publisher.
Identifiers: LCCN 2024044685 | ISBN 9780806195407 (hardcover ; acid-free paper)
Subjects: LCSH: Anderson, Robert, 1805–1871. | United States—History—Civil War, 1861–1865—
    Biography. | Generals—United States—Biography. | United States. Army—Biography. | Fort
    Sumter (Charleston, S.C.)—Siege, 1861. | Charleston (S.C.)—History—Civil War, 1861–1865.
Classification: LCC E467.1.A545 M66 2025 | DDC 973.7092 [B]—dc23/eng/20250203
LC record available at https://lccn.loc.gov/2024044685

Hero of Fort Sumter: The Extraordinary Life of Robert Anderson is Volume 80 in the Campaigns
and Commanders series.

The paper in this book meets the guidelines for permanence and durability of the Committee on
Production Guidelines for Book Longevity of the Council on Library Resources, Inc. ∞

For
Beth

I could not do any of this without you.

Long after Fort Sumter shall have crumbled away, brightly will stand forth the example of Anderson as that of a soldier true to his standard and of an American true to his country.

—Senator John J. Crittenden, Kentucky

CONTENTS

Acknowledgments

I have received much kindness and support in the writing of this book. I would like to thank the librarians and staff at the Library of Congress, the United States Military Academy Library, the Filson Center, the P. K. Yonge Library at the University of Florida, and the United States Army Military History Institute, Carlisle Barracks. All were extremely helpful and friendly. I also need to thank my home institution, Florida State College at Jacksonville. My fellow faculty have always been motivating and helpful. The librarians were willing to help in any way I asked, and I am always amazed at their ability to track down the most obscure sources. The administration has been very supportive of my work. And, of course, my students, whose curiosity always pushes me to dig deeper.

The University of Oklahoma Press has been a pleasure to work with. I highly recommend them to any author. Last, but not least, I have to thank the National Phil Kearny Society. Without them this project would not have been nearly as much fun.

Introduction

A walk through the oak-shrouded cemetery of the United States Military Academy along the beautiful banks of the Hudson River is a tour through our nation's past. Buried near the old cadet chapel are luminaries of America's military history, such as George Armstrong Custer, Lucius Clay, Sylvanus Thayer, Winfield Scott, and "Vinegar Joe" Stillwell.

One of the largest stones is a rather modern-looking granite monument. Carved on the reverse is "Fort Sumter, 1861." It is the grave of Major General Robert Anderson. On top is a sword draped in a flag. It appears as if it had been casually left, not meticulously carved out of stone. The writing on the back of the stone is fitting. Robert Anderson is forever linked with Fort Sumter and the events of the first days of the Civil War. Like Custer and the Little Bighorn or Pickett and his famous charge, Anderson is frozen in one time and place. He served his nation for almost forty years, from South America to Maine, through four wars, eventually reaching the rank of major general. Yet he always remains Major Anderson of Fort Sumter.

The events of Fort Sumter in the winter and spring of 1861 marked a major turning point in American history. Many books have been written on the battle and the political intrigues that surrounded it. Most recently, best-selling author Erik Larson added his name to the list of writers who have told the story. Much like earlier authors, Larson only gives Anderson's background and character a few pages. This can lead to misconceptions about his motivations and, thus, the events themselves. Anderson is a central figure to the start of the Civil War. That his training and experience are rarely given much space and his post-Charleston actions are ignored is a disservice to a patriotic public servant and our understanding of American history. His calm leadership and bold action in Charleston on the eve of the Civil War changed the course of American history. To understand those events, one has to understand Anderson. Like anyone, Anderson was a culmination of his life experiences.

Robert Anderson was raised in the home of a Revolutionary War veteran. He and his brothers all served the nation in different ways. As a boy, Anderson saw past and future presidents pass through his Kentucky home as well as a fair number of explorers, war heroes, and the occasional Supreme Court justice. With his training at West Point and his service to the nation's flag, Anderson was a patriot to the core.

Anderson's military experience also exposed him to some rather unpleasant things. As an officer during Indian removal, he witnessed societies uprooted and ways of life destroyed. He cradled a wounded infant in one arm as the child's mother died in his other arm. He lived through the intense suffering of the Trail of Tears. He served during the Mexican War. His battery fired into the city during the siege of Vera Cruz, and he witnessed the terrible destruction and suffering.

These experiences, along with others, naturally colored his view of war. He loved his country, but he saw the physical and psychological damage done by war. While in a city that welcomed the conflict, his decisions at Charleston were motivated by the desire to avoid the destruction and bloodshed that the American Civil War brought. His calm leadership and bold action caused the nation to rally around the man and the Union cause. Had Anderson meekly surrendered or acted aggressively the Northern states would not have been as supportive of Lincoln in those first critical years of the war.

In the West Point cemetery, a small white stone, broken from its base, leans against Anderson's massive marker. It is the tombstone of his devoted wife, Eliza. That her marker is broken and leaning against her husband's is fitting. A woman who constantly struggled with health issues, her identity became completely intertwined with that of her husband, even more than the average nineteenth-century woman. She outlived her husband by more than thirty years and spent most of that time defending his historical reputation,

Facing Anderson's monument is an equally large marker. Underneath it is his daughter, Eba Lawton, and her husband, a wealthy New York City banker. As a Gilded Age socialite and president of several New York genealogical societies, Mrs. Lawton took up her mother's mantle. Despite her herculean efforts, Anderson fell into obscurity. His loyalties became mischaracterized, and his contributions were forgotten.

One does not have to be a devoted daughter to see that his story should be told for his sake and ours. Anderson's life bridged the new republic of Jefferson and the end of antebellum America. To try to understand Robert Anderson is to try to understand his America. The two cannot be separated.

CHAPTER 1

ON THE OHIO AND THE HUDSON

On June 14, 1805, Robert Anderson was born near the frontier town of Louisville, Kentucky. His was one of the first families of Kentucky, as close
to aristocracy as one could find on the banks of the wild Ohio River. He was
the son of Richard Clough Anderson and Sarah Marshall Anderson. Richard
Anderson was a hero of the American Revolution and a leader of the growing
city. Sarah Marshall Anderson was from an elite Virginia family that included
the famous jurist Chief Justice John Marshall.

Richard Anderson was from Hanover County, Virginia. He left Virginia
at sixteen to work for a local merchant as the supercargo, the merchant's
shipboard agent. It was in this position that Anderson witnessed the Boston
Tea Party in 1773. When war broke out, the twenty-six-year-old Anderson
joined the Patriot cause and was appointed captain of the newly created Fifth
Virginia Continentals. Anderson took part in Washington's famous crossing
of the Delaware River and saw his first action at the battles of Trenton and
Princeton. He was wounded at Princeton and carried to a hospital in Philadelphia. As was too often the case, the military hospital was more dangerous
than the battlefield. Anderson contracted smallpox and carried its scars for
the rest of his life.[1]

After the Battle of Brandywine, Anderson was promoted to major of the
First Virginia. He led his men at the Battle of Monmouth. Although it was
an indecisive battle, it was a moral victory for the Continental Army. They
fought a professional British force to a standstill in European style. Ordered
south, Anderson took part in the failed assault on Savannah in October 1778.
American and French casualties numbered nearly eight hundred. One out of
every five men on the Patriot side were either killed or wounded.[2] During the
attack on the British stronghold, the Polish hero Casimir Pulaski was killed.
According to family tradition, Anderson cradled the dying Pulaski in his last
hours and was given his sword in thanks.[3]

Anderson was next sent to Charleston to help defend that city against a British onslaught. He was one of the over fifty-five hundred men captured by the British when the city surrendered. Anderson was a prisoner of war for nine months. After his exchange, he served with General Daniel Morgan and the Marquis de Lafayette. By the war's end, Anderson had been promoted to lieutenant-colonel in the Continental Army and brigadier general of the Virginia militia. However, he would always prefer to be called "colonel." He was rewarded for his services with the position of surveyor-general of Virginia's western territory.[4]

Anderson settled in the small collection of log huts known as Louisville. It was still part of Virginia and was a station settlement. The settlers worked their land during the day, taking turns standing guard over their neighbors, constantly vigilant for Indian attacks. At night, everyone slept within the wooden walls of Fort Nelson.[5]

Louisville was a frontier settlement named after the king of France, who had helped the new nation gain its independence. Since the Indigenous Nations of Kentucky did not recognize Britain's power to cede their land to the new American nation, Indian attacks were frequent in Louisville and the surrounding area. Colonel Anderson's fighting days were not over. Before the decisive Battle of Fallen Timbers and then the War of 1812, Indian attacks were a normal part of life for most settlers. As an older man, he entertained his children and grandchildren with exciting tales of battling the "savages."[6]

Anderson's move to Kentucky should not be considered a second-rate posting on the frontier. Kentucky was the fastest-growing region in the decade following the Revolution.[7] Louisville quickly grew into an important trade center because of its location on the Ohio River. Before the 1803 Louisiana Purchase, Louisville was an official US port of entry. In this bustling, growing city, Colonel Anderson was a man of influence. He became involved in the shipping trade on the Ohio and Mississippi Rivers and even owned a ship in the transatlantic trade. With the addition of the Louisiana Territory, Louisville only grew in size and importance. However, at the start of the new century, its population was only around 1,000, including 165 slaves. By 1807, there were eleven retail stores, three taverns, and a newspaper.[8] A police force was established in 1810 when the town hired two watchmen. In 1803, Meriwether Lewis and Richard Anderson's brother-in-law, William Clark, traveled through Louisville on their way to launch their famous expedition. This growing town on the Ohio River was, at the start of the century, the starting point for westward expansion.[9]

In 1789, Richard Anderson, his wife of two years, and their first son left Louisville and its muddy streets and busy docks to build a home ten miles away that he named Soldier's Retreat. It was a two-story, sixteen-room home of gray limestone with three-foot-thick walls. Designed by the colonel himself, it was a fortress. Its main feature was the long dark interior hallway with no outside access except the heavy wooden black walnut front doors. There were no trees close to the house; there were only six trees on the entire three acres that surrounded the home. No enemy force would be able to sneak up on Soldier's Retreat. Anderson had lived and fought in enough wooden stockades to appreciate a fortress that could not be set on fire.[10] One cannot help but notice how fitting it is that a man whose career and place in history are so tied to stone walls was born inside what was probably the only stone fort in Kentucky.

There was fear among the children and their friends that the long, dark hallway was haunted, and there must have been dread and anxiety when the Jefferson County militia rallied there to deal with Indian raids or even the threat of British invasion during the War of 1812. Although the thick stone walls must have been reassuring, they could not have helped but be a reminder of the danger of living on what was still the frontier.[11]

Mostly, however, those who grew up there remembered Soldier's Retreat as a happy place. Its halls and rooms were always filled with children. Robert was the eighth of twelve children. He was his father's third son and his mother's second. He had five older sisters. Richard Anderson's first wife, Elizabeth Clark, died in 1795. He married again four years later. His second wife, Sarah Marshall, was the niece of Chief Justice of the Supreme Court John Marshall. Only twenty-three years old at the time of their marriage, she would outlive her older husband by several decades. Anderson's oldest son would remember his father as a kind and affectionate man, and he hoped that his own son "may have virtue enough to look at me with the feelings with which I now look at my father."[12] Anderson's first wife, a Clark, was from a family most associated with the westward movement. His second wife, a Marshall, was from a family associated with the eastern establishment.

Besides the Andersons, the children of friends and neighbors were constant guests, and the children of Anderson's twenty slaves were the playmates of their owner's children. Included among the guests were the children of a local tobacco planter, Colonel Richard Taylor, whose eight children included future president Zachary Taylor. Young Zachary left Louisville to serve in the army before Robert was born, but he was friends with Robert's older siblings.[13]

On the second floor of Soldier's Retreat was a twenty-by-forty-foot ballroom where all the children, including the neighbors, were taught to dance. The Andersons hired a professional teacher for these events. The children learned to dance to the music of a slave fiddler. Watching the proceedings from the side but never participating was the senior Anderson in his silk stockings and knee breeches. When fashion changed during the era of Jefferson, Anderson continued to dress as he would have at a 1775 Mount Vernon dinner party.[14]

Anderson was an avid hunter, and the hunting parties he led, made up of boys as young as eight, were extremely popular. These boys, Robert included, became crack shots as they learned to shoot squirrels and other small game. Anderson would also lead quail hunting parties. Quail are not the brightest animals and are easily trapped. Anderson would instruct the boys to choose the two largest, healthiest-looking birds from the trap and release them. He was a farsighted conservationist in a land teeming with wildlife.[15]

Colonel Anderson was an early follower of the temperance movement. Initially, the movement was not against the use of all alcohol, just distilled liquors. Wine and beer were preferable to the hard stuff. Anderson grew grapes and produced wine in an attempt to convert an area now famous for its bourbon into a wine-drinking region. It was anything but successful, but the children loved the grapes from his vineyard.[16]

Besides the garden and orchard kept by his gardener, a Polish veteran of the revolution, Anderson also grew corn for his large herd of pigs. Nearly a hundred were killed at the first frost each year for the family's consumption and the local market. As was the tradition on the southern frontier, Soldier's Retreat was the scene of corn shuckings. The long, tedious job of removing the husk was turned into a social event by bringing the community together. Games were held, music was played, and a good time was generally had by all.[17]

Behind the main house were the quarters for Anderson's twenty slaves and an office for the overseer.[18] The children called the male slaves "uncle," and they all had nicknames for the Anderson children. For some reason, the slaves called young Robert "Marse Cob." Colonel Anderson tried to limit familiarity. However, the children of the slaves played with the Anderson children and their friends. The game of prisoner's base was a favorite. As is the nature of young boys, fights would break out. When this occurred, Colonel Anderson took it quite seriously. He would hold court, listen to all sides, and render judgment. The party found at fault was punished regardless of race. Neighbors complained that Anderson's kind treatment of his slaves was ruining all slaves. According to his younger brother, Robert left the state for West Point before the worst elements of chattel slavery and its enforcement would arrive in Kentucky, and that was why Robert Anderson did not become the antislavery advocate that his siblings, who remained in Kentucky, became.[19]

The Colonel was a popular figure, and among his guests at Soldier's Retreat were the Marquis de Lafayette, Andrew Jackson, Henry Clay, James Madison, and Aaron Burr. The uncles of the older children, William and George Rogers

Clark, were regulars. Among the occasional visitors was an old enemy, Chief Little Turtle of the Miami, who was responsible for one of the worst defeats the US Army ever suffered, the St. Claire Massacre. The Anderson children had at least passing acquaintances with some of the most important figures of the history of the young republic and, if they desired, could call on important men to advance their careers.[20]

As were most of the elites of Virginia in the Revolutionary era, Richard C. Anderson was an Episcopalian. Since there was no Episcopal church in Jefferson County, the children were sent to the Union Sunday School. It was taught and attended by Baptists, Lutherans, Episcopalians, Methodists, and Presbyterians. According to his brother Charles, Robert, of all the children, had "the strongest religious temperament." The Colonel's "sole personal effort was to make his sons first patriots and good citizens and next moral and most especially veracious men. Not merely truthful men in all their words but in all their actions."[21]

Colonel Anderson had diverse business interests. He speculated in land, produced crops and livestock, and even owned an ill-fated merchant vessel, the two-masted *Carolina*, which operated in the Caribbean. His government position as a surveyor and his pension produced a steady income and, along with Soldier's Retreat, made Anderson a wealthy man. However, it was Anderson's lifelong regret that he had not attended college. He would make sure that all of his six sons received college educations and his six daughters attended elite boarding schools.[22] In the days before scholarships, student loans, or grants, this was a costly undertaking.

When the children could learn no more from their parents, they were sent to a privately run school on the road to Louisville, Uncle Tompkin's School. When Robert was fourteen years old and could learn no more from Uncle Tompkin, he was sent to the Buck Pond Academy near Versailles, Kentucky, about sixty miles away from home. The school had a reputation as the best classical academy in Kentucky. For fifty-four dollars a year, Robert Anderson was prepared for a university education.[23]

One of the first things that young Robert learned was that Uncle Tompkin's school had not prepared him for the more rigorous Buck Pond Academy. He complained in a letter to his younger brother that all the young men from the Louisville school had to be "put back." In this letter, Anderson begins with the complaint that was in so many of his letters throughout his life. He was not receiving enough letters.[24]

Louis Marshall, Robert Anderson's great-uncle on his mother's side, ran the school. Marshall's father had also served with Colonel Anderson in the revolution. When Marshall promised to look after Robert's education, there were few people the family trusted more.[25]

By the time Robert arrived in April 1819, Dr. Marshall had passed control of the school over to W. R. "Dominic" Thompson, his longtime assistant. Marshall promised the Colonel, however, that his son was in good hands and that he would keep a very close eye on the boy's education.[26]

Classes met at Marshall's estate, but the students lived with families in the area. Anderson and several other boys lived in the home of a local man named Burgan. According to Anderson, Burgan was from New Jersey and was devoutly religious. After dinner each night, he led the boys in prayer for half an hour. Anderson complained that his knees were always sore from this exercise.[27]

The Burgan home was about a mile and a half away from the school. Anderson did not mind; it was "a very pleasant walk." The school's curriculum was mainly the Latin classics. Anderson studied Caesar and Ovid during his first year. He lamented the lack of "English books" to read while at school; the Burgan home only contained the Bible and prayer books, and while at Buck Pond, it was only Latin. The students only spent half a day at school. They were expected to read and prepare for their examinations the rest of the time. A student who was lax in his studies could expect a blow from a rattan cane as the result of an incorrect response.[28]

While Anderson was at school, a religious awakening swept the county. It affected Mr. Burgan and many of the students at the school. Many of Anderson's classmates gave "satisfactory evidence of their conversion" at Pisgah Presbyterian Church, a dry-stacked-stone little building constructed in 1812. There is no evidence that Anderson took part, but it would not have been out of character.[29] Whether he publicly gave evidence or not, it surely affected this young boy away from home.

Anderson remained at Buck Pond for only two years. In July 1821, at the age of fifteen, the United States Military Academy at West Point, New York, accepted his application. Whether West Point was Anderson's idea or his father thrust it upon him is unclear. That Anderson spent almost his entire adult life in the army makes a strong argument that a military career was his plan, as does the fact that he was the only one of Richard Anderson's sons to attend the Academy. As well, the fact that he was the son of a Revolutionary War veteran and, as a boy, spent a great deal of time in the presence of war heroes argues that the army would have been a career choice that he made on his own. However, there is evidence that West Point was not wholly his decision. West Point was the only free education available in the country, and the Anderson family had the political clout to secure an appointment. One can imagine the senior Anderson informing his son of his chosen career path, as was the case with

William T. Sherman and Ulysses S. Grant. Anderson later wrote that he was a "soldier by chance rather than choice."[30] This statement could mean that the opportunity was unexpected but not forced upon him.

Richard Clough Anderson Jr., Robert's older brother of seventeen years, was a congressman between 1817 and 1821 before he returned to Kentucky to serve in the state legislature. While in Washington, he became friends with Secretary of War John C. Calhoun, who offered to secure a position for Robert if his father "desired it." On July 13, 1820, the senior Anderson wrote to the secretary of war, asking for a place for his son at West Point. The letter must have been only a formality because Anderson makes no argument as to why his son should be accepted. His name is Robert Anderson, "don't know what else you need."[31] Anderson was accepted and informed that he must immediately notify the War Department that he planned to attend. It was the first of many orders from the War Department. On March 1, 1821, Anderson wrote Calhoun that he would report to the United States Military Academy as ordered.[32]

The trip from Louisville to West Point would have been an arduous journey. The first leg of the voyage would have been a pleasant and exciting adventure. Steamboat travel on the Ohio River was relatively new. He could have ridden in relative comfort at least as far as Pittsburgh. It was an exciting adventure for a fifteen-year-old who had never gone more than eighty miles away from home. From Pittsburgh, he would have gone overland to New York City, primarily by stage and sometimes over routes that had changed very little from when Daniel Boone had made the trip in the other direction.

On reaching New York City, a city with a population of over 123,000 compared to around the 4,000 who lived in Louisville, Anderson traveled by boat up the Hudson to West Point. Like most West Point cadets, the fifteen-year-old Anderson probably spent at least a day exploring the exciting city. The Ohio River Valley can be beautiful; anyone visiting Louisville should take advantage of one of the old paddlewheel riverboats that still cruise the Ohio. However, nothing can compare to the beauty of the Hudson River Valley. It was soon after Anderson made his trip up the Hudson that the beauty of that same area struck the artist Thomas Cole so profoundly that he launched what became the first school of American art that attempted to capture the beauty of nature on canvas.[33] Young Anderson was not as impressed as Cole. He wrote his sister, "The Academy was the most dreary place in the world, nothing but hills and rocks." In defense of the natural beauty of West Point, he wrote this after having spent his first winter at the Academy.[34]

The Hudson River steamer made the thirty-seven-mile trip from New York City to West Point in a few hours. Anderson and the other cadets streaming in during the late spring were loaded onto a small boat and dropped at the little pier; the steamer did not yet dignify West Point with a full-fledged stop. The Academy stands at the top of a high cliff overlooking the river. Like all new cadets, Anderson was not sure exactly what he had gotten into and must have been intimidated by the gray stone buildings staring down at him. A sentry on duty directed him to the top of the hill. Anderson could have dragged his trunk to the top to report or paid the porter to take it up when there was enough for a full load. The porter was a one-armed veteran whose reward for his service was this concession.[35]

The institution that Robert Anderson was about to enter had just recently experienced a radical change. The United States Military Academy was only three years older than Anderson. Although West Point, as the Academy came to be known, officially opened in 1802 with the unlikely support of President Thomas Jefferson, the push for a military academy had begun under George Washington. Most American officers during the American Revolution had a great deal of respect for the European officers who joined the cause. They were professionals who received rigorous training in military academies. Their expertise convinced many American officers, including Washington and future secretary of war Henry Knox, that a national military academy was necessary for the young nation. Although men like Richard Clough Anderson may have supported the idea of a national military academy, the country at large was less than receptive. Besides viewing it as an unnecessary expense, there was the fear that an educated military class would lead to the creation of a European-style aristocracy.[36]

President Jefferson's motives are still debated. Trained engineers helping build America and then moving back into the army when needed did fit with the Jeffersonian ideal of a militia army. Jefferson also inherited an army dominated by men with Federalist leanings. A military academy that required an appointment from a Congress dominated by men of the same political mindset would definitely be appealing, and it would perhaps create an officer corps that better reflected the general population.[37]

When young Robert Anderson left Kentucky for the Academy, it was not as respected an institution as it would be for later generations. The first decade of the Academy was difficult and problematic. It began with only ten cadets and seven officers. These officers and cadets could be stationed anywhere in the country at the army's discretion and had to find their own lodgings. It was a far cry from the modern Academy. Discipline was lax, and the academics were questionable.[38] This was, of course, about to change.

Although Major Sylvanus Thayer was West Point's fifth superintendent, he is considered the "Father of the Military Academy." The Massachusetts-born

Thayer graduated from Dartmouth in 1807 and had his heart set on a military career. As a student, the young Thayer followed the campaigns of Napoleon in the nation's newspapers. General Benjamin Pierce, a family friend, helped secure an appointment to West Point from President James Madison. The academic rigor of West Point was nowhere near what it would be under Thayer. He completed his course of study in one year and earned his commission. After serving in the Corps of Engineers, he was an assistant professor of mathematics at West Point for one year. He became superintendent in 1817.[39]

Newly elected president James Monroe visited the Academy in June 1817. He was very upset about the lax culture at West Point. Not only was discipline poor, but there were also serious questions about academic standards and accusations of the misappropriation of funds. Thayer had just returned from a fact-finding mission to Europe on the question of military education, a rarity with the usually extremely economical Democratic-Republicans in charge. He was the perfect choice to restore integrity and high standards to the institution.[40]

Cadets who had served at least one year under the outgoing Alden Partridge were not happy with the changes Thayer brought. There were several revolts and attempts to remove the new superintendent. With the president's support, Thayer quickly overcame any resistance from cadets or their well-connected families.

Thayer based his program on the French model of military education. In the first half of the nineteenth century, the French Army was the ideal of soldiers throughout the Western world. Not even Napoleon's eventual defeat would sour the prestige of the French Army. Thayer instituted a merit roll system. Cadets earned demerits for poor conduct and earned points in the classroom and drill field. The cadets were ranked by their number of points. The army used this ranking to assign the cadet, upon graduation, to a branch. The top cadets would become engineers, and the poorest-performing cadets were infantry. The students were divided into small sections based on ability and taught by an assistant professor who was usually an army officer and a recent graduate. The professors did not often teach but directed the assistant professors.[41]

Perhaps the most challenging aspect of the Academy was the final examination. Over a two-week period, each cadet eligible for graduation had to pass a five-hour oral examination. The questions asked dealt with all aspects of the cadet's education. An outside board, along with faculty, examined the potential graduates. In 1835, when Anderson was on the opposite side of the examiners' table, he created a list of forty-seven possible questions to ask his students on the subject of artillery. One of these questions asked cadets to "illustrate ricochet and enfilading fire, determine the angle of projection and initial velocity in both cases, and the limits of the height of a work that may be reached by ricochet."[42]

The board of examination was the undoing of many potential army officers over the years. One cadet whose military career ended during this grueling five-hour session was James McNeill Whistler. In a story the famous artist liked to tell during dinner parties, he failed the chemistry portion of the exam when he misidentified silicon as a gas. He often told his guests, "If silicon had been a gas, I would have been a general."[43]

Thayer also introduced a significant change in the Academy's organization when he created the Corps of Cadets. Each cadet earned a rank dependent on his class standing. The top cadet of the senior class was the First Captain, and the lowest remained a private. To lead the Corps of Cadets, Thayer appointed a regular army officer as commandant of cadets. The commandant's responsibility was discipline and military subjects, such as tactics and drill.[44]

President James Monroe also had a different view of the role West Point should play within the army. On March 2, 1821, Monroe signed the Military Establishment Act. The law, put forward by Secretary of War John C. Calhoun, significantly cut the size of the US Army. It reduced the officer corps by about 20 percent and the enlisted ranks by more than half. The law created a rank-heavy institution. The idea behind this was that when war came, and the army's numbers swelled with volunteers, the officers trained in peacetime would take command of the new men. The army's top generals, including Andrew Jackson, Winfield Scott, and Edmund Gaines—three men who rarely agreed on anything—had championed this idea of an expandable army.[45]

In his report to Congress on the Military Establishment Act, Secretary Calhoun argued that "in the present state of military science," it was imperative to the nation's "independence and safety" "to create and perpetuate military skill and experience." To achieve this, it was necessary to have a "body of officers, sufficiently numerous, and well instructed in every branch of duty."[46]

These new officers would not be men like Andrew Jackson or Jacob Brown, the two senior officers of the army of the day who had proven to be very talented amateurs. These officers would be professionals trained along European lines. Theoretically, the only way to the top was to master the set body of knowledge as you gain seniority. This was by no means a perfect system. It was, however, the system that fifteen-year-old Robert Anderson entered as a new cadet in July 1821. His West Point class would be the first to begin under this new professional army.

The Academy in that year was only a handful of buildings. The largest structures were the two dormitories sitting at right angles of one another, still used as cadet barracks more than two hundred years later. One was three stories, the other four. To the west of the barracks was the two-story academic building.

The mess hall was beyond it. For the new cadets, these four buildings and the parade ground would be their world for the next four years.[47]

Anderson's acceptance to West Point was conditional, as it was with all new cadets, upon passing an examination. Thayer and the professors gave the exam orally. It was basic, meant only to screen out illiterates. According to the form letter Anderson received from the War Department, he "must be able to read distinctly and pronounce correctly, to write a fair legible hand, and to perform the various operations of arithmetic." Even with the simplicity of the entrance requirements, between 30 and 60 percent of the potential cadets each year had to be rejected.[48] This was not the case for Anderson. With his classical background, the low entrance standards must have given him pause about his chosen path. If it did, he did not have much time to dwell. The entire corps of cadets was being organized for a march.

The Grand March, as it was sometimes called, was the idea of Thayer's new commandant of cadets, Major William Jenkins Worth. He had only been on the job for one year when Anderson's class arrived. Worth was an impressive figure and made a lasting impression on the teenage cadets in their uncomfortable and ill-fitting new uniforms. Only eleven years older than Cadet Anderson, Worth was a decorated veteran of the War of 1812. He was described as "tall, handsome, and a splendid horseman, he was physically the ideal soldier."[49] The cadets who served under Worth gave him as much credit for creating antebellum West Point as they did Thayer.

The march was one way that Worth put his stamp on West Point. It was the second of its kind. The previous summer, the cadet corps had made a similar march to Philadelphia. These marches had two distinct purposes. One was educational, and the other was political. A six-hundred-mile march would instill discipline and physical stamina into the cadets. Throughout the early nineteenth century, West Point was always in danger of being shut down. Not only was it an expensive endeavor, but its critics claimed that a military elite was being formed on the banks of the Hudson with tax dollars from small farmers who could never hope to pay for a formal education for their sons. The marches served as excellent public relations. At most places where the corps halted, Worth gave speeches about patriotic duty with the cadets in gray as his backdrop. Worth and the cadets helped create a sense that West Point and its disciplined cadets were a symbol of national pride.

Major Worth loaded the 235 cadets onboard two steamboats on July 20, 1821. The hundred-mile trip to Albany took one day. The cadets enjoyed the company of the passengers, including many young women traveling from New York City. On landing, the cadets marched to the capitol, where after a review, the lieutenant governor and many other dignitaries of the New York state government greeted them.[50]

The Corps of Cadets averaged around twenty miles a day on the march to Boston, arriving on August 7. They were followed by a wagon train that carried most of the equipment; each cadet carried a rifle, knapsack, and a blanket roll. On Boston Commons, a five-hundred-square-foot area was set aside for their encampment. Local militia companies fed and entertained the cadets. They were invited to visit Harvard University, where they performed close-order drill for the scholars. They also spent one night on the Bunker Hill battlefield.[51]

The corps marched south to Quincy and visited former president John Adams. The cadets drilled as the aged legend watched from his front porch. Adams then delivered one of his last speeches. The speech, written in his own shaky hand, is preserved in the West Point Archives. He extolled the military virtues of the Revolutionary generation. Real glory, according to Adams, "arises from wisdom and benevolence. There can be no solid glory but that which springs from equity and humanity from the constant observance of prudence, temperance, and fortitude." To Adams, there was no glory in the conquests of Alexander or Caesar because there was no justice in their cause. They fought for "ambition of conquest" and "desire of wealth." Although Adams was using examples from the ancient world, there could have been little doubt to his audience that he was addressing the dangerous influence that Napoleon would have had on the young men before him studying the art of war.[52]

After the speech, the eighty-six-year-old former president shook the hands of each of the cadets. John K. Findlay, one class ahead of Anderson, remarked sixty years later that seeing Adams was one of the most memorable events of his life. He "touched the hand that had signed the Declaration of Independence. I heard the voice (now feeble from age) which hurled the defiance of thirteen feeble colonies to one of the mightiest powers on the globe."[53]

The cadets then marched south to New London, Connecticut, where they caught a steamer, which returned them to New York City and then back to West Point. They arrived on August 21 after spending more than a month on the march. The summer march must have had a significant impact on the cadets. The three-hundred-mile march instilled discipline, camaraderie, and physical fitness. At every stop, the cadets heard speeches about the greatness of the nation, the army, and West Point. Cadets, like young Robert Anderson, must have returned to West Point with an overpowering belief in duty, honor, and country.[54]

Anderson was a typical cadet in most ways. Like the others with him at West Point, Anderson longed for more letters from friends and family.

Although some cadets were from Kentucky, he did not know them until he arrived at the Academy. He complained about the officers and instructors over him. Of the many officers on "the Point," Anderson told his sister that Thayer and Colonel Jared Mansfield, the professor of mathematics, "are the only gentlemen."[55] These were harsh words from Robert Anderson, who was very reserved with criticisms.

Like all cadets, Anderson was assigned to one of the barracks by the adjutant. The rooms were basic. The second- and third-year cadets would have shown Anderson and the other new cadets what was expected of them. The culture of hazing had not yet developed, and Thayer was determined it would not. A cadet could be dismissed for even conspiring to give the new cadets the silent treatment.[56]

West Point was the beginning of a regimented life for Anderson. Reveille was at 5 a.m. The beating of drums called the students to "fall in" in front of the barracks. The cadets were then marched to breakfast, followed by drill on the Academy's now-famous parade ground. No cadet who has left us his memories of West Point has ever had anything kind to say about the food served. Classes began at 8 a.m. and concluded at 2 p.m. Then came artillery drill until four in the afternoon. Weather permitting, after training, there was a period for outdoor recreation. Following dinner, the time until 10 p.m. was dedicated to personal study.[57]

The vast majority of Anderson's education would have occurred in a building called the Academy. This structure contained the original chapel, the chemistry and physics laboratory, the engineering and mathematics departments, the library, and the adjutant's office. Chalkboards covered the mathematics rooms. Most of the beautiful buildings that make up what most people consider the historic campus of West Point were still a decade in the future.[58]

Anderson and the other cadets were instructed in artillery by a West Point graduate and army officer, Zebina J. D. Kinsley. He had entered the Academy as a cadet during the War of 1812. Kinsley spent his entire military career at West Point. "Old Zeb" was not popular with the cadets. He was in charge of the South Barracks, and they accused him of attending to his duties "too zealously." When he left the army in 1835, he opened Kinsley's Classical and Mathematical School not far from the campus. His replacement was Robert Anderson.[59]

The discipline was strict. Besides the list of what cadets had to do, there was a long list of what they could not do. During Anderson's four years at the Academy, nearly one hundred cadets were dismissed. Fighting and dueling were strictly forbidden. So were alcohol and gambling. To ensure there was no gambling, all card games were banned. Food and cooking were not allowed in the barracks. The infraction that tended to snare the most cadets was leaving the post without permission, which was rarely, if ever, given. The favorite destination for cadets was the infamous Benny Haven's Public House, where the cadets could buy a meal or, more likely, have a few too many drinks. The first record of Benny Haven's in the West Point disciplinary records does not appear until Anderson's senior year; it may have been on the scene much earlier.[60] Whether Anderson snuck away to visit Benny Haven's or any other off-campus venue is unknown; however, it would have been unlike the highly dutiful Anderson to have been a regular visitor.

Anderson received a unique education. Not only was West Point the only engineering school in the nation, but it was also the only school that offered what we would call a practical college education in the United States. The colleges and universities of early nineteenth-century America taught philosophy, classical literature, and ancient Greek and Latin. The philosophy was that students learned how to think and properly view the world, and the baser knowledge could be acquired on their own. The point of that kind of education was not vocational training but to make the students better people. The idea of West Point was to give the graduates the skills to make them better officers. Cadet Anderson and his classmates learned French. The thought of teaching a language that was still in use was abhorrent to other American colleges. Anderson also learned engineering, chemistry, physics, and the technicalities of army life. He took meticulous notes on military law and courts-martial. This would benefit his career as he was often called upon to participate in those legal proceedings.

On July 4, 1825, Cadet Robert Anderson of the State of Kentucky was presented with his diploma. Signed by Thayer, Worth, and the entire Academy staff, the document stated that the cadet had "been carefully examined on all the branches of the arts, sciences and of literature taught at the United States Military Academy" and "has been judged worthy to earn the degree."[61]

Anderson graduated a respectable fifteenth out of a class of thirty-six. The top of the class was Alexander Bache, who served as the head of the US Coast Survey, mapping the US coastline, and was one of the founders of what would become the National Academy of Science. Bache has been called the most imminent scientist of the antebellum period. The goat of the class, a term that would emerge much later for the lowest-ranking member of the class, was Samuel Allston. Allston served a decade in the army, mostly on frontier posts. He died of natural causes within two weeks of resigning from the army. Among his classmates was Charles F. Smith, who might have gone on to greatness in the Civil War had he not died of an infection on the eve of the Battle of Shiloh. Among Anderson's closest friends was Benjamin Huger. From one of the best families in Charleston, Huger and Anderson would serve together often during the next three and a half decades.

Barely twenty years old, Robert Anderson was now a second lieutenant in the Third United States Artillery. The Third was commanded by Colonel Walker Armistead, whose brother was famous for the defense of Fort McHenry during the War of 1812. Colonel Armistead's then eight-year-old son, Lewis, would be killed leading his brigade at the Battle of Gettysburg. The Third was assigned to defend American harbors between Annapolis, Maryland, and Charleston, South Carolina. However, Anderson's first service to the United States would be much further from home.

CHAPTER 2

La Gran Colombia

While Robert was finishing his final year at West Point, his oldest brother, Richard Clough Anderson Jr., was already making history. In 1802, he left Kentucky to study law at William and Mary College. During the War of 1812, Anderson was a member of the House of Representatives. He also practiced law in Lexington, which included a great deal of criminal work. Anderson does not seem to have been fulfilled by this work. Defending a drunk charged with abusing his horse was not his idea of service to his nation.[1]

Anderson was relieved when President James Monroe appointed him America's first minister to the newly independent nation of Colombia. Under Spanish rule, the modern countries of Colombia, Venezuela, Ecuador, Panama, and parts of Peru and Guyana made up the Viceroyalty of New Granada. After the defeat of the Spanish Army, the viceroyalty became the Republic of Colombia, with Simón Bolívar as its first president. Modern historians refer to this new republic as La Gran Colombia to distinguish it from the much smaller modern nation of Colombia. It was short-lived. By 1830, nationalist and political factions broke it into several different countries.[2]

Anderson spent two and a half years in Colombia. While there, he successfully negotiated a trade agreement and a treaty for suppression of the international slave trade. The treaty allowed American ships to stop Colombian ships suspected of participating in the trade.[3] In another issue close to the heart of Secretary of State John Quincy Adams, American citizens would have religious freedom while in Colombia and Colombian citizens would enjoy the same protections in the United States. The treaty was considered a success. Americans celebrated and honored Anderson. Louisville gave him a public dinner, and major newspapers across the country wrote glowing stories about him.[4]

The minister returned home in 1825 after the death of his wife, Elizabeth, in Bogotá. It was on this return trip that Adams, now President Adams, asked Anderson to be one of the two US representatives at the Congress of Panama.

The meeting, scheduled for the summer of 1826, was organized by President Bolívar. He invited all the newly independent nations of Central and South America and the Caribbean. Bolívar feared that the Holy Alliance would aid Spain in the reconquest of her former colonies. It was not an unreasonable fear. Prussia, Russia, Austria, and France had openly discussed doing just that for many years. It was the reason behind President Monroe's famous doctrine. Bolívar hoped a military alliance and perhaps even a union might be formed among the Latin American countries. Great Britain and the United States, two nations that had made a public stand against intervention by the Holy Alliance, were also invited.[5]

The newly inaugurated President Adams accepted the invitation and named Anderson and John Sergeant of Pennsylvania as representatives. Anderson was a natural choice as he was already assigned to Colombia. Sergeant, a former member of the House of Representatives, was a close ally of the Adams administration. The two appointments, which had to be confirmed by the US Senate, set off the first of many fights for the new president. The 1824 election had ended in the infamous Corrupt Bargain, which Andrew Jackson and his supporters believed had unjustly cost him the White House. Whether there was any truth to the claim, Jackson's men would battle Adams and his administration on practically every issue for the next four years. Adams's acceptance of Bolívar's invitation was only the first of many conflicts between what was emerging as a two-party state. The Era of Good Feelings was over.[6]

There was more than just partisan bickering behind the congressional debates over the Panama Congress. Those who opposed sending a delegation had other reasons besides the fact that John Quincy Adams supported it. Southerners like John Randolph from Virginia and John C. Calhoun from South Carolina were concerned about the effect the conference might have on slavery. The rules of diplomacy might force the American delegation to deal with other races on an equal basis. There was a rumor that a joint attack on Spanish-held Cuba would be planned. The liberation of that large slaveholding island might motivate US slaves to revolt.

There were other reasons for the opposition to be alarmed. Congressmen, including future presidents James Buchanan and Martin Van Buren, were concerned that American attendance might lead to the type of foreign entanglement that George Washington had so famously warned about in his farewell address. They and other critics believed the Panama Congress would lead to war with Spain. Both sides thought the other was only being partisan.[7]

The Senate confirmation vote was a close 24 to 19. The vote in the House of Representatives to provide the necessary funds was 134 to 60. Anderson would not learn that he had been confirmed by Congress until he was already at his post in Colombia.[8] Regardless of what the Senate voted, Anderson was the minister to Colombia and would need to return whether he was attending the Panama Congress or not. Sergeant waited until Congress approved his appointment. Unlike Anderson, he would have had no reason to go if Congress had refused his appointment. Sergeant further delayed his trip until the end of the summer to avoid the worst season for tropical diseases. By the time he agreed to leave, the Panama Congress had already met. Secretary of State Clay sent orders to Anderson to remain in the Colombian capital and send word to the Panama Congress asking them to delay the meeting or move to a healthier climate. The message did not arrive until after he had left for Panama, a delay that would prove costly to the American minister.[9]

When Robert graduated from West Point, his brother Richard asked him to join him in Colombia. Although Anderson was now a commissioned officer in the US Army, he could delay reporting to the Third Artillery until he returned. An officer serving on detached duty was common in the antebellum army. Ambassador Anderson had no problem getting his younger brother assigned to the State Department and the mission to Colombia. After all, his influence had secured Anderson his position at West Point. Aside from his many political connections, it probably did not hurt that he had been a classmate of General Winfield Scott at William and Mary.[10]

Freshly minted lieutenant Robert Anderson was able to return to Louisville for a short visit, and like generations of soldiers before and after him, he proudly showed his family and friends the new uniform. The trip would have been much easier and quicker than the one he had made four years earlier, thanks to the expanding canal system of the growing nation. Lieutenant Anderson arrived at the same time that his oldest brother was visiting. Richard C. Anderson Jr. was settling his motherless children in boarding schools in Kentucky before he returned to South America. Whether he had already planned to recruit Robert to serve as his assistant or whether the idea struck him when he saw the young army officer at Soldier's Retreat is not known.[11]

As two of his sons were returning to the East Coast, Colonel Anderson decided to return to Virginia after more than a forty-year absence. He must have sensed that the end was near and wanted to see the places of his youth one last time. His oldest son recorded in his diary that during this trip, it became apparent that his father's memory and judgment were starting to "decay." The Anderson brothers were facing the same difficulties as anyone with aging parents.[12]

In September, Richard was still having difficulty booking passage to Colombia. He would not succeed until late October. Packet ships that made regularly scheduled trips were a relatively new idea. Before this, a passenger would have to wait until a ship had made enough business arrangements to fill its manifest and ensure a profitable journey. While packet ships regularly ran from major American cities to each other and Europe, scheduled trips to South America were in the distant future. Robert did not seem to mind the delay. While in New York City, the dashing young officer was invited to many fashionable parties. Anderson found himself "surrounded by the most captivating galaxy of beauty" but was unmoved and only asked to be introduced to one young lady; at least, that was what he wrote his sister.[13]

Both of the brothers were seasick for most of the voyage to Colombia. It was a miserable three-week journey to Cartagena. They suffered through storms and periods of no wind. After landing at Cartagena, they would have to travel overland to reach the Ric Magdalena, where they could catch a steamboat south to Bogotá, the capital.[14]

The small party—Richard C. Anderson Jr., his assistant Robert, and a second assistant, Denis Hite—spent sixteen days in Cartagena. Ambassador Anderson had work to do in this important port city. He met with European consuls and officials from the Colombian government. His primary reason for remaining was probably the hope that he would receive instructions from Washington about the Panama Congress, but none came. Robert Anderson was able to do a little sightseeing while in Cartagena. The city did not impress him. In a letter to a cousin, Anderson described his impressions of the city. As a recent graduate of West Point, he was interested in the country's military history. He visited the sites of the disastrous British invasion during Queen Anne's War. Anderson wrote that little had changed since Admiral Vernon and General Wentworth had visited it ninety years earlier. With the eyes of a young man from a young nation, he saw as serious drawbacks what other visitors might see as charming. Anderson commented on the beauty of the cathedrals of Cartagena, which were "very spacious and bountifully supplied with huge carvings gilded with gold and pictures of saints and images and holy relics." Like all of us, Anderson was a product of his education and upbringing. As a good Episcopalian, Anderson had a severe bias, and what he saw convinced him that "the Roman Catholic Religion is daily becoming weaker in this country. As the inhabitants become more enlightened, they must give way to some more simple mode of worship." He was still a very young man, and as he sat through a Catholic Mass, he paid as much attention to the young women and their "finest worked French stockings" as he did the service.[15]

The letters Anderson wrote from Colombia are very revealing about his character. There are plenty of examples of a young man taking himself just a little too seriously; in a letter to his sister Maria, Anderson wrote, "Duty must call me from my pleasure. I am to become an actor on the world stage."[16] Yet one might cut young Anderson a little slack since he would indeed become an actor on the world stage, at least for a brief moment.

The initial stage on the trek to the national capital, Bogotá, was Turbaco, about ten miles southeast. The party traveled on horseback, and the luggage followed much slower by mule. Robert complained that the saddle on his horse was old enough to have been used by Columbus.[17]

Because of the poor conditions of the roads, the party did not arrive until late on the evening of November 23, 1825, the day they left Cartagena. They stayed and ate dinner at the home of Doña Juana. Richard C. Anderson described the home as a "neat, clean looking negro hut, with three rooms. A decent house for this country." His brother was more impressed by the food served by the "widow lady," specifically the good chocolate that she served.[18]

The next stage of the trip was to the region of Arjona, roughly another ten miles to the southeast. Before they left Turbaco, the party learned that a senior Colombian general, also on his way to Bogotá, had confiscated the mules carrying their luggage. Richard Anderson had to use his diplomatic credentials with the local alcalde to get the mules returned. To Richard Anderson, this incident showed the shocking lack of freedom in Colombia that a man's possessions could be so easily seized. Since the two parties were traveling to Bogotá on the same route at the same time, relations must have been strained. Unfortunately, neither of the Anderson brothers leaves us their opinion of a man as interesting as General and Admiral José Padilla, a hero of the wars against Spain.[19]

As they traveled across rough roads unsuitable for a carriage, wagon, or any wheeled vehicle, the young West Point graduate could not help but see the world through his training as an engineer. Anderson wrote with just "a little labor and skill employed, carriages might be able to travel with perfect ease and safety" and that with the building of a few ditches, the rainy season would not be nearly as destructive.[20]

As they traveled through the interior of Colombia, they passed through villages with structures made of bamboo and palm leaves. Most of the land was cleared and tilled, but when they were in untouched areas, Robert Anderson took the opportunity to play naturalist. He described in letters home beautiful parrots and exotic lizards that he saw as he made off-road excursions. He was impressed with the country's natural beauty but did not care for the climate, as he was "afraid that it is very well calculated to make a man lazy."[21]

The party arrived at Barrancas at sunset on November 26, 1825. From Barrancas, they would catch a steamboat to carry them to central Colombia. No one knew when the boat would arrive, and a large party of foreigners with business in the capital began to congregate. As they waited for the boat, the Americans and Europeans did what they could to entertain themselves. A group of

Englishmen organized mule races. Some went hunting, and many hands of cards were played while they waited.[22]

The boat finally arrived on December 6, 1825. It must have struck Robert Anderson that he was on the shores of the ice-bound Hudson only a year before, and now he was slowly moving down the tropical Magdalena River. The steamboat would have been either the *Santander* or the *Bolivar*. Juan Bernardo Elbers owned the two ships. He was a German businessman who had been awarded the monopoly on steamboat traffic on the river by the Colombian government. Steamboat traffic on the river had only begun that year, and there were still many issues for Elbers's company to work out.[23]

Whichever boat it was, she carried between forty-five and sixty passengers. There was only one large cabin, and the female passengers occupied it while the men slept on the deck either in hammocks or on cots. During the day, the passengers played cards and chess, practiced their marksmanship, and complained about the conditions on board. The mosquitoes were unbearable, and the food and drink, including the water, were unpleasant.[24]

The steamboat was slowed by sandbars, shifting islands, and the unpredictability of the river. Not only did the boat run aground numerous times, but midway through the journey, they began to run out of wood for the boilers. The captain, a man named Batis, would anchor in the middle of the river and send some of the crew ashore to cut wood. The fresh-cut wood did not produce enough steam as dried wood or coal, and the boat continued to fight the current at only a fraction of its potential speed.[25]

Tropical diseases also affected the passengers. Both of the Anderson brothers became ill but recovered during the voyage. Colonel John Hamilton, one of the British commissioners to Colombia, died either of yellow fever or typhoid during the journey. Not knowing the cause, most of his possessions and the silverware and cups he used were thrown into the river.[26]

The Anderson brothers of Louisville, Kentucky, spent New Year's Day 1826 on a steamboat in the Colombian jungle. Although Robert did not leave us a description of this voyage, Richard must have been poor company on this day. His journal was filled with the kind of self-reflection common among middle-aged men on their birthdays and other events that mark the passage of time.[27]

As they neared Bogotá, the weather became milder, although, as the senior Anderson pointed out, January in Colombia was still "equal to our warmest summer weather in Kentucky." The mosquitoes were not as overpowering, and there were fewer crocodiles in the river.

On January 7, the party learned from a boat going downriver that San Juan de Ulloa had fallen to Mexican forces.[28] The sixteenth-century fortress was the last stronghold of Spain in the newly independent nation of Mexico. It was highly unlikely that Robert Anderson would have predicted that he would be fighting a war against Mexico in twenty years—and would command an American garrison in that fortress.

On January 17, 1826, the boat finally arrived near Hondo, where the travelers would disembark and make the rest of the journey overland to Bogotá. They had spent an unpleasant six weeks on the Magdalena River. The entire party had been sick for at least part of the journey. Robert suffered from a terrible headache for most of the trip. Richard, however, was unable to wait for the boat to reach its destination. About six miles short of the town of Hondo, he hired a local in a canoe to carry him the rest of the way. This allowed him to arrive enough ahead of the rest of the passengers to rent mules to take his party to Bogotá. There were just enough mules in town for the Andersons and a few others to make the trip. Everyone else would have to wait.[29] This was obviously not Richard Anderson's first trip to South America.

The trip to Bogotá took another four days. The roads and accommodations were even worse than those from Cartagena to the river had been. Growing ever impatient, Richard struck out alone toward Bogotá on the third day, leaving Robert alone to bring up the baggage. Richard was disappointed when he finally reached the capital. There was no official or personal correspondence waiting for him. He was deeply concerned about how his children were doing in Louisville and hoped to have word from them waiting for him—although since the Anderson brothers had so much difficulty reaching Bogotá, it seems slightly unreasonable to expect the mail to have beaten them there.[30]

The city of Bogotá sits on a plateau over eighty-six hundred feet above sea level. It is in the shadow of mountains averaging over seventeen thousand feet tall. Under the Spanish, the city had been the capital of New Grenada. After the revolution, it remained the capital of the newly independent Gran Colombia. The presidential residence was the former palace of the viceroy. The city was made up of narrow paved streets that formed blocks in the Spanish New World style. Bogotá at the time occupied less than two square miles and housed a population of around thirty thousand. The Catholic Church dominated the public landscape with its twenty-six churches, seven monasteries, and three colleges. The public buildings had thick walls and heavy supports because of the numerous earthquakes that shook the city. The houses were low for the same reason; a two-story home was very uncommon. The capital rarely impressed English-speaking visitors. They were struck most by the filthy streets and the beggars who flooded in from the surrounding villages instead of the natural beauty surrounding the city.[31]

Although the ambassador was still feeling ill after the voyage from Cartagena, he still had a great deal of work to do. He met with Colombia's secretary of foreign affairs to discuss an agreement about import duties. The government had also instructed Richard Anderson to attempt to dissuade Colombia and Mexico from using military force to liberate Cuba. The United States wanted to purchase Cuba from the Spanish, an obvious impossibility if Cuba were independent. Anderson was unhappy with his instructions. He felt "every belligerent has a right to annoy and distress its enemy in every practicable way." He would do his duty. He convinced Colombia to suspend the Cuba operation "in deference to the U.S."[32]

Richard Anderson also had to deal with the legally awkward problem of James Chaytor. Although a Virginian, Chaytor was what President Adams called one of those "Baltimore pirates." Chaytor had been captain of the privateer *Independencia del Sud*. Chaytor, a veteran of the War of 1812, captured Spanish shipping first in the employ of Argentina and then Colombia. He was now looking to return to the United States. His days as a privateer had ruined him financially. Chaytor had too closely followed international law and did not profit nearly as much as some of his less scrupulous contemporaries. Chaytor was coming to Anderson because he was in strict violation of the US Neutrality Act of 1818, and he wanted to know how likely it was that the new administration would prosecute him [33]

Robert Anderson spent most of his time in Bogotá in bed. Struck with chills and fever, he would relapse many times while in Colombia. Although neither he nor his brother mentions his malady by name, he was more than likely suffering from malaria. It would affect his health for the rest of his life—although on at least one occasion, his brother blamed Robert's overindulgence in "sweet things" at an official dinner as the cause of his discomfort.[34]

More than a month after arriving in Bogotá, Robert was finally well enough to leave his bed. On February 27, Robert Anderson made the diplomatic rounds with his brother. They paid official visits to Colombia's vice president, the ambassador from Mexico, and Britain's representative in Colombia. It was a cold, rainy day, and Robert was in his sickbed again as soon as they had finished the day's work. It would be another two weeks before he would be well enough to leave their residence. Richard took him to the horse races. Although he was from Louisville, this may have been Robert's first exposure to the sport, at least on a large scale.[35]

In March, Robert traveled to a village outside Bogotá to partake in "warm baths" to fight his illness. It had, at least, a short-term effect as "he considered himself quite well" afterward. On his return to Bogotá, Anderson took a much deeper interest in Colombia and her people. He worked his way through a book on Colombian geography in Spanish, collected and catalogued rocks, and sketched the dress of native Colombians.[36]

On February 28, the elder Anderson brother learned from the newspapers that the US Senate had finally taken up the issue of authorizing his mission to the Congress of Panama. It would not be until March 22 that the Senate finally confirmed Richard Anderson and John Sergeant of Pennsylvania to represent the United States in Panama. The news reached the brothers in Bogotá, and they set off on the long-anticipated trip to Panama on June 11, 1826. Richard Anderson believed in the mission and was ready to leave. He decided to refuse the ambassadorship to Colombia if he were put in a position of choosing between the two.[37]

The party had to retrace their travels back to Cartagena. They would proceed downriver on the same steamboat that had brought them. An easier voyage was expected since they were not fighting the current. It was by no means a comfortable trip. The temperature remained in the high nineties, they ran aground numerous times, and the mosquitoes and other biting insects did not seem to care whether a boat was traveling upstream or down.[38]

As they steamed downriver, the captain was racing against a falling river. On June 26, 1826, the ship got stuck on another sandbar, and the prospects of freeing her seemed slim. After a few days stuck on the sandbar, they began to run out of food. The passengers were obliged to go ashore to hunt for food. On the third day, trapped on the sandbar, driving rain fell. It was not enough to lift the boat, only enough to make everyone a little more miserable. Passengers began to abandon the steamboat for passing canoes. On July 3, the Anderson party and several others boarded a *champan,* a flat-bottomed riverboat.[39]

Robert Anderson spent his nation's fiftieth birthday in a small village along the river. They purchased a few chickens and eggs from the locals and, with a little coffee, had a very limited brunch as a celebration.[40]

On July 8, they arrived at Barrancas, where they had begun their river voyage eight months earlier. Once again, they began the grueling overland trip to Cartagena. On July 11, they reached the town of Turbaco, about ten miles from Cartagena. Hite was sent ahead with the baggage. Richard Anderson had begun to feel ill, with a fever and a headache. This was probably yellow fever, and he took mercury chloride tablets, commonly known as calomel pills, an already controversial cure for the disease.[41]

The secretary, Hite, returned a few days later with word from the American consul at Cartagena, J. M. MacPherson, that they should remain where they were. There was a yellow fever outbreak in the city. He also informed Anderson that the only vessel that could carry them to Panama from Cartagena at this point was the mail boat. Macpherson believed it would be below Richard Anderson's dignity to travel on such a small vessel, a rather odd statement since Anderson had just traveled downriver in a boat pushed with a pole.[42]

Richard Anderson was determined to go on. It was his duty to reach the Congress of Panama. His landlady was also ready for him to move on as yellow fever victims are not the most welcome tenants. On July 12, he sent Robert and Hite ahead to prepare for the voyage to Panama. Richard Anderson arrived in Cartagena two days later. His illness grew worse, and he died on the night of July 24.[43]

John Sergeant did not leave the United States until his confirmation by the Senate. He would not arrive in time to attend the Congress of Panama. That neither of the American representatives attended the meeting made very little difference. In the end, the Congress of Panama was a failure. After meeting for only a few weeks, the delegates decided to reconvene at Tacubaya, Mexico, a healthier climate with better accommodations for the representatives. The Tacubaya meeting never took place, and with the death of Bolívar, the idea of pan-American cooperation passed away for more than seventy years.[44]

Robert Anderson returned home early in August 1826. After a short stay in Washington, DC, where Henry Clay's wife caught him up on Anderson family news, he returned home to Louisville for a short visit before reporting to the army. It was the last time he saw his father. Colonel Anderson, the Revolutionary War hero, died in his bed that November. The two men spent their final hours together working on a biography of the Colonel that would later be published by one of his grandchildren. They probably spent some time mourning the loss of a son and older brother.[45]

Robert Anderson's South America experience was short, difficult, and ultimately tragic. The damage to Anderson's health would plague him for the rest of his life. However, the training Robert Anderson received from his brother was as important as what he learned at the Academy. The nineteenth-century military officer was as much a diplomat as a warrior. Many times in Anderson's career, he would see his role as an army officer as preventing war, not waging it. His brother would be the first of many influences who would foster the importance of peaceful solutions.

CHAPTER 3

SOLDIER IN TRAINING

Lieutenant Robert Anderson, on his return from South America, was assigned to the Third United States Artillery and sent to Fortress Monroe in Virginia. The Third Artillery was relatively new when Anderson joined. It was founded in 1821 with the same army reorganization that had revolutionized West Point. Secretary of War Calhoun divided the artillery branch into four regiments. Each regiment was subdivided into nine companies, each designated with a letter.[1]

Fortress Monroe was also part of Calhoun's military reorganization. Although Fortress Monroe was relatively new—construction had begun in 1819, and the first garrison arrived in 1823—there has been a fort of some kind at Old Point Comfort at the entrance of the James River since 1609. The War of 1812 made it evident that a better system of coastal defense was needed. Fortress Monroe was the largest of all the forts built as part of what would come to be known as the Third System of Fortifications. Its ten-foot-thick walls surrounded nearly sixty acres. Surrounded by an eight-foot-deep moat, Fortress Monroe was almost an island within an island. Designed by a former aide of Napoleon, the "Gibraltar of the Chesapeake" was meant to hold 412 heavy guns and 2,625 men, although there would be fewer than fifty guns there during its first decade of existence.[2]

Besides the critical need to defend the Atlantic coast from a repeat of the British attack of the War of 1812, Secretary Calhoun had another, more specialized mission for Fortress Monroe. He designated it as the Artillery School of Practice. This was the army's first specialist school and one of the few formal types of post–West Point education that existed until after the Civil War. Calhoun's plan called for ten artillery companies out of the four regiments to rotate through the school. New graduates from West Point would be stationed at Fortress Monroe for a year.[3]

When Second Lieutenant Robert Anderson arrived at his new duty station, the twenty-two-year-old was of average build for the early nineteenth century.

SOLDIER IN TRAINING   29

He stood slightly less than five-feet-eight, and as he wrote his sister, the steady supply of ducks and oysters at Old Point Comfort had caused his weight to rise to 133 pounds.[4] His fellow officer, Erasmus Keyes, described him as

> well built. His shoulders were sloping, and the tailor found it easy to fit him with a coat. His face was rather long, his forehead high and narrow, and the expression of his hazel eyes were such that they could always be seen when his face was in sight. His hair was dark and straight, and was cropped close, and his beard clean shaved. He was popular among citizens, to whom his salutations were cordial, and with whom he maintained extensive friendly relations.[5]

On station at Fortress Monroe, the young artillery officer was getting a clear idea of what the routine of his army life would be. It was natural for him to begin questioning whether this was the right career path for him. In the poetic style of the day, Anderson wrote his sister that he was unsure "what port should I direct my bark! Whether it be best to leave all to fortuitous circumstances or form boldly attempt to manage for myself. I cannot determine."[6]

Anderson chose to remain in the US Army, although there were countless lucrative opportunities in "the more diversified life of a citizen." As a West Point graduate, Anderson was a formally trained engineer, and many of his fellow graduates had done quite well with those skills in the ever-expanding American economy. He was, however, satisfied with army life, and his pay was sufficient. He admitted to his sister that any desire to leave was simply due to homesickness and the lingering thought that great monetary success lay outside the army.[7]

Boredom may also have had something to do with Anderson's questioning of his career choice. After the initial training, there was a great deal of downtime in the antebellum army. With no major conflicts during the thirty years between the War of 1812 and the Mexican War and with ever-constricting budgets, these years were relatively quiet. During one of his two stints in the US Army, Edgar Allan Poe described his time serving at the Fortress as allowing him ample time to take in the sun, walk on the beach, and follow his literary pursuits.[8]

Anderson would show the kind of self-discipline that all successful people have. He did not spend his leisure time collecting shells, like Poe did, or hunting and fishing as other officers did. He spent at least part of his free time translating French works on the military arts into English.[9] This served the dual purpose of continuing his military education but also improving his skills in the French language. These two skills would help set him apart from many of his contemporaries in the old army.

With the small size of the army and the vast amount of country it was spread over, men like young Lieutenant Anderson were called upon to meet many emergencies that were not in their job description or part of the training as artillery officers. One such event happened in 1827 and made a splash in the nation's newspapers. In 1905, General George Gordon Greenough gave an address at West Point on what would have been Anderson's one hundredth birthday. A fellow West Pointer and artilleryman, Greenough was a cadet at the Academy during the Fort Sumter crisis. As part of his speech praising Anderson's patriotic service, he told how the young Anderson had been sent with his command to capture a pirate ship that bad weather had driven into Hampton Roads. "His fearless onslaught soon made him master of the vessel," and the pirate leader "shot himself dead on the deck to escape capture."[10] The image of the young officer leading his men in rowboats across the channel to storm the ship in a fierce hand-to-hand struggle with bloodthirsty pirates is a novelist's dream, especially considering it is the first action of the story's hero. Unfortunately for the historian, the story told by Greenough is a little misleading.

The pirate in question was a fifty-five-year-old Frenchman named Alexander Tardy. He was a small man who carried a small cane. His modus operandi was to pose as a passenger, poison the crew and other passengers, and seize control of the ship. It is an idea he tried a few times with little success. On two separate occasions, Tardy posed as a doctor and poisoned the galley's sugar bowl. The rest of the passengers and the crew only got sick instead of dying. When an investigation discovered the poison, Tardy was suspected. In both cases, he was able to shift blame to the cook. In both cases, the cook was Black, and the ships' final destinations were southern ports where paranoia existed over Black cooks using poison. Whether this was just Tardy's good luck or the result of preplanning is unknown. The city of Charleston, South Carolina, even hung one of the unfortunate men.[11]

In 1827, Tardy used slightly modified tactics to seize the brig *Crawford*. He hired three Spanish sailors, Pepe, Couro, and Feliz, to kill the rest of the crew as soon as they became incapacitated by the poison. The only man who survived was the first mate, Edward Dobson, who agreed to navigate the ship for them. The four pirates were not skilled enough to reach port without his help. It was common practice to keep the skill of navigation away from common sailors for just this reason. Dobson was shrewder than his captives. He not only anchored the *Crawford* under the guns of Fortress Monroe, but when he lowered the ship's boat so that Tardy could go ashore, Dobson was able to escape into the current that quickly took him directly to shore. According to the newspaper account, the astonished Tardy called after the escaping Dobson and asked if he meant to betray them. Dobson's response was not recorded.[12]

Tardy cut his throat to avoid capture and a likely trip to the gallows. The other three fled into the Virginia countryside. The insurance company rewarded Dobson with five hundred dollars for saving the ship and the cargo. Anderson was tasked with securing the ship after the action was over. Of course, when Anderson and his men rowed across to the *Crawford,* they had no way of knowing that Tardy was dead and his confederates had fled. As they climbed aboard, they could have been facing an ambush.[13]

Anderson was called to testify in the trial of the surviving pirates. Since piracy on the high seas was a federal crime, the trial would occur in the US District Court. In 1827, the Supreme Court justices still rode the circuit, hearing criminal and civil cases, not just appeals at the highest level. The Chief Justice of the Supreme Court would sit in judgment of the three pirates. This was not a case that required one of the great legal minds of the nineteenth century. The three men were quickly found guilty and sentenced to death.

When the trial was over, Anderson was called in front of the judge. Chief Justice John Marshall was the cousin of Anderson's mother. Marshall complained to the young man that he had to find out through court proceedings that the son of his cousin and a dear friend, Richard C. Anderson, was in town.[14] It was unlikely Anderson failed to call on Marshall out of rudeness. His extreme propriety may have kept him from having contact with the judge in a case in which Anderson was testifying, regardless of how minor his testimony was.

Anderson's posting at Fortress Monroe was only temporary. His next assignment was as different from West Point and Fortress Monroe as possible. Lieutenant Robert Anderson was transferred to the army barracks in Baton Rouge. In 1828, the future capital of Louisiana was a strategically important position. Not only did it sit on the Mississippi River, but it was only 150 miles from America's southwestern border. In 1819, when construction began on the buildings that Anderson would call home for the next several years, the plan was to erect a fortress similar to the big forts on the East Coast. The successful completion of Mexico's War of Independence removed the Spanish Empire from Louisiana's border. A stone fortress able to withstand a siege from a modern army seemed unnecessary. The interior buildings were completed in 1825 after yellow fever and malaria outbreaks caused many delays. They were not protected by the thick stone walls and casemates, as was Fortress Monroe. The four two-story brick buildings were meant to serve as an arsenal, a barracks, and—also for the same purpose the earlier post had done during the Creek Indian War and Andrew Jackson's campaign against the British during the War of 1812—as an assembly point for militia and new soldiers.

The Pentagon Barracks, as Baton Rouge's military post was called, was occupied by the Fourth United States Infantry. The Fourth was one of the seven infantry regiments authorized during Calhoun's reorganization. Its roughly one thousand men were scattered from America's western border with Mexico, to the Atlantic coast of the Florida Territory. At the time of reorganization, its commanding officer was the fourth in seniority among the eight colonels commanding infantry regiments, hence its designation.[15]

Although only midway on the seniority list, the Fourth Infantry's commanding officer, Colonel Duncan Lamont Clinch, got the posting he wanted: the Florida Territory. Originally from North Carolina, Clinch joined the army in 1808 when he was twenty-one. The tension was high, and war with Great Britain was likely when Clinch set aside life as a country gentleman for the army. When war did break out four years later, Lieutenant Clinch was promoted to lieutenant colonel and given command of an infantry battalion. Unfortunately for his career, Clinch did not see any action in the war. Men with less seniority, like Winfield Scott, became generals and national heroes. A former dinner guest at Soldier's Retreat, Andrew Jackson, who had no military experience worth mentioning, became a general in the regular army and president of the United States, thanks to his combat experience in the War of 1812.

Although not as glorious as a war against British regulars, Colonel Clinch saw action on America's southern border in what became known as the First Seminole War. The war culminated in General Jackson's invasion of Spanish Florida and America's acquisition of Florida in exchange for giving up its claim, based on the Louisiana Purchase, on Spanish territory between the Rio Grande and the Sabine River. Clinch would play an important role in the development of American Florida.

Colonel Clinch invested his limited funds in land near Saint Marys, a small town on the Florida-Georgia border. Along with five slaves he imported from North Carolina, Clinch laid the groundwork for a highly profitable plantation. Further attaching himself to the local community, Clinch married the daughter of a wealthy and respected local landowner, John Houstoun McIntosh. As army life took Clinch around the Southeast, his young bride stayed at Saint Marys, mostly at her parents' plantation. In 1821, she gave birth to their first child, named after her mother, Eliza Bayard Clinch.[16]

Unfortunately, Anderson did not record in his letters to family and friends his initial impression of Colonel Clinch, a man who would play an essential role in his life and, in many aspects, would be as much a role model as Anderson's father. Clinch was a successful military man with a growing family. He was a wealthy landowner and had the respect of the community. These became Anderson's goals.

Anderson arrived in Baton Rouge in the spring of 1828. It was a small town of only around fifteen hundred people sitting about forty feet above the muddy

General Duncan Lamont Clinch, 1836. Clinch was Anderson's father-in-law and a US representative from Georgia . Courtesy of the Library of Congress, LC-DIG-cwpb-06860.

Mississippi. It was an international town, although not as much as New Orleans. There were Spanish and French families who predated American annexation in 1810.[17] There were several German families, enslaved Africans working the growing number of sugar plantations in the area, and Native American tribes on the outskirts of town.[18]

Although the fastest route to his new posting would have been by ship to New Orleans, Anderson was, as was customary in the army, given the time to travel overland to Louisville to see his family. It was Anderson's first trip to Louisville since his father's death. It was also Anderson's last visit to his boyhood home, Soldier's Retreat. The family sold the six-hundred-acre estate later that year, and the new owners demolished the stone building in 1840.[19]

Anderson did not have enough time to attend his older brother's wedding in Cincinnati. Larz married Catherine Longworth. She was the daughter of a Cincinnati millionaire, banker, and winemaker. Nicholas Longworth introduced winemaking to the Ohio Valley and profited greatly from the endeavor, something Larz's father had unsuccessfully tried. Larz Anderson would use his newfound wealth and influence to become a successful Ohio politician. Larz took his and Robert's widowed mother to live with him and his new bride in Cincinnati.[20]

Anderson would travel down the Ohio River to the Mississippi and then to Baton Rouge. He described the post to his sister as "a very pleasant situation, and one of the most delightful winter residences in the country." The warmer seasons were, however, incredibly unhealthy. Tropical diseases, such as malaria and yellow fever, were still a problem in most of the American South, especially along the swampy areas of the southern banks of the Mississippi River.

Anderson's attention turned to his personal life and desire to marry. Perhaps it was the example of his slightly older brother Larz, or maybe it was gentle pressure from his mother, or perhaps it was just the loneliness of life on an isolated military post that drove Anderson. Maybe the example of the post commander's young and happy family motivated him. He lamented in letters to his sisters and mother that he had yet to find a bride. "They say I look for perfection, but that like the philosopher's stone, it is not to be found." He offered a different theory for his failure to find a wife. "I am too easily pleased that I am doomed to singledom. I find so many charming ladies that before I can decide which will suit me the best, up comes some other lovers who are not genteel enough to let me even hope to marry any of the bunch but seem to me to marry without courting."[21]

Although he did not know it, he had already met his future bride when he wrote those words. Colonel Clinch's eldest daughter Eliza was only six years old when she met her future husband. She was not initially impressed by the young artillery officer. Near the post was a fenced-in park. There was a small lake frequented by deer, swan, and geese. It was quite a privilege for the post's children to play inside. When the young Eliza went to the deer park, she was accompanied by a chaperone, Lieutenant Robert Anderson. As the commanding officer's daughter, her safety would have been of keen interest to the men and officers. Anyone who has ever lived in Louisiana knows that it is safe to assume that even the smallest body of water has the potential of an alligator or poisonous snake lurking near the surface. The young Miss Clinch did not understand the potential danger. To her, he was only an annoyance, keeping her from feeding the geese and throwing sticks at the deer.[22]

Anderson spent three relatively uneventful years in Baton Rouge. His responsibility was logistical support. He was tasked with ensuring the arsenal was prepared to equip a field army. Anderson was also responsible for ensuring that the cannons at Fort St. Philip and Fort Jackson were equipped and prepared to prevent an enemy navy from sailing up the Mississippi River. It was a quiet posting and did not offer any opportunity for a young officer to make his mark and advance his career. The business of the post would occasionally carry him to New Orleans. Anderson was not overly impressed with the bustling port city or its residents. It was, as Anderson described it, a "city of strangers" whose only goals were to make money, "to spend it and to be seen."[23]

Although Anderson was unhappy at Pentagon Barracks, he was satisfied with his career choice. His family had offered him Soldier's Retreat along with its 300 acres, more than enough to qualify him as a gentleman farmer.[24] He passed on the offer. His officer's commission offered job security. Plantations went bankrupt if they were mismanaged or the owner had bad luck. Anderson wanted to continue his army career, just not in Louisiana. Advancements in the antebellum army came very slow, and if an officer was not careful, his career could stall in a quiet post for decades. An army career had to be carefully managed. He wrote several requests for a transfer to a position that offered a greater chance of upward mobility. He wrote his West Point classmate Charles F. Smith, then an Academy instructor, to feel out the possibility of returning there.[25]

In 1831, his request for a transfer was granted, and the army sent him to Jefferson Barracks in St. Louis. It was a frontier post, but it was much closer to Louisville and a much preferable climate to Anderson than Louisiana. Anderson shied away from using contacts and influence to get what he wanted. Still, it could not have hurt that the commanding general in the West, headquartered at Jefferson Barracks, was a close friend of the family, Henry Atkinson. Because of his posting at Jefferson Barracks, Anderson would see the first battle of his military career. On September 30, 1831, he handed over the responsibility of the ordnance at the Baton Rouge arsenal and Fort St. Philips to another officer and headed north toward his first of many dates with history.[26]

CHAPTER 4

RELUCTANT WARRIOR

Robert Anderson's training from West Point to his early years as a subaltern prepared him to fight a war on the Western European model. This was true for all the officers in the antebellum army. Instead, they found themselves spread across half of a continent and fighting a different kind of enemy with which many young officers, like Anderson, came to sympathize. He was at the knife's edge of territorial expansion and saw the "misery and suffering" of not only the Indians but also "our inhabitants on the frontier."[1]

Anderson's first experience in Indian warfare as a soldier was the conflict that came to be called the Black Hawk War. Named after the old Sauk warrior, the conflict's origins were much more complicated than is often presented. It was not the Sauk response to the infamous Indian Removal Law. Its origins long predated the passage of that law.

The chain of events that set off the Black Hawk War began the year before Anderson was born. Following the murder of three white settlers, representatives of the Sauk and Mesquakies signed a treaty with the territorial governor, William Henry Harrison, in 1804. They feared retribution from the United States since they were unable and unwilling to hand over the perpetrators. The Sauk warriors who committed the murders claimed the victims trespassed on their territory. The four Sauk chiefs and one Mesquakie chief hoped to gain a pardon for the young warriors. The plan was to purchase forgiveness with goods and money, an accepted native practice. The chiefs ceded over fifteen million acres of western Illinois, southern Wisconsin, and northeastern Missouri, essentially all their land east of the Mississippi River. Besides the pardons, the Mesquakies and Sauk received over two thousand dollars worth of goods and an annual payment of one thousand dollars worth of goods. It is doubtful that they realized how much land they traded. When the delegates returned home, they reported that they had only traded the disputed land in

Missouri, which had led to the situation in the first place. If that had been the deal, it might not have been bad.[2]

More than twenty years passed before the Mesquakies and Sauk were dispelled of the mistaken idea of what they had sold. One of the unique features of the treaty was that the tribes would not have to leave until American settlers arrived in the area. This did not happen until the late 1820s when the lead mining industry took off in the region. The influx of miners created a series of conflicts between the new settlers and the many Native groups in the area.

These conflicts caused Illinois governor Ninian Edwards to demand that the federal government remove all Indians from the land given up in the 1804 treaty. Even though the signatories represented only two of the more than half a dozen nations in the region, the governor had enough support in Washington, DC. The violent incidents had gained enough national attention that President John Adams ordered the 1804 Treaty to be enforced. All Native Americans were to be moved west of the Mississippi River.

The crisis caused the Mesquakies and Sauk nations to split into two. One faction led by the fifty-year-old Keokuk accepted the situation. Traditionally, they spent the winter hunting west of the Mississippi River and returned to their lands in the east to plant corn in the spring. All that was required was that they not return in the spring of 1831. The leader of the group that refused the treaty and would return was Ma-Ka-Tai-Me-She-Kia-Kiak, more commonly known as Black Hawk. In his mid-sixties, the old warrior was a veteran of the War of 1812 and fought with the famous Tecumseh. After the war, he maintained good relations with the British, earning the nickname for his followers, the British Band.

The British Band consisted of about three hundred warriors and their families. When they returned after the winter hunt in 1831, the new Illinois governor, John Reynolds, called up the Illinois militia and requested the US Army. When a force under the command of General Edmund Gaines arrived, Black Hawk and his people retired across the Mississippi and agreed not to return.

White settlers were not the only problem the Sauk and Mesquakies faced. In 1830, the Sioux and Menominee killed ten Mesquakie men as they traveled to Prairie du Chien. The following year, the Mesquakies retaliated. They attacked a Menominee camp of about forty people located a mile and a half north of Fort Crawford. The more than a hundred Mesquakie warriors caught them entirely by surprise. When it was over, ten men, four women, and nine children were dead. The Menominee reached out to their allies to aid them in seeking revenge. They also asked the United States. The Menominee appealed to Joseph Street, the Indian agent at Fort Crawford, to help them get justice. Unsure how to respond, Street contacted his superiors. That, of course, was not a quick process in the 1830s.[3]

When the spring of 1832 arrived, the situation was more favorable to Black Hawk than when he and his people had agreed not to return. A Ho-Chunk mystic named White Cloud began preaching resistance. He attracted followers from many groups and, in 1832, joined with Black Hawk, who now had a fighting force of over six hundred men. When the expanded British Band arrived at Saukenuk, known today as Rock Island, Illinois, the governor called up the state militia and again requested aid from the US Army.

As the events leading to federal intervention played out, one of Lieutenant Anderson's many requests for a transfer was answered. He was ordered to the St. Louis Arsenal. The wild frontier town had a population of only about seven thousand. The fur trade was the primary industry. The city was similar to his boyhood home of Louisville.

The arsenal employed roughly twenty-five soldiers and civilians. It was about three miles south of the city. These men manufactured and repaired muskets, pistols, and carriages for artillery pieces. There were also more than fifteen thousand cannonballs ready to be issued to the army or militia companies. Unlike at Baton Rouge, Anderson was not in command of the arsenal. That honor fell to Lieutenant Richard B. Lee, a fellow West Pointer. Lee's career never rivaled his more famous cousin Robert E. Lee. He did not make much of an impression on Anderson either. When Anderson wrote about these events forty years later, he got Lee's name wrong.[4]

Also in St. Louis was Jefferson Barracks. It was the home of the Infantry School of Practice, the infantry's version of the school Anderson attended at Fortress Monroe. It was not as successful as Fortress Monroe in its training because the men were constantly needed for duty on the frontier. The post's commander was Brevet Brigadier General Henry Atkinson. The North Carolina native had served in the army since 1808. He was a veteran of the War of 1812 but had spent most of his career in the West successfully treating with native tribes. He founded Jefferson Barracks in 1826 and would spend most of his remaining career in command there. Atkinson was a family friend and may have helped Lieutenant Anderson get the posting at the arsenal.

On March 17, 1832, Atkinson was ordered to take part of his command four hundred miles up the Mississippi River to Fort Crawford. He was to force the Mesquakie and Sauk to hand over those responsible for the Menominee killings. No mention of Black Hawk and his British Band was in the original orders, but many American officials suspected him in the deaths. As Atkinson prepared his six infantry companies for the move north, Anderson volunteered to accompany him. Anderson followed proper army protocol and requested permission from his commanding officer to volunteer. Atkinson gratefully accepted Anderson's offer. The general knew that he would soon have many Illinois state militia forces under his command, and a West Point–trained officer to help him manage the influx of amateurs would be a welcome addition. It did not hurt that Atkinson knew and trusted Anderson. General Atkinson made Anderson his assistant inspector general. The duty consisted of ensuring the smooth operation of the force. It required a detail-oriented individual, well versed in military rules, regulations, and procedures—a perfect position for Anderson.[5]

In the early morning of April 8, 1832, General Atkinson loaded his six infantry companies and one artilleryman onboard two steamboats for the four-day cruise up the Mississippi River to Fort Armstrong on Rock Island in northern Illinois. The men and officers with their equipment did not have much room in the two boats, and many were probably towed behind on barges. The *Enterprise* and *Chieftain* were only about sixty to seventy feet long and fifteen feet wide at their beam. The advantage of the two vessels was their shallow draft, which allowed them to operate in less than three feet of water, and their powerful steam engines that could fight the river's current.

The *Enterprise* already had a long and storied past when Atkinson pressed her into service. In 1815, the US government hired the privately owned boat to carry ammunition to General Jackson for the critical Battle of New Orleans. Perhaps more importantly, she had proven that steamboat navigation of the entire Mississippi River was both possible and practical. By 1832, there were larger and more powerful boats on the Mississippi, but the *Enterprise* was still plying her trade.[6]

In the days before massive dredging and constant maintenance projects by the Corps of Engineers, a trip on the Mississippi was a dangerous undertaking. Underwater hazards abounded, from shifting sandbars to full-sized trees racing downriver from collapsed banks. The pilots who worked the river memorized every bend and studied every ripple on the surface for hidden dangers. Although the river was much more powerful in Louisiana and Mississippi, it could be more dangerous along the route Anderson traveled as the pilots had much less room to maneuver. The tiny flotilla arrived at Fort Armstrong at midnight. Traveling on the river after sunset was a dangerous prospect. Whether Atkinson pushed cautious pilots to steam through the night for military necessity or the ships' owners were in a rush to unload the army for more profitable customers, we can only speculate.

Built in 1816, Fort Armstrong was a solid wooden fort on the southern tip of 946-acre Rock Island. The strategically important island was just a little farther north of where the Rock River, which originated deep in Wisconsin, flowed into the Mississippi. It was a critical crossroads.

When Atkinson arrived at the island, new intelligence was waiting for him. Black Hawk and his British Band had once again returned to the area. Dealing with Black Hawk had not been why Atkinson had left St. Louis. It was not, however, in Atkinson's opinion, a different crisis. He assumed that those responsible for the Menominee Massacre were with Black Hawk and his people.[7]

At Fort Armstrong, Anderson received a letter he had been hoping for: from Dennis Hart Mahan, a classmate at West Point. Earlier that year, Mahan had accepted the position of professor of engineering. He resigned his commission in the army to take the job at West Point permanently, or at least until his death almost forty years later. In this position, Mahan had more effect on West Point, and thus the army, than perhaps anyone except for Thayer. Nearly every Civil War general was a student of Mahan. He was offering Anderson the position of assistant professor of engineering. The appointment was a great opportunity for a young officer with an eye on his career. The position would allow him to make contacts with some of the most influential people in the US Army and the government.

Two significant issues made accepting the position a difficult matter. When Anderson had first expressed interest in the position, he was in a lonely, boring post in what must have seemed a career dead-end. Now he was in the middle of the action with a position of extreme importance, perhaps second only to the commander himself. Aside from the positive good that his position with Atkinson would do for his career, this was just the type of adventure and excitement for which a young man chose the army as a career.

The second problem was in the offer itself. After several years of studying French military academies, Mahan believed that West Point's faculty's transitory nature was a detriment. Mahan had resigned his commission to dedicate his life to the Academy. While he did not expect Anderson to do the same, he expected him to commit to a long tenure.[8] Anderson had envisioned his return to West Point as one chapter in a storied military career, not as the final destination. It was a commitment he was not ready to make. He turned down this opportunity but would eventually serve as an assistant professor at West Point anyway, though not under the soon-to-be-legendary Mahan.

The respectfully written letter declining the honor would have to wait. Anderson had to give his complete attention to the problem at hand. He was with Atkinson when the general met with Sauk and Mesquakie leaders. They confirmed that the people sought were among the six hundred people with Black Hawk.

In Robert Anderson's long career as an army officer, he served with the antebellum army's great commanders in war and peace. Each shaped who he would be as a commander. Sometimes the most important lessons are what not to do. Unfortunately, this was the case with General Atkinson and the Black Hawk War. Atkinson was an old hand with Indian affairs. He had spent the last twenty years negotiating treaties with the tribes along the Missouri River. He gained their respect and the nickname "White Beaver," the origin of which is lost. Unfortunately, during the summer of 1832, he made several miscalculations that led many of his contemporaries and modern scholars to argue that Atkinson fought an unnecessary war.[9]

General Henry "White Beaver" Atkinson made two perhaps faulty assumptions. First, he assumed Black Hawk was going to fight. Black Hawk wrote that he never intended to take up arms against the US Army. Of course, that was written with a white man's aid, and for a white audience. Nevertheless, besides Black Hawk's words, other evidence suggests that Black Hawk's intentions were not warlike. The presence of women and children suggests this was not a war party. The Sauk, like most Eastern Woodland Nations, had separate leadership for war and peace. Both were there on the Rock River, so even if Black Hawk had decided on war, the decision would not have been entirely his. Their presence would have made it more likely that White Beaver could have negotiated a peaceful settlement.

The second potentially faulty assumption was linked to the first. Atkinson feared that his six companies of infantry might not have been adequate to defeat Black Hawk. This led him to seek aid from John Reynolds, governor of Illinois. Reynolds, a longtime politician, had served in every branch of the Illinois government and in the US Congress. He had been a frontier scout in the War of 1812. Governor Reynolds delivered more than twenty-one hundred militiamen, although not all would serve directly under Atkinson. Atkinson's request greatly complicated the situation and made it much more challenging to negotiate a peaceful solution, which his record showed was his preferred conclusion. In the letter to Reynolds, which soon became public, the general wrote, "The Frontier is in great danger" and that "the regular force under my command is too small." The letter let loose panic on the frontier and—along with a large number of untrained, excited militiamen—made a peaceful solution impossible.

As assistant inspector general, the militia was Anderson's responsibility. Reynolds made him a colonel in the Illinois militia to prevent issues caused by Anderson's lowly regular army rank. Anderson's responsibility was the equipping, disciplining, and general management of a few thousand frontiersmen. He was in charge of everything but leading the men into combat. In other words, Anderson had the most challenging job but with no chance for glory.

Among the wild frontiersmen whom Anderson swore into federal service was twenty-three-year-old Abraham Lincoln. He was the newly elected captain of the New Salem, Illinois, militia company. Lincoln and his sixty-nine mounted volunteers were armed with thirty muskets, which probably saw service in the War of 1812. These men were very different from the West Point cadets or army regulars with whom Anderson was used to dealing.

Thirty years later, when Lincoln was president, Anderson did not remember meeting him. Anderson made more of an impression, as the future president recalled Anderson when the two men met again in the White House. Although Lincoln never saw action and on the campaign trail would belittle his service in the Black Hawk War, it was invaluable training. Lincoln was a country boy with no experience in army discipline. One day, he would be the commander in chief of a military force overwhelmingly made up of country boys experiencing military life and discipline for the first time.[10]

After the nearly seventeen hundred militia were mustered into service and Anderson filled out the massive amount of necessary paperwork in his neat, efficient handwriting, Atkinson began his pursuit of Black Hawk up the Rock River. The army regulars, Atkinson, his staff, and a couple of militia companies slowly made their way up the river by keelboat. Around fifteen hundred mounted Illinois volunteers traveled along the river. The old family friend Colonel Zachary Taylor commanded the infantrymen in the boats.

The mounted volunteers were under General Samuel Whiteside. Originally from North Carolina, Whiteside led a scout company in the War of 1812, mainly against Britain's Native allies. Like many frontiersmen, conflict with the Natives was personal. When he was a boy, his brother was killed in an Indian raid while he and his mother survived by hiding in the woods.

Traveling with Whiteside was Governor Reynolds. He carried the rank of major general of volunteers. When they reached Dixon's Ferry, about sixty miles away from Rock Island, they met a force of 275 mounted volunteers under the command of Major Isaiah Stillman. The successful store owner and militia officer was awaiting further orders when General Whiteside's force arrived on May 12, 1832. Governor Reynolds took advantage of the fact that Stillman and his men were not yet sworn into federal service. As militia, they were under his command, not Atkinson's. Since Reynolds had been sworn into federal service, this should have been a distinction without a difference. But in his role as governor, Reynolds sent Stillman and his men on an independent mission. Stillman's men were to rush ahead and attack Black Hawk and his force. Whiteside tried to convince the governor of the folly of this idea. As an officer of militia and an experienced soldier, he knew the quality of recently organized militia units. Rushing them forward to attack an enemy of unknown strength was a recipe for disaster. Reynolds could not be persuaded that his plan would end badly, and he ordered Major Stillman forward.[11]

When a party of Black Hawk's men attempted to meet under a flag of truce, the scared and undisciplined militia opened fire and launched a disorganized charge. The Sauk and Mesquakie force beat them back. In an attempt to regain control of his men, Stillman ordered them to withdraw, a difficult maneuver in the best circumstances. It turned into a panicked retreat that came to be known as Stillman's Run. The Black Hawk War had begun. There was no going back. Stillman and Governor Reynolds both defended their reputations in print, mostly blaming the other for bad decisions. Both also exaggerated the size of the enemy force. The fifty-sixty Sauk and Mesquakie warriors turned into a few thousand in the letters they sent to the newspapers. The regulars naturally blamed the Illinois men for starting the war and convincing Black Hawk's men and other Natives who might have remained neutral that the Americans could be defeated.[12]

Both forces returned to the battlefield at different times in the days that followed. Black Hawk sent men to gather the supplies abandoned by the fleeing enemy, including eight kegs of powder and three hundred pounds of lead for bullets. Among the Illinois men sent to bury their fellow militiamen was Abraham Lincoln.

Although Atkinson's officers, including Colonel Taylor and Lieutenant Anderson, blamed the militia entirely for the disaster, the army high command viewed the whole situation as Atkinson's mess. President Jackson lost confidence in Atkinson. It was an election year, and Jackson wanted the problem dealt with quickly and efficiently. Major General Winfield Scott was on his way to take control. Scott, a hero of the War of 1812, would not arrive in time to take part in the war. Asiatic cholera broke out among the men he was bringing by ship through the Great Lakes. By the time they arrived in the Michigan Territory, he had only three hundred men out of his original force of thirteen hundred fit for duty. He and his staff pushed westward to take part in the action but did not arrive in time. Although he and his relief force did not affect the war's outcome, it had a considerable impact on the region. Deserters from Scott's force spread the disease throughout the Midwest. The dead bodies that had been dumped overboard from his four plague ships washed ashore for the rest of the summer. The human toll was almost incalculable. Small fishing and farming communities were completely wiped out, with no one left to report the loss.[15]

Black Hawk was probably as surprised as anyone at how events played out. Although he had stumbled into a victory, and other villages frustrated with American expansion flocked to his banner, he had no illusions that he could defeat the Americans. Tecumseh, his old leader, even with the full support of the British, had failed. It was evident to Black Hawk that he would receive no aid from his former British allies. His strategy remained one of avoiding battle with White Beaver and his force.

Settlers in Illinois and the Michigan territory—in 1832, the modern states of Michigan, Wisconsin, and Iowa—faced sporadic attacks. Black Hawk sent some of these raids to draw attention away from his main body. Others were independent groups trying to aid Black Hawk or were taking advantage of the chaos for revenge or plunder. More militia units were raised to defend the towns and isolated farms. Nearly two hundred whites and an equal number of Indians were killed during the scattered fighting. Of the new militia units, the most successful was a group of mounted militia under the command of Henry Dodge. They were from the lead mine region of the Michigan territory, what is today western Wisconsin. Colonel Dodge and Atkinson had served together in other emergencies with the Native tribes. Atkinson trusted the colonel's judgment. At Atkinson's request, Congress authorized the creation of the Battalion of Mounted Rangers with Dodge in command.

It was not until late June that Atkinson resumed the pursuit of Black Hawk and the British Band. Atkinson had reorganized his army. There were new militiamen for Anderson to swear in and organize. New regulars arrived, both infantry and Dodge's mounted men. There were also twelve hundred mounted Illinois militia under the command of General James Henry. The infantry was under the command of Colonel Jacob Fry; Colonel Taylor had been left in charge of Fort Crawford. The Northwest Army, as Atkinson's army was designated, was roughly three thousand men moving northward along the rough terrain of the Rock River Valley. It processed extremely slowly and cautiously, making on average only five or six miles a day. Besides traveling over the wild and swampy country, the army built a defensive position complete with wooden breastworks at the end of each day, forcing them to stop well before sunset to set up their elaborate camp. Black Hawk would later claim that he could have stopped to plant and raise corn and still avoid his pursuers.[14]

As Black Hawk progressed north along the Rock River, he attacked and looted small farmsteads, including the occasional small fort that residents had built for their defense. Between the small engagements and desertion, his force was shrinking. He had lost over 10 percent of his three-hundred-man fighting force. He was also running desperately low on food. They began eating their horses and anything else they could scrounge.

Despite the Northwest Army's slow speed, they gained on Black Hawk. Mounted warriors were only a portion of his people. Women, children, and the elderly kept them from moving quickly. As they moved into what is now Wisconsin, Atkinson's force was only three days behind. There was plenty of evidence for the US Army and local militia that they were on the right path.

They continued to find abandoned camps, horse carcasses, and starved Natives along their way. On July 8, they may have been as close as a few miles behind Black Hawk. It was at this point that an old, one-eyed Ho Chuck chief, Decori, came into the army's camp and convinced General Atkinson, despite the overwhelming evidence to the contrary, that Black Hawk and his force had changed direction and were now heading south. Atkinson ordered his army to turn around and begin retracing their steps.

After two days of marching in the wrong direction, the army was beginning to fall apart. Provisions were running low, and nearly half the mounted volunteers were now on foot due to improper care of their mounts. Atkinson ordered the sick and those on foot back toward Dixon's Ferry. He sent Dodge and Henry's command to Fort Winnebago, about seventy miles away. Atkinson, Anderson, and Fry's four hundred regulars marched to the shores of Lake Koshkonong and a recently constructed fort.

Both Dodge's and Henry's command and Atkinson's force learned of Black Hawk's location at about the same time. When Dodge's and Henry's force arrived at Fort Winnebago on July 12, Pierre Paquette, the local agent for the American Fur Company, informed them that Black Hawk was to the east on the Rock River. At roughly the same time, a patrol from Atkinson's force under the command of Captain William S. Harney rediscovered Black Hawk's trail.

With Paquette guiding them, Henry and Dodge renewed the pursuit. Between Dodge's regulars and Henry's militia, they only had about 570 useable horses. They had suffered injuries and loss when an Indian raid had stampeded the horses when they first arrived at Fort Winnebago. It took Henry and Dodge three days to reach the Rock River. The path led through swamps and thick underbrush. On reaching the river, they once again found an abandoned camp, but they were on the elusive Black Hawk's trail. He was moving west. In order to close the distance, the horsemen abandoned unnecessary equipment. Wagons, tents, and coffee pots were left scattered on the trail. They were only a few miles behind their target. The men slept in the rain and ate raw meat and flour because the rain was too heavy to have a fire.

After two days, Dodge's and Henry's force had ridden their horses to near exhaustion. Their pace slowed with each hour, but as Black Hawk's people were nearly worn out, the Americans kept closing the gap. Atkinson, Anderson, and the regular infantry were catching up as well. The combined trail of Henry, Dodge, and Black Hawk was becoming increasingly easy to follow.

Dodge's dragoons and Henry's volunteers made contact with the British Band as they crossed the Wisconsin River. In what came to be known as the Battle of Wisconsin Heights, Dodge and Henry dismounted their troops and attacked with bayonets in the pouring rain. In what can only be described as a rearguard action, Black Hawk's men took position on the bluffs overlooking the river. The majority of the natives forded the river as the warriors were driven slowly back toward the river. They took heavy losses crossing the river but, once on the opposite bank, took a position on the opposing bluffs. The regulars and volunteers could not cross without serious casualties.

Henry gave the order to stand down, and his exhausted men laid down and slept on what had been the battlefield only moments before. One man was killed and eight wounded. Based on scalps taken by his Native allies and militia and the number of bodies left on the field, Dodge estimated that Black Hawk's losses were about forty.[15]

As Black Hawk continued northwest toward the Mississippi River, Dodge and Henry fell back to the south to meet with Atkinson's advancing force and gain fresh supplies and mounts for their exhausted men.

On July 25, Atkinson's army crossed the Wisconsin River. It was apparent that Black Hawk was attempting to cross the Mississippi to Sauk territory. The entire conflict was based on Black Hawk's refusal to do just that, but to allow him to do so without being defeated would have been a loss for Atkinson and an invitation for Black Hawk to return the following spring. The Northwest Army continued north in pursuit across sometimes hilly and sometimes swampy land in the summer heat. Black Hawk was increasingly easy to follow. As his people tried to make good their escape, they left behind a trail of men who had succumbed to their wounds from Wisconsin Heights and emaciated men, women, and children who just sat down to wait for death. It was "scenes of distress and misery exceeding any" Anderson "ever expected to see in our happy land."[16]

Atkinson was only a day behind when Black Hawk's band reached the Mississippi about five miles south of the Bad Axe River. As Black Hawk slowly moved his people across on the few canoes available, they had the bad luck of running into the *Warrior*. Despite its fierce name, the *Warrior* was no fighting vessel. She was a paddlewheel steamboat owned and commanded by Joseph Throckmorton. He and his boat had been hired into federal service. With two crew members and twenty-three soldiers, the *Warrior* carried supplies and messages up the Mississippi. Throckmorton was returning south from informing Atkinson's Sioux allies that Black Hawk was moving west. On the trip, Throckmorton met another group of Sioux who informed him that Black Hawk and his people were crossing the river.

When Throckmorton placed the *Warrior* in the path of the retreating natives, Black Hawk raised a white flag. He called for Throckmorton to send a boat ashore so that he could discuss terms. Although many historians of the conflict believed Black Hawk's sincerity and saw a lost opportunity to avoid the upcoming battle, Throckmorton thought it was an obvious trick to capture the *Warrior*'s boat. Further raising his suspicions was Black Hawk's refusal to come out to the *Warrior* in one of his canoes. Throckmorton responded with his cannon. The men on the shore fired back with their muskets. The soldiers aboard the *Warrior* and Black Hawk's men spent the next hour firing across the water at each other. When the *Warrior* began to run low on firewood for her boiler, Throckmorton weighed anchor and returned south to Fort Crawford. One of the soldiers aboard took a musket ball in the leg. Throckmorton reported twenty-three killed on the shore. Considering that none of his people ever set foot on dry land, that number seems dubious.

The following day, Atkinson launched his thirteen hundred men against the bloodied remnants of Black Hawk's force. His command had been strengthened by the arrival of four hundred regulars under Colonel Zachary Taylor. This would be twenty-seven-year-old Robert Anderson's first taste of combat.

Caught between the river and the enemy, the outnumbered Sauk and Mesquakie did not stand much chance. As they had done at the Battle of Wisconsin Heights, Black Hawk's men attempted to fight a holding action as the rest escaped across the river. Unfortunately for Black Hawk's people, the *Warrior* returned to block their escape.

Atkinson lost 7 men killed and 17 wounded. Their opponents lost 150 killed and 40 captured. The number killed was difficult to determine as many were shot trying to swim the river. Most of those who did make it across were hunted down and killed by America's Sioux allies. Of the prisoners taken on the battlefield, all but one were women and children. Black Hawk was spared those fates temporarily as he was away searching for aid when the final battle took place. Black Hawk turned himself in to the Ho-Chunk chief, Decori, who later claimed to have captured Black Hawk.

Among the wounded and dead were a mother and her child. A musket ball passed through the infant's arm and killed the mother. It was from her dead arms that Anderson plucked the child. The army surgeon saved the child's life but not the arm. Many newspapers published the account of Anderson and the child, a little bit of humanity in an otherwise brutal story.[17]

Anderson was not just upset about the death and destruction. He was also disappointed that war was not like what he had studied at West Point. He complained to his brother Larz that the Sauk and Mesquakie "are only seen when they raise to fire upon you or to fly." To Anderson, it was not "worthy" of being called a fight.[18]

The misery of the battle and "the suffering of the inhabitants on the frontier" left him depressed about frontier warfare. It did not sour him on his chosen profession, however. The Black Hawk War was a boost to his career. He was now a combat veteran with letters of commendation from his general.

From the battlefield, Atkinson's army moved to Dixon's Ferry. It was now Anderson's job to muster the volunteers out of service. Detailed reports had to be kept so that men could be paid. Atkinson returned to St. Louis. When Scott arrived at Fort Armstrong, everything was his responsibility. Atkinson sent Anderson to the new commander with dispatches and a transfer to Scott's command.

Scott placed Anderson in charge of the prisoners. In this capacity, it was his job to travel to Fort Crawford and take possession of Black Hawk and other high-ranking prisoners being held by Colonel Taylor. Anderson and a small detachment of guards were carried north on the *Warrior.* Unfortunately, Scott had not escaped cholera. He had brought it with him. Within a day of setting out, the symptoms of the dreaded disease began to appear among the soldiers on the *Warrior.* Anderson did his best for his men. The *Warrior* put into the Gelena River. Anderson took a small boat to the town. The local doctor had served in the war and gladly returned with Anderson to minister to the soldiers.[19]

By the time the party reached Fort Crawford, Anderson was sick. He did not distance himself from his sick men as other officers would have. According to William Clark—the former explorer, a relative of Anderson's, and Indian commissioner for the region—in a letter to Scott, Anderson nursed his sick men day and night.[20] Colonel Taylor discharged his prisoners to Anderson's custody. Taylor assigned his assistant to aid Anderson on his mission. Colonel Taylor was probably relieved to send his adjutant Jefferson Davis away as the young lieutenant was becoming too friendly with his daughter.

When Davis and Anderson returned to Fort Armstrong, cholera was raging. Nearly twenty men had already died. Scott sent the *Warrior* and its passengers to Jefferson Barracks. After Black Hawk, William Clark, and General Atkinson agreed to terms, Black Hawk was sent on his famous tour of the East Coast cities and his meeting with the great war chief, Andrew Jackson.

On his return to the St. Louis Arsenal, a still-sick Anderson continued to take care of his men with cholera. A few years after leaving St. Louis, a dozen German immigrants who served under him wrote a letter thanking Anderson for "the care, humanity, and kindness" he showed them and "the benevolent manner he took care of them."[21] The disease eventually ran its course. Anderson and his men returned to the daily routine of duty at the arsenal. The excitement of the Black Hawk War was finished. However, contrary to his wishes, Anderson was not done with frontier warfare.

CHAPTER 5

THE FLORIDA WAR

A fter the conclusion of the Black Hawk War, First Lieutenant Robert Anderson spent another year at the St. Louis Arsenal. He was twenty-seven years old, and friends and fellow officers were getting married while the first streaks of gray were showing in his black hair. He complained to his sister that he met "many charming ladies," but before he could make up his mind, other men swept in "to marry without courting." Of course, part of his difficulties may have come from the promise to his mother only to marry a woman from Virginia or Kentucky.[1]

In May 1833, the army sent Anderson to Washington, DC, to serve as acting adjutant general of subsistence. It was not the type of position that won glory and honor. Nor was it a position that made one popular with his fellow officers. Officers often had to pay out of their pockets for equipment, food, and other necessities and then seek reimbursement from the army. It was one of Anderson's duties to approve or disapprove these requests. It was a necessary position, and Anderson did his service without complaint. He wrote many letters in his career to this same office, requesting reimbursement. It was only temporary duty, and after a year of pushing papers, he was again with an artillery company.[2]

While in the nation's capital, Anderson paid a courtesy call on an old family friend, President Andrew Jackson. Jackson's office was crowded, and the president was extremely busy with his other visitors when Anderson arrived. Anderson wrote to his brother-in-law that the president "looked well and in better spirits than I expected to find him, hourly and constantly harassed as he is."[3]

How closely Anderson followed politics at this point, we do not know. He rarely discussed politics in his letters to friends and family. Most likely, his political leanings were Whiggish. His father had been an old Federalist, his eldest brother served with John Quincy Adams, and his other brothers would be staunch Republicans when that party formed. His professional associations also spoke of Whiggery. Like any national organization, the army tended to support the political party that favored a strong central government.[4] The men who would be Anderson's mentors during his career, Winfield Scott and Duncan Clinch, were leading Whig politicians.

At the end of 1833, Anderson received orders to report to Fort Constitution near Portsmouth, New Hampshire. The twenty-year-old masonry fort was the latest fortification defending Portsmouth and the Piscataqua River, dating back to the mid-seventeenth century. Unless war broke out with a European power, there was little chance there would be any action. He was second in command over thirty enlisted men. Anderson's adversaries were boredom and the weather. He exchanged many letters with his family, always ending his letters with a request for more mail. The winters on the North Atlantic coast were like nothing like the Kentuckian had ever seen. The fort was too far away from the town for Anderson to take part in the town's social life. He traveled to Portsmouth on Sundays as Jackson had made that day a holiday for the entire army as part of his military reforms. Although Anderson would always be a strong supporter of the rights and welfare of the enlisted men, he had doubts about that particular reform. There was not much to do on Sundays in Portsmouth as the service at the Congregationalist Church could take all day. As a child of the frontier, where they could only make it to church at best once a month, a weekly service seemed odd to Anderson. It bothered him that the New Englanders thought they were better Christians because of it.[5] As the son of an early temperance supporter, Anderson was probably happy to see the whiskey ration replaced with coffee and sugar.

Before he had spent an entire year in New Hampshire, Anderson's application to transfer to West Point had been accepted. He arrived in 1835 as the Academy's assistant artillery instructor. It was a lesser position than Mahan had offered him, but it was also only temporary. Little had changed since Anderson had been a cadet. His duties included classroom and field instruction and commanding the handful of enlisted artillerymen stationed at West Point. In December, Z. D. Kinsley, the instructor of artillery, resigned his commission for a civilian teaching position, making Anderson the senior instructor. Anderson had taken the position with the idea of learning from Kinsley and now had to teach himself advanced artillery as he taught his cadets the basics. Among those students were George Meade of Gettysburg fame; George Thomas, the Rock of Chickamauga; William T. Sherman; and P. G. T. Beauregard, who would face Anderson across the battle lines at Charleston Harbor in 1861.[6]

The year 1838 would bring an end to Anderson's time at West Point. His prior record and professional connections could have landed him almost any position he wanted. Per a new US law, Anderson could have served in a more comfortable staff position while still gaining seniority with his regiment, truly the best of both worlds. General Scott, among others, suggested that Anderson take advantage of this option. Anderson, however, strongly believed that it was in the army's best interest that officers did not spend too much time away from their regiments. This was especially true since he had been promoted to captain. He would command a company, and his place should be with his men because "as experience has shown none but the captain feels that interest and pride in the welfare and condition of the company which are essential to make the soldiers contented and efficient."[7] Returning to his company meant Florida and war. He was offered another term at West Point. The army saw Anderson as an officer too valuable to send to the swamps. That his company would be in harm's way only strengthened his belief that their captain should be with them. Unlike Anderson, many officers resigned their commissions to avoid service in Florida, a crisis that some members of Congress used to question the necessity of a military academy.

Orders were issued, and Anderson was recalled to the Third Artillery. He would have to fight another frontier war. Company D, Third Artillery, was already near the New River Settlement, the future location of Fort Lauderdale. By 1837, the war had been raging for almost two years. More than two hundred US soldiers had been killed, out of force of under seventy-five hundred men, including members of the Third Artillery and classmates from the Academy.[8]

The origins of the conflict are complex and controversial. The Seminoles arrived in Florida in the late eighteenth century. They were mainly from the Creek Nation, who moved south from Alabama, Georgia, and Tennessee because they favored an alliance with Spain over Britain. Not all Seminoles were former Creeks. There was a large group of what were called Black Seminoles. In 1835, there may have been over a thousand Seminoles of African descent. Their origins were diverse, from those who escaped from white owners and sought refuge with the Seminoles to those stolen in raids into Georgia and Alabama and even a small minority purchased by the Seminoles. There were even those descended from freedmen from the early Spanish period.[9]

When Florida became US territory in 1821, problems between settlers and Seminoles began almost instantly. The Seminoles were successful cattle ranchers, having adopted the herds left behind by the departing Spaniards. Questions of ownership caused many conflicts. Slave raiders kidnapped Black Seminoles. Although there were many runaway slaves with the Seminoles, these slave catchers rarely cared if they got the right person. When Seminoles entered a white settlement, it was common for an unscrupulous merchant to ply the unwary Seminole with liquor. When the poor Seminole awoke the next day from his drunken stupor, he would be informed that he had sold his musket and his horse, a Seminole man's most important possessions, for a few drinks. The aggrieved Seminole, in return, would steal cattle or horses from the nearest homestead to recoup his losses. This set off an ugly chain reaction that did not end well for anyone.[10]

It became evident to the Florida territorial government that a buffer was needed between the Seminoles and the large number of white settlers streaming into the territory if widespread violence was to be prevented. The United States initially attempted to create a Seminole reservation in the southern part of the peninsula.

The 1823 Treaty of Moultrie Creek was doomed to failure for many reasons. Mainly, Seminole leadership spoke for and had as much control over their people as the federal government had over the settlers flooding into Florida. The Seminoles discovered they did not particularly like their new land, and paying the promised funds was not a priority of the US Congress.

However, in 1830, another solution presented itself. While Robert Anderson was still in Baton Rouge, the nation was absorbed in the debate over a new law. An Act to Provide for an Exchange of Lands with the Indians Residing in any of the States or Territories and for the Removal West of the River Mississippi was more commonly known as the Indian Removal Act. The law was another tool to push the Amerindians further west. Although it continued a pattern established with the first European settlers to the New World, the Indian Removal Act has been inaccurately portrayed as a turning point in history as opposed to a continuation. The policy had and would continue to lead to conflicts that fell to the US Army to fight.

Anderson's opinion of Indian removal was most likely mixed. He grew up on the frontier, raised by an old Indian fighter, in a house specifically designed to withstand a siege. It is unlikely that he left Kentucky without some negative feelings toward Indians. However, Anderson would later write with sympathy toward the Natives and their fate, especially after his experience with Black Hawk. He was also sympathetic to the plight of the settlers in that conflict. Perhaps he felt like many that a buffer between the two groups would be better for all.

The strongest argument that Anderson was against the law was his party affiliation. When Congress voted in favor of the bill, it was strictly along party lines. Regardless of region, the Democratic Party solidly supported removal, while the Whigs were firmly opposed even in the South and West.

The law, as written, could be viewed as innocent enough. It authorized the president to trade unowned land in the West for Native American–owned land on the condition that Natives resettle on their new land. The law promised that the western land would be "forever secure" for "their heirs or successors." There was no mention in the bill of using force or punishment if the Native nations refused to bargain. That its opponents so bitterly opposed its passage showed that there was much more to the bill than what was written on the page. They correctly predicted that Jackson and the state governments would use the law to commit abuse and fraud. Government officials, federal and state, misled or threatened Indian leaders. As well, Indian signatories often traded land that was not theirs to exchange. Federal agents were often willing accomplices, and the Democratic Congress ratified the treaties with little concern over such legal niceties.

In Florida, the US government put forward a treaty that called for the Seminoles to rejoin the Creek Nation in modern Oklahoma. Relations between the Creeks and Seminoles had only deteriorated since their split. The treaty of Payne's Landing allowed a delegation of Seminole leaders to travel west to inspect the land and speak to Creek leaders. In either poor planning or an abundance of honesty, the seven Seminole chiefs were taken to Oklahoma in the middle of winter, not the best time to sell Oklahoma real estate. While in the West, the chiefs signed the Treaty of Fort Gibson, which was highly problematic. Signing a new agreement was not the reason these men traveled to Oklahoma. What had been decided in Florida was that they would inspect the land, meet with Creek leaders in the area, and then report back to a conference of Seminole chiefs—who then, and only then, would decide. Now the United States had a treaty that stated all Seminoles had agreed to accept the terms of Payne's Landing. When the delegation returned to Florida, they quickly distanced themselves from the agreement. They claimed they were lied to or pressured, or the signatures were forgeries. That the agent who oversaw the trip was later removed from his post for embezzlement speaks volumes.

The underhanded methods of achieving the final agreement soured most Seminoles on the deal and sabotaged any hope of convincing them to accept the move without force. Another obstacle to Seminole acceptance of the treaty was the future of the Black Seminoles. The Black Seminoles feared whites would attempt to reclaim former slaves during the move or that the Creek would claim them as their own property. Regardless of the issues with the Treaty of Fort Gibson and the lack of acceptance among the Seminole people, the US Congress ratified the treaty. The Seminoles were now required to leave Florida by January 1836.

General Duncan Clinch, Anderson's former commander, was in charge of all US troops in Florida. It was his responsibility to move the Seminoles by force if need be. Clinch was a Florida landowner and veteran of many years in the area. He fought in the First Seminole War in 1817–1818. Clinch understood the Seminoles' fears. He also knew the influence of the Black Seminoles. He pleaded with the government to address Seminole concerns but to no avail. Clinch also tried hard to convince the Seminoles that they must agree to a mass movement by the spring 1836.

As the deadline approached, it was becoming obvious that although some Seminoles were preparing to leave, the younger leaders and their people would not be forced out without a fight. Warriors sent their women and children to the safety of the deep woods, which was not a good sign. Violence throughout the region grew. Small settlers and isolated sugar plantations were attacked. General Clinch began preparing the Florida territory for war. Part of Clinch's preparations was to move the majority of the garrison from Fort King, near modern Ocala, to his own plantation twenty miles away. As the men fortified what was now Fort Drane, only one hundred men defended Fort King. A company of the Third Artillery, under the command of Major Francis Langhorne Dade, was ordered to march north from Fort Brooke on Tampa Bay to reinforce the weakened Fort King.

Seminole warriors, under the combined leadership of Halpatter Tustenuggee, Osceola, and Ote Emathla, devised an audacious three-pronged attack against US forces. If successful, they hoped to convince the United States that Seminole land would not be worth the cost. The plan was to ambush Dade's men as they marched north, surprise and overrun Fort King, and lure Clinch and his command into the field and an ambush. Clinch was successfully lured into battle, but the Seminoles were not able to defeat his forces. Nor were they able to overrun Fort King—although they had partial success in killing Wiley Thomas, the government agent who had helped craft the removal treaties. The real success came against Dade. He and the 107 men of his command were about fifty miles south of Fort King when they marched into an ambush by almost 200 Seminoles. Dade's command held out for almost four hours, long enough to construct a triangular breastwork out of pine trees and bring their six-pounder cannon into action. It was not enough. The Seminoles killed all but two men, who survived only because they were left for dead. The United States and the Seminole Nation were now at war. President Jackson ordered to the front Winfield Scott with nine companies of regulars.[11]

Robert "Buck" Buchanan, a friend and fellow West Point graduate, wrote Anderson just after news of the Dade Massacre reached the rest of the country. Buchanan was one of the few people, if not the only person, who called Robert Anderson "Bob." As did most officers of the old army, Buck's and Bob's careers would cross paths many times from West Point to the Civil War. Although Buchanan's career spanned more than forty years and he was in every major battle fought by the Army of the Potomac, he is mostly remembered as the strict disciplinarian who drove Ulysses Grant from the army in 1853.

Buchanan called the death of Dade and his men a "wanton sacrifice of valuable lives to the mean niggardly policy of the government." In this conflict and others, it was a common opinion in the army that Congress's attempts to save money left the army unprepared when war came. Men like themselves, the men and officers with Dade, paid the cost. Anderson echoed this opinion in a letter to his mother: "In our Indian warfare, how shameful that inadequate preparations had been made to put down at once the threatened hostilities. Oh no, we must keep quiet until the blood of our butchered brothers and the defenseless families call aloud for vengeance, and then, and not until then, do we put on our armor and repair valiantly to the blood-stained field." Buchanan was stationed in New Orleans and was preparing to be shipped to Florida. His role would be similar to Anderson's in the Black Hawk War, swearing in volunteers to federal service.[12]

The Dade Massacre was the topic of conversation at West Point. The Seminoles had killed friends and former classmates. If the war lasted long enough, new graduates would be sent there, and instructors would get a new duty assignment when their tours at the Academy were done. However, few people at the Academy would have given Florida much thought beyond sympathy for the fallen and professional curiosity. The idea that the conflict would last long enough for anyone not currently assigned to the Southeast to see action there was ludicrous. The great General Winfield Scott was on his way to Florida with regular infantry, and volunteer units from Southern states would soon pour into Florida. The Seminoles could not last long under so much pressure.

The belief was that the Seminoles stood even less chance than Black Hawk had. That was not what happened. The US military was facing its longest, most costly Indian war. Initially, the American strategy had been to fight a major battle that would convince the Seminoles to accept their fate. It was a strategy with a history of success. It was the strategy of Anthony Wayne at Fallen Timbers, Andrew Jackson at Horseshoe Bend, and most recently Henry Atkinson at Bad Ax. The Seminoles refused to add their name to the list. After destroying Dade's force and fighting Clinch on the Withlacoochee, the Seminoles adopted hit-and-run tactics. They went where the army was not. They struck sugar plantations, army supply wagons, isolated farmsteads, and even the occasional lighthouse.

Scott grew frustrated at his inability to bring a sizeable force of Seminoles to battle. Nothing in his experience or training, nor that of his West Point–trained subordinates, prepared him to fight a guerilla war. Realizing there was no glory or potential for advancement in Florida, he passed command to the territorial governor of Florida, Richard Keith Call. Governor Call was a veteran of the Battle of Horseshoe Bend, the decisive battle of the Creek Indian War. He continued unsuccessfully to try to bring the Seminoles to a similar battle.

When it became clear that the war was not helping his political career, Call passed command back to the Regulars. Brigadier General Thomas S. Jesup assumed control of all US and volunteer troops in Florida. A native of Virginia, Jesup enlisted in the army in 1808. During the War of 1812, he quickly rose through the ranks. Jesup was with Scott in the famous Battle of Chippewa, where he was wounded multiple times. He ended the war as a colonel and was promoted to general three years later.

In 1818, Secretary of War John C. Calhoun made Jesup quartermaster general of the US Army. Jesup reorganized and modernized the Quartermaster Corps, earning the nickname "Father of the Quartermaster Corps." As so many of the army's problems in Florida were logistical, Jesup was a good choice. His entry into the conflict marked a significant shift in American strategy. He also made some controversial decisions. His first was recruiting five hundred Creek and Cherokee militiamen from Georgia and Alabama. Although they would prove helpful in the war—considering that one of the Seminole's major concerns was the fact they were being forced to rejoin the Creek Nation—bringing the Creek into the conflict may not have been the wisest idea.

Although General Jesup's preferred strategy was to compromise with the Seminoles, his orders were clear: the Seminoles were to be removed, leaving him little room to negotiate. Instead, his strategy was to drive the Seminoles south. There would be as many as nine columns moving simultaneously, a very complex undertaking in the days when armies communicated by messenger.[13] Once he drove the Seminoles into the Everglades, the army would take up a defensive line, trapping them in that great swamp. At that point, the Seminoles' only options were starvation, surrender, or fighting the battle the US Army had long been trying to instigate.

Jesup's strategy was already in effect when, in November 1837, Anderson received his orders to report to the Florida Territory. He took the usual ferry from West Point down the Hudson to New York City and then a ship south to the growing river town of Jacksonville. From there, he took one of the Army's steamboats up the slow-moving St. John's River. His blue wool uniform would have been comfortable on the river in early January. Soldiers and equipment headed toward the front lines crowded the boat. On reaching Lake George, the men and equipment were unloaded and continued the rest of the trip by wagon and horseback, and on foot.[14]

The new year of 1838 found Lieutenant Anderson in an area very different from his boyhood home. On January 5, Anderson recorded on a small pocket

calendar that they passed the remnants of Fort McNeil, a couple of small buildings surrounded by a wooden stockade. It was abandoned only ten days after
its completion. A scouting party discovered that the fort was only three miles
from the navigable southern end of the St. John's River. A waterfront location
was a preferable place to build a fort. Fort McNeil was replaced by Fort Taylor,
a few miles southeast. It was not yet finished when Anderson arrived. Commanding the fort and overseeing its construction was Lieutenant Henry W.
Fowler. Anderson was able to practice some of the engineering skills he had
learned as a cadet. He spent a couple of days overseeing construction of the
fort's wharf.[15]

After a couple of days of construction work, Anderson got his first taste of
war in Florida. Fowler led Anderson and the men of the First and Third Artillery on an eight-day trek through cypress swamps. Besides alligators, cougars,
mud, and the cypress roots that make travel so difficult over that country, the
column saw nothing. The terrain tore their clothing to shreds, and the wet
conditions destroyed their leather shoes. The men arrived at their destination
barefoot and in rags.

On January 16, they arrived at the recently completed Fort Floyd. Anderson's
fellow Kentuckian Zachary Taylor built it about twenty miles north of Lake
Okeechobee. They continued the trek and camped at the site of Colonel Taylor's
victory at the Battle of Lake Okeechobee. Taylor's force of over a thousand men
had fought a Seminole party of about four hundred led by Halpatter Tustenuggee and Holata Micco, or Alligator and Billy Bowlegs as they were known to
the Americans. Although the battle would make Taylor a national figure and
be hailed in the press as an American victory, the Seminoles had achieved the
desired effect of bleeding the American force at a small cost to themselves.[16]

The small group continued eastward to join General Jesup. He had pulled
together a force of more than fifteen hundred men at Jupiter Inlet. Included in
this large force were nearly four hundred men of the Third Artillery under the
command of Colonel William Gates. Anderson commanded one of the five
companies of the Third. Six hundred US Army dragoons were under Colonel
Willam S. Harney, and five hundred Tennessee and Alabama volunteers were
under Major William Lauderdale. There were also just under a hundred Delaware and Shawnee warriors.[17]

On the morning of January 24, 1838, thirty mounted dragoons operating as
scouts in front of Jesup's main force were fired upon by Seminoles concealed in
a large wooded piece of high ground next to the Loxahatchee Creek. The situation was very similar to the one faced by Colonel Taylor a few weeks earlier. The
Seminoles had chosen an excellent defensive position and lured the American
army into an attack. The dragoons initially dismounted to offer battle to the

Seminoles led by Abiaka, known as Sam Jones. Although outnumbered, Captain William Fulton and his dragoons carried the new Colt carbines. With the ability to fire six .52-caliber bullets as fast as a man could pull the trigger, they were confident they could hold their position.[18]

When the dragoons realized the numbers they were facing and that Abiaka was deploying his men to surround and cut off their small number, they fell back four miles to the main body. Jesup, like Taylor the month before, rushed his men forward. After years of pursuit, the US Army would oblige when the Seminoles were willing to give battle.

The Seminole position was surrounded by deep undergrowth, swamp, and the Loxahatchee Creek. Abiaka had massed his force at the one ford that provided the only access to the Seminoles' location. Although most of the artillerymen were being used as red-legged infantry, so-called for the red stripe on their uniform pants designating them as artillery, there was artillery in the battle. From across the creek, members of the Third fired a twelve-pounder howitzer, designed to be dismantled and carried by pack horses, a cumbersome six-pounder, and Congreve rockets. Made famous for their "red glare" during the defense of Fort McHenry, Congreve rockets were adopted by the army for use in Florida. An individual rocket weighed only twenty-four pounds and needed just a fifteen-foot guide pole to launch it, giving it the appearance of a giant bottle rocket. They were much easier to move through the Florida woods than a nine-hundred-pound cannon, but the rockets were not nearly as effective. They were a psychological weapon, and there are no recorded instances of them causing any casualties.[19]

On this day, the artillery was used to good effect, driving the Seminoles back from their original position. The main body was now behind a thirty-foot section of the creek. While the artillery still fired their cannon and rockets toward an enemy they could not see, the mounted Tennesseans and Colonel William S. Harney's dragoons attempted to cross. When the Tennesseans reached the water's edge, the Seminoles launched a volley of fire into them. The volunteers wavered and began to fall back. At this point, General Jesup rode to the front, dismounted, and waved his pistol in the air to rally the troops. He might have been successful had he not been shot in the face. Fortunately for the general, it was a minor wound. The musket ball struck his eyeglasses and glanced across his left cheek. Jesup calmly picked up his broken glasses and followed the volunteers to the rear.[20]

Harney and his dragoons pushed forward. The creek was deeper than they had supposed, and they were forced to swim across under fire. The cartridges in the cylinders of their new Colt carbines were ruined by the time they had crossed through the black swamp water. The Seminoles, however, did not know that and began to fall back as the dragoons emerged from the water. The Seminoles disappeared into the vegetation, and the battle was over as quickly as it had begun.

Anderson and Lieutenant William Davidson led a company of the Third Artillery in pursuit of the Seminoles for several miles with no success. Although Davidson survived the Battle of Loxahatchee without a scratch, he was one of many of Anderson's fellow West Pointers who would not survive the war.

In one of the largest battles of the Second Seminole War, Jesup had lost nine men with another twenty-nine wounded. Three of the wounded were from the Third. As usual, Seminole casualties were unknown beyond the single body found on the battlefield.

Between the wounded and the need to resupply, Jesup's army was in no position to continue the pursuit of the Seminoles. They returned to Jupiter Inlet, five miles away, where the navy could supply them. Most of Jesup's command was on the wrong side of the creek. Once again, Anderson had a chance to practice his engineering skills, as he was tasked with building a bridge across the Loxahatchee. He carried the job out quickly, and by the twenty-sixth, Jesup's command was on the shore of the Atlantic Ocean. That evening, the navy arrived with food and other supplies, and carried the seriously wounded to St. Augustine. The remaining men began the construction of Fort Jupiter.

Jesup's strategy was beginning to bear fruit. On February 7, two important chiefs, Halleck Hajo and Tuskegee, came forward under a white flag to discuss terms. Jesup proposed that if the Seminoles remained in the southernmost end of Florida, they could stay in the territory. This was a suggestion made to Jesup by his senior officers after the Battle of Loxahatchee. Jesup and many officers felt they had driven the Seminoles onto land no one else wanted. Further, fighting seemed an unnecessary waste of lives.

The proposition was agreeable to the Seminoles. Now Jesup had to sell the idea to his superiors. He sat at his field desk and wrote to the secretary of war as Fort Jupiter was constructed around him. Jesup's aide, Lieutenant Thomas B. Linnard, carried the message to Washington. There was little to do but wait for his return. Construction was completed on Fort Jupiter. If Washington accepted Jesup's plan, the fort would be an important post, sitting on the northern edge of Seminole land. Supplies arrived, including several barrels of shoes to replace the ones that had disintegrated during the long marches through the cypress swamps.

Even though Jesup had a poor record of honoring the white flag, the Seminoles trusted his truce and moved their camp near Fort Jupiter. Nearly six hundred Seminoles and more than a thousand soldiers waited together for the response from President Martin Van Buren. Jesup's officers were invited to attend Seminole celebrations as long as they provided the alcohol. It seems extremely unlikely that Anderson took as active a role in the festivities as the younger officers. His dignity as an army officer, an Episcopalian, and a Kentucky gentleman would have prevented that. He did use the opportunity of their proximity to learn a little Muscogee and Mikasuki, the languages the Seminoles spoke. To Anderson's credit, he understood that pointing at an object and asking *Noikte* (What's that) might not produce the most accurate results.[21]

A distraction more appealing to the professional-minded Anderson was the arrival of the twenty-two-year-old inventor and industrialist Samuel Colt. The war had temporarily saved his company. Colt brought samples of his new pistol, which he hoped to sell to the army. A firing range was set up, and the officers were allowed to try the revolvers. Opinions were mixed, with most not quite sure about the new technology compared to the reliable single-shot muzzleloader Model 1805, the standard army sidearm since before most of them were born.[22]

On March 17, after more than a month of waiting, official word arrived from Secretary of War Joel Poinsett. The reaction was not what Jesup and his officers had hoped for. According to Poinsett, the army's job was to carry out the wishes of Congress and the president, not to judge the quality of the land. He also made it clear that a failure to remove the Seminoles was the professional failing of Jesup. The general called a council with the Seminole leadership. They must have predicted the response, as none appeared. As he had done with Osceola previously in the war, Jesup decided to violate the truce and seize the Seminoles before they disappeared again into the wilderness. Colonel David Twiggs and his Second Dragoons captured 151 warriors and more than 350 noncombatants. Considering Jesup's reputation, that the Seminoles were not prepared for this seems to show that these Seminoles, at least, were resigned to their fate.[23]

More US forces arrived in the area for what Jesup believed would be mopping up operations. Unlike the Black Hawk War, there would be no final event that marked the end of the Second Seminole War. Holatoochee informed Jesup there were fewer than two hundred warriors at large. He even agreed to go into the woods to convince Alligator, Halpetter Tustenuggee, to submit. This he successfully did. Alligator and more than one hundred of his followers surrendered.

The end was in sight, but the war continued for another four years. Abiaka and Arpeika were reportedly in the Everglades along the New River, south of Jesup's position at Fort Jupiter. Abiaka—Sam Jones as he was known to Florida's white settlers, or the Devil as the soldiers called him—was among the few senior war leaders still in the field and had been a pain in Jesup's side since he first took command.

Jesup sent Lieutenant Colonel James Bankhead with six hundred men of the First and Fourth Artillery and two hundred Tennessee volunteers commanded by Major William Lauderdale. They were preceded by a force of sailors and soldiers in boats under Lieutenant Levi Powell of the US Navy. The soldiers were Company D of the Third Artillery, commanded by Anderson. Powell was a veteran of swamp warfare.

The area was suffering from a drought, which made travel more difficult. The water became too shallow for the men to ride in the boats but still too wet and muddy to walk. The men loaded their equipment into the boats and shoved them through the muck and the aptly named sawgrass. The dirty, miserable group had not traveled far when they discovered the Seminoles' trail leading to a piece of high ground. Powell sent word back to Bankhead, who brought his force up in the same deliberate manner. It was no place for horses.[24]

On March 22, 1838, the force of nearly eight hundred men reached the Seminole's encampment. It was a position very similar to the one they had taken at the Battle of Lake Okeechobee and the recent Battle of Loxahatchee. Colonel Bankhead unfurled the white flag in order to offer Sam Jones a chance to surrender. The Seminole leader responded by firing at the flag bearer. Bankhead began to deploy his troops for battle. In a textbook move, he kept a third of his force in the center to hold the Seminoles in place while the rest of his men attempted to move around the flanks. Powell, Anderson, and their men were given the right flank. The water was deeper here, and they could use the boats. As soon as they were in rifle range, the Seminoles fired on them. Powell responded with one of the four-pounder cannons mounted in the bows of his boats. The Seminoles, seeing Bankhead's strategy, withdrew before they could be surrounded. They left behind twenty good canoes, gunpowder, and cooked provisions.[25]

After making the military's first incursion into the Everglades, a place the Seminoles believed the army could not operate, Bankhead and his men returned to Fort Jupiter. Powell returned to Fort Dallas, the future site of Miami. Waiting for Anderson were orders from Jesup to travel to Fort Lauderdale with his company.

At Fort Lauderdale, Anderson and his men spent the next week completing work on the post's walls.[26] As they labored in the South Florida sun, a major change occurred in the command of the Army of the South. Jesup asked to be relieved of duty. As the size of the Seminoles opposing them shrank, so would Jesup's command. With the yellow fever and malaria season beginning and the command no longer requiring a general officer, it made sense to pass the command to a junior officer. Colonel Zachary Taylor, who had received much praise from the press for his victory at the Battle of Lake Okeechobee, was now in command. To prevent complications with state forces, Taylor was given the brevet rank of brigadier general.

As Jesup waited for the slow bureaucracy of the War Department to finalize his request, he continued his pursuit of Sam Jones. He ordered Lieutenant Colonel Harney to pursue him into the Everglades. With two hundred men, Harney traveled overland from Jupiter Inlet sixty miles south to Fort Lauderdale. Harney learned from a Seminole who had surrendered that Sam Jones's camp could be reached easiest from south of the Miami River. Harney, having no respect for volunteers, took only army regulars with him to Fort Dallas, including Anderson. Harney's Dragoons, armed with the new Colt carbines, traveled by steamer to the mouth of the Miami. Anderson and the artillery company, on horseback and armed with the standard army muskets, traveled overland fifteen miles to the rendezvous.[27]

It was a wet trip. They had to cross much swampy land and swim the horses across at least one river. At Fort Dallas, on the New River, they camped at Richard Fitzpatrick's sugar plantation. The army occupied the plantation throughout the war. Anderson took a special interest in what was growing. Besides sugar, Fitzpatrick had many acres of tropical fruit trees. The plantation was a turnkey business. Fitzpatrick spent most of his time in Key West and the territorial capital, Tallahassee.[28] A plantation was an investment that would allow an army officer to increase his wealth while still serving his country. Anderson had many models. Zachary Taylor owned a sizeable plantation in Louisiana, and Anderson's future father-in-law, Clinch, owned plantations in north Florida and South Georgia.

There were not enough small boats at Fort Dallas to carry his entire force. Harney, Anderson, and nearly one hundred other men sailed south in fifteen boats, hugging the coastline. The forty-eight dragoons and fifty-five artillerymen searched for signs of recent Seminole activity. After sailing about twenty miles, they discovered tracks leading southwest into the interior. Harney led the men on foot into a mangrove swamp. After about two hours of trudging in the tropical heat, they found Sam Jones's camp in a stand of pine trees. According to Harney's report, there were seventy-five warriors and their families. Anderson's notes that there were fifteen. The men fled, leaving behind women, children, and supplies. For two and a half hours, the soldiers chased after the Seminoles, who occasionally paused to fire from the cover of a pine tree. The Seminoles outpaced the soldiers and disappeared into the wilderness. None of Harney's men were wounded, but they were all exhausted. He ordered a return to Fort Dallas. They carried back twenty-five prisoners, a wounded Seminole warrior, and souvenirs from the Seminole camp. Anderson claimed a pair of alligator-skin moccasins.[29]

The war was not nearly as close to being over as Jesup believed. He left Florida in April 1838, and the war would not end until 1842. When the United States decided to stop prosecuting the war, the situation was very similar to what it had been when Jesup suggested a truce. Several hundred Seminoles remained in the Everglades.

The army was sent to other trouble spots. A potential war with Britain brewed on the Canadian border, and the Cherokee Nation was about to be removed from its traditional homeland. Anderson would soon see service on both fronts.

CHAPTER 6

TRAGEDY AND
DIPLOMATIC TRAINING

On May 11, 1838, Brevet Captain Robert Anderson received orders to join General Winfield Scott in another campaign of Indian removal. From Key Biscayne, Anderson traveled on mail and supply boats to St. Augustine. The little craft hugged the coast, and Anderson complained about being "nearly tormented to death by flies."[1] On May 16, he arrived in the city, an old Spanish settlement, which must have reminded him of his time in Colombia.

From St. Augustine, he caught a ship and was in Charleston in two days. From there, he began to move west to take part in the infamous Trail of Tears. On June 16, 1838, he reached Athens, Tennessee, General Scott's headquarters and the site of the Eastern Division of the Cherokee Agency. Scott had arrived a month earlier. His orders were to remove the Cherokee from their traditional homeland in Tennessee, North Carolina, Georgia, and Alabama. Anderson was one of Scott's four aides-de-camp: two regulars and two volunteers. Scott had roughly seven thousand men, regulars, and volunteers to complete his mission of moving more than fifteen thousand Cherokee to the Indian territory.

Like the Seminoles, the Cherokees were the victims of a flawed treaty. In the Treaty of New Echota, the US government paid five million dollars for all Cherokee land in the Southeast. It had been negotiated and signed by twenty Cherokees with no legitimate authority to speak for the Cherokee Nation.

Although long the victims of land-hungry settlers, the Cherokee resisted differently from the Seminoles. Since their first contact with Europeans, the Cherokee had adopted many aspects of Western culture, at least those they saw as an improvement. They had adopted a written language, which they used to write a constitution and publish a newspaper. Instead of taking up arms, as did so many other groups, the leadership of the Cherokee took their grievances to the courts. Cases against the state of Georgia and the federal government slowly made their way to the US Supreme Court. Here, Anderson's cousin, Chief Justice John Marshall, disappointed the Cherokees' hope for justice. The Cherokee Nation had the dubious honor of being victimized by all the branches of the federal government, not to mention the state of Georgia. On the orders of President Martin Van Buren, it was now up to Scott, Anderson, and the army to forcibly move them west.

It was not a proud moment in US history or for the army. It was also a low point in Winfield Scott's and Anderson's military careers. On May 10, 1838, Scott issued two orders that launched what has come to be known as the Trail of Tears. Scott first issued a message to the Cherokee people. He asked them, especially the leaders and warriors, to peacefully accept the situation. He also placed the blame for the current situation on the Cherokee. According to Scott, they had two years to prepare and had done nothing toward that goal. Now they would have to be on the move before the month was over.[2]

Scott next issued an order to the army and the state volunteer units under his command, spelling out the situation. Fifteen thousand Cherokee were to be moved west, four-fifths of whom "are opposed or have become averse to a distant immigration, and although none are in actual hostilities with the United States or threaten a resistance by arms, yet the troops will probably be obliged to cover the whole country they inhabit, in order to make prisoners and to march or to transport the prisoners." Scott continued with strict instructions to his officers and men to carry out their duty with kindness and humanity. Scott took this stance because he respected the Cherokee "for the advances they have made in Christianity and Civilization." He also predicted that "acts of harshness and cruelty on the part of our troops, may lead ... to a general war and carnage," which he wanted to avoid on a humanitarian level but also because it would make the army's task much more difficult.[3] Unfortunately for most Cherokee, Scott could not enforce his humanitarian policies. The Cherokee were victimized by civilians, soldiers (regulars and volunteers), and their fellow Cherokee.

Anderson was sympathetic toward the Cherokee. As he wrote to his mother when he first arrived,

Here, what sobs are heard, what sorrows swell the heart and moisten the eyes at the idea of leaving the old family residence, the garden from which so many fragrant roses have been plucked rapidly away. These are griefs that all have felt, and some felt keenly. But they are transitory and slight when compared with those which agitate the breasts of the Cherokees. They go but not [of] their own free will and choice. The treaty under the provisions of which they are emigrated was not approved by their people, they go, compelled by stern unyielding necessity. Their homes are required by the whites, and they must seek others in a distant and strange land. With a heart susceptible to friendship and perhaps love, I cannot but feel warmly for these poor people. Would to heaven that it was in my power to aid in exciting in their bosoms the kind feelings which I entertain for them. The country to which they go has many things to render it preferable to this. And after a few years, I hope that they will be convinced that they have been benefitted by the change.[4]

A man of his time, Anderson had more sympathy for the Cherokee than he did for the Seminoles or the nations he encountered during the Black Hawk War. He saw the Cherokee as having made "considerable gains in civilization." He saw the improvement in the treatment of Cherokee women as a sign of this, as he witnessed a man tying his wife's shoe or helping her carry the children. He jokingly told his mother that although he was the only brother not yet married and gray was starting to show in his hair, she should not worry about a Cherokee daughter-in-law. His "sympathies have not taken that turn."[5]

Anderson spent this campaign at a desk, unlike in the Seminole and Black Hawk Wars, where Anderson was on the front line with the occasional musket ball whizzing a little too close past his head. Anderson was assistant adjutant general and was mostly at Eastern Division Headquarters, where he primarily dealt with procuring supplies and other logistical issues, civilian complaints, and even an accusation of murder. He could do little for that complaint but pass word forward to the accused's eventual destination.[6]

While dealing with the minutia of the unglorified task of Cherokee removal, Anderson's previous work gained him a small degree of fame in army circles that would help further his chosen career path. While at West Point, Anderson began to translate the French Army manual for field artillery. The highly technical and comprehensive document dealt with everything from how to lead horses, maintenance, maneuvering, and crossing bad ground to handling the weapons in combat. Anything a soldier needed to know about field artillery was included in its 164 pages. The project was close to the heart of the commanding general and thus good for Anderson's career. On completion, Anderson sent the translation to the War Department, where three senior artillery officers reviewed it. With minor changes to fit the American situation, the committee would adopt the French work as the official manual of the US Army. It would guide the American artillerists on the battlefields of Mexico and, with a few updates, both the Union and Confederate Armies. A few times, the manual would give him respite from the tedious work with the Cherokee. He would travel to Washington to meet with the committee, both in his role as the translator and as an active-duty artillery officer.

Anderson got his final relief from America's conflicts with its indigenous peoples when he was called to the Canadian border in 1841. In the shadow of potential war and amid angry and scared civilians, Anderson would learn lessons that would serve him in Charleston twenty years later.

The Canadian/US border between Lake Ontario and the Atlantic was an area of growing tension in the 1830s and 1840s. The American and British negotiators who drew the border in 1783 operated with flawed maps, and were not overly concerned at the time as it was a sparsely populated area of little value. By the 1830s, it was a different story. The completion of the Erie Canal and the discovery of excellent pockets of farmland created population growth on both sides. Now there was significant financial interest in exactly where the border was.

The political situation north of the border was becoming more complicated. Americans who had settled in the area brought their republican ideals with them and their distrust of the British. Even without the American presence, a natural independence streak runs in those who settle in rugged country. There was a growing push for self-rule in the region. Repeating their mistakes with the thirteen colonies to the south, Parliament responded with harsh regulations, shutting the door on any possibility of local control. Just as in 1775, the results were rebellion.

US citizens in that border country were drawn to the conflict. It was the same volunteering spirit that had brought Americans to the Texas War of Independence. Motives varied, but the plight of independent-minded people fighting a tyrant awoke the "Spirit of '76" in many, while others acted in what they saw as their country's best interest. An independent Canada might join the Union. Even if it did not, a Republic of Canada would offer strategic and economic advantages.

Rebellion broke out in November 1837. Canadian rebels and Americans launched attacks against the cities of Hamilton and Toronto. Under the Scottish-born Canadian revolutionary William Lyon Mackenzie, a small force went to Buffalo, New York, to recruit more Americans. With a promise of three hundred acres and a cash bounty, he recruited almost a thousand men and, along with some of his men, seized Navy Island, just north of Niagara Falls.

While at Navy Island, the rebel encampment was being supplied by the steamer *Caroline*. During the night of December 29, 1837, the British crossed the river, seized the *Caroline*, drove its occupants ashore, and sank the ship in the middle of the river. A bystander watching from the shore was the victim of a stray bullet during the action. The *Caroline* incident led many Americans to demand action. British troops had invaded our sovereign soil, and an

American was dead. The British action became worse in the retelling. It was not long before the death toll had risen to more than twenty-five poor souls who were sent to their deaths over Niagara Falls in the flaming wreck of the *Caroline*.[7]

The state of New York was ready for war. President Martin Van Buren, a New Yorker, did not want a conflict. While the United States had twice been victorious against Great Britain, those victories had come at a great price. The Seminoles had proven a handful for the army, and the recent Texas War of Independence might mean war with Mexico. It was no time for a conflict with the leading world power.

Van Buren sent his commanding general, Winfield Scott, to the border to prevent war. As local militias organized and governors issued orders, Scott had no legal authority to tell them to stand down. And even if he did, Scott did not have the military strength to enforce it. He was traveling only with a small staff.

To Anderson, this was General Scott's greatest moment. Within walking distance of the battlefields where Scott had proven his bravery against the British in the War of 1812, his six-feet-four-inch frame in a beautifully tailored uniform, Scott, in the overly dramatic fashion he was known for, preached the patriotic duty of peace to the militia.

The dramatics worked. War was avoided for the time being. All might have remained calm had it not been for drunken boasting in a New York bar. Alexander McCleod had been in the Canadian militia unit that had sunk the *Caroline*. In February 1841, he was in Lewiston, a small town near Niagara Falls. After a few too many drinks at the local bar, he began telling the other patrons about his role in the *Caroline* incident. The locals were impressed but not in the way McCleod had hoped. He was soon in jail with an angry mob outside and the city prosecutor preparing a case of murder against him.[8]

McCleod had unwittingly created an international incident. The British had the unenviable choice of officially announcing that the invasion of US territory and the destruction of the private property of a US citizen was a British military operation or allowing one of their citizens to be executed for murder.

Henry Fox, the British ambassador in Washington, angrily demanded that McCleod be released. To Fox, this was an issue between nations, not an issue of local jurisdiction. For President Martin Van Buren, it was a little more complicated. There were international considerations. There were also the political problems of an angry mob many Americans felt was in the right and a New York governor from the opposing party looking to use the situation to gain points against a Democratic president. Ironically the Whig governor using a stringent states' rights argument was Abraham Lincoln's future secretary of state, William Seward.[9]

General Winfield Scott during the Mexican War. Scott served as Anderson's mentor throughout his military career. Courtesy of the Library of Congress, LC-USZ62-57637.

If the situation had solely been in the professional hands of Van Buren and Prime Minister William Lamb, there would have been little chance of this turning into an armed conflict. The fear was that angry citizens, Canadian or American, would take up arms. If there was an attempt to free McLeod from the Lockport jail, either to rescue him or to dispense frontier justice, it could lead to war. The president sent his peacemaker Winfield Scott to the border once again.

Scott rescued Anderson from the tedious and distasteful Cherokee duty and called him north to serve as one of his aide-de-camps. Anderson quickly handed over his responsibilities to a subordinate and was in Washington by the first week of March 1841. After a short meeting with the officers examining his book, he headed to New York City to report to General Scott. Scott and his staff took a steamboat up the Hudson to New Hamburg and a stage to Albany. They arrived at the state capital on March 16 and planned to continue across the state to Lockport. They were delayed several days waiting for US attorney general

John J. Crittenden, a fellow Kentuckian, to arrive. A close friend of Scott's, Crittenden was there to brief the general on the legal aspects of the McLeod case.[10]

The delayed departure and a fall on the ice put the already prickly Scott in a bad mood. Serving on Scott's staff was difficult even when he was in a good mood. Scott was a senior general and expected his subordinates to treat him as such. His exacting needs were to be met, whether refilling his water glass with a hint of gin or his apple fritters at the exact right temperature. If David, his enslaved body servant, was not immediately available, his West Point–educated staff officers would have to meet the big man's needs.[11]

Scott took himself extremely seriously and expected those around him to do so as well. This attitude did not make Anderson dislike his senior. He respected the man and believed it was "due to one who has done such good and great service to his country." During their travels, Anderson once referred to his senior as being in a "huff." The general dressed down his subordinate to the point that Anderson even apologized in his personal journal.[12]

The indiscretion aside, General Scott liked Anderson and helped shepherd his career. He suggested Anderson translate the French artillery works as he had done with infantry tactics early in his career. A fellow officer described Anderson as having "minute punctuality in all the duties, habits, and relations in life." Scott respected this type of professionalism in his subordinates. The same officer described Anderson as a man of no vices and "honest and conscientious as it is possible for a man to be."[13] Standing only five-feet-eight, he would have made the six-feet-four Scott look even larger, something the vain general would have appreciated. As a bonus, as a man raised by Virginians, Anderson's pronunciations would have been to Scott's standards. He would not have had to correct him as he did so many junior officers, especially those from northern states.

On Sunday, March 21, the little group left Albany for Lockport. The three hundred miles by stagecoach took nearly a week, with stops in Auburn, Seneca Falls, Palmyra, and Rochester. Seneca Falls was not to the party's liking: "dirty house—bad dinner." One positive moment on this trip over bad roads in thirty-degree weather was that Anderson sighted the first robin, a sign that spring was coming.[14]

After learning that McLeod's case would be reviewed by the State Supreme Court before the trial, postponing the potential crisis, they took the extra time to tour some local battlefields of the War of 1812. The modern historian can only envy these officers as they walked the ground, which still resembled the battlefields of thirty years prior, with General Scott explaining the intricacies of the actions. Short of actual combat, it is hard to imagine a better military education for Anderson and the other officers. Scott kept them entertained with humorous anecdotes. Some of these stories the men had heard many times, and according to Anderson, the story of Private Boyd of Townson's Artillery was an army favorite. Unfortunately, that story has been lost to time. They also had the opportunity to observe British troops in formation. Anderson was not impressed with their drill, writing that although they were pleased with themselves, they were "not well instructed."[15]

On Thursday, March 25, they reached Niagara Falls and saw the spectacular view from the American side of the river. At a dinner held in the general's honor, the guests were entertained by Henri Gourand, recently from Paris. He was an apprentice of the famous Louis Daguerre, developer of the daguerreotype, an early forerunner of the photograph. Gourand had ten thousand of the copper plates treated with a silver solution. Although the daguerreotype's most practical use was for portraits, he planned to capture "various points of interest" in the country, perhaps the first landscape photographer. He planned to sell the images for fifteen dollars a plate. Anderson was interested and would have purchased some if they had been ready, the first signs of interest in collecting art, which he later did as an investment. Unfortunately for Gourand, the plan did not work. An impoverished Gourand would later write, "The daguerreotype will hardly afford sustenance for satisfying a tame hare."[16]

General Scott and his entourage would spend the next several months traveling the US/Canadian border. They ventured as far east as Maine and as far west as Detroit. They traveled by rail, stagecoach, and steamship, never spending more than a night in one place. Scott met with local militia and civic leaders, sometimes addressing rooms full of armed, angry, and scared men. He also met with British and Canadian leaders preparing to respond to an American incursion with their own strike. Scott was carrying out the herculean task of calming a thousand miles of the border. The election of William Henry Harrison made the job more difficult. After twelve years of either Jackson or Van Buren, the country had elected its first Whig president. Not only was this a change in the political philosophy of the commander in chief, but unlike Van Buren, Harrison was a veteran of the last war with Britain. This fact must have given pause to those north of the border during this crisis.

Although he never commented on presidential politics in his letters, Anderson surely approved of the new resident of the White House. Harrison was similar to Anderson's father. They were both former Virginians whose careers took them to the frontier. Anderson did not vote in the 1840 election. He held the opinion, as did so many antebellum officers, that as instruments of the government, it was undemocratic for them to have a say.

Neither Anderson nor anyone else had much time to celebrate the first Whig president. Between the long inauguration parade and ceremony in poor weather and the stress of the flood of Whig job seekers, illness claimed the seventy-one-year-old president's life within a month. Anderson was in Rochester, New York, when he heard the news. He marched in the city's procession and attended church services for the first American president to die in office.

On November 22, Scott, his staff, and Brigadier General John E. Wool inspected New York Harbor's outer defenses. Major General Scot handed over his trusted subordinate and the Canadian situation to General Wool. Anderson had been part of Scott's staff since May 1838. During his time with Scott, the lessons he learned were not those of a warrior but were more like those he learned from his brother, the statesman, on their mission to South America. Scott taught Anderson that an officer had to be a diplomat and a fighting man. To Anderson, Scott had prevented war with Britain, and "if justice is meted out by posterity, add a brighter wreath to his brow than worn by any warrior of his time."[17] General Scott must have believed that Anderson had learned his lessons well because he sent his protégé to the spot where violence might still break out and undo all of Scott's work.

Anderson traveled to Utica to deal with the potential problems from the McCleod trial. A company of US regulars and a violent hailstorm two days before the end of the trial helped to quell any thoughts of a violent response to the not-guilty verdict. Along with one of his lieutenants and the county sheriff, Anderson escorted McCleod and his lawyer to the Canadian border without incident.[18]

With the peaceful conclusion of the McCleod incident, Anderson's duty under Wool became much more routine. He traveled just as much as before, inspecting forts and army posts, but the stress of potential war was removed. He was able to visit friends at West Point and even occasionally dine with Scott in New York City. This duty also gave him increased availability to serve on the board, examining his artillery manual.[19]

The more routine duty also gave Anderson time to devote to two pursuits very close to his heart, a spouse and the creation of a retirement home for US soldiers. Anderson was in his early thirties. As he often commented on in his letters, streaks of gray were showing up in his hair. He was fast approaching the age when a man got labeled a confirmed bachelor, and marriage would become nearly impossible. His mother, sisters, and sisters-in-law often asked him why he had not made the leap. His letters to them always contain an excuse for his single status. He complained that as the age gap between him and the eligible women grew, they began taking him less seriously "and take with me liberties they would not toward one of less experience."[20]

Fearing he would lose his opportunity to become a family man, Anderson adopted a new strategy. He would approach a young lady with whom he had family connections so that he could meet with her outside a situation where there would be other suitors. He also had to act quickly while she was still available.

The young lady he approached was Eliza Clinch, the oldest daughter of General Duncan Clinch. He had first met Eliza when he served under her father at the Baton Rouge arsenal. She was only six, and Anderson's stiff military protocol and overprotectiveness had so put her off that when he came to visit her ten years later, the sixteen-year-old Eliza almost refused to see him.[21]

Eliza Clinch had a rough childhood. She spent most of her youth on army posts in the Deep South. She had lost her mother at a young age and a stepmother. Miss Clinch was a positive social match for any army officer. Clinch was not only a well-respected former military man and wealthy plantation owner but also a member of Congress representing Georgia.

Unfortunately, we know next to nothing about the courtship of Robert and Eliza. We know about his formal visit to her Philadelphia boarding school, the first time he saw her as an adult, through an interview she gave a New York newspaper as an old widow. What happened romantically between that meeting and the wedding four years later, we can only speculate. As Anderson moved around military posts in New York and New England, we can assume he and his future bride must have kept up a lively correspondence. None of those letters survive. When Eba Anderson Lawton published her father's letters to her mother during the Mexican War, she scrubbed anything personal from them. She most likely removed the letters from their courtship from her father's papers. We do have a few hints of their relationship from other sources. In letters to his mother and sisters, there are references to her being a sickly young woman. He referred to her as being bedridden, unable to walk, and under the care of a doctor. He mentions a spinal disorder, but there are no details.[22] Perhaps her health issues were why there were no more age-appropriate suitors. The young, sickly wife likely appealed to Anderson's protective nature.

Their March 26, 1845, wedding was a major social event in New York City. President John Tyler was in attendance, and General Scott gave away the bride. Her father was too ill to make the voyage from Savannah. This was most likely a favor to Anderson, not the Clinch family, as Scott probably still held a grudge against General Clinch for testifying in favor of Scott's rival, General Edmund Gaines, in the court of inquiry over the handling of the Second Seminole War.

The newly married couple spent only a little time in New York before he was transferred to Fort Moultrie in Charleston. Before the year was out and they arrived in Charleston, seventeen-year-old Eliza gave birth to the first of four children. Eliza McIntosh Anderson, whom her father called Eba, would spend much of her adult life preserving her father's legacy.

The legacy Anderson would have preferred to be remembered for did not occur in Charleston Harbor. The mid-nineteenth century was a period of reform movements of all kinds. A religious man like Anderson was not immune. The reform Anderson put his efforts toward was the fate of old soldiers. The life of a nineteenth-century army officer was hard. Anderson and his fellow officers made many sacrifices. Life for the enlisted man was even more difficult with fewer incentives.

The difficulty of army life and the many better opportunities a growing America offered made recruiting men a hard task. The men who made the enlisted ranks their home were from the lowest classes of society, who were unable or unwilling to do other work. The stereotypes most Americans held of enlisted men were drunks, loafers, incompetents, or all three. Army officers often shared this view.

When an enlisted man finished his career, he most often had nothing to show for it. Of course, the idea of a pension or retirement is a modern invention, and most men became dependent on their families when they were too old to work. The soldier rarely had even that or skills that he could transfer to civilian life. There was an opportunity for old soldiers to serve as ordnance sergeants. In forts or arsenals that did not have a garrison, an ordnance sergeant was a combination maintenance man and security guard. This was not retirement but a job. Even so, there were not enough of those positions for the thousands of men no longer young enough to serve. Those who, in Anderson's complaint, were "worn out in service, destroyed in constitution, and unfitted by his habits, for embarking in a new pursuit, he must be discharged and thrown an outcast upon society."[23]

Anderson campaigned for the creation of a retirement home for enlisted men. The result would be the United States Soldiers' Home. In 1914, Anderson's daughter published a full-length book arguing that this was the sole idea and creation of her father. The modern historian owes a debt to Mrs. Eba Anderson Lawton. The massive Robert Anderson collection at the Library of Congress is a wealth of information on the nineteenth-century army, and it was created by her as a tribute to her father. Unfortunately, I must disagree with her in the case of the Soldier's Home. She proves beyond a doubt that her father was a driving force behind the creation of the soldiers' retirement home. However, the idea predated Anderson. It had been put forth officially as early as 1827 by the secretary of war, for Revolutionary War veterans. Secretary James Barbour based his suggestion on similar institutions in Britain and France.

Even though it was not Robert Anderson's original idea, he worked tirelessly to bring it about. He wrote letters to representatives in Congress. He convinced his commanding officers at each new posting to write similar letters. He got fellow officers to sign petitions. He kept the idea alive among the decision-makers. However, it would take the war with Mexico to bring about the creation of the Soldier's Home. That event was fast approaching.

CHAPTER 7

THE MEXICAN WAR

When Captain Robert Anderson and his young family arrived in Charleston in 1845, it was a growing hub of activity. It had a population of over forty thousand. The first twenty cadets of the Citadel had only just begun their education. Many of the city's famous landmarks were under construction. The wealth that was building Charleston came from the rice plantations and their slave labor.

Charleston's defense relied on the thirty-year-old Fort Moultrie on Sullivan's Island. By the time the Andersons arrived, the army had strengthened the fortification and upgraded the guns. Along with Castle Pinckney, built on a small island a mile from downtown Charleston, the two forts were intended to defend the city from an invasion fleet. In 1845, the cutting-edge fortification that would anchor Charleston's defense and be the center of a great national tragedy was at its earliest stage of construction. Ships still dumped tons of granite from New Hampshire quarries into the bay to make the artificial island.

The Andersons made their home on Sullivan's Island. According to one of its most famous former residents, Edgar Allan Poe, who had been stationed at Fort Moultrie during his short time in the army, Sullivan's Island was "very singular." The island "consists of little else than sea sand" and was "separated from the mainland by a scarcely perceptible creek, oozing its way through a wilderness of reeds and slime." In summer, "the island was inhabited by the fugitives from Charleston, dust, and fever."[1]

Despite Poe's unflattering descriptions of the island, it was a popular resort destination for the elite of Charleston. The sea breezes over the island were a welcome relief from the heat and smell of Charleston in the summertime. The best families owned cottages on the island. The center of activity was a two-story hotel called the Moultrie House. Complete with a bowling alley and shooting gallery, it was one of the South's most famous resorts. Army officers had long been a staple of social life on Sullivan's Island, and a short stroll to

Fort Moultrie to listen to the regimental band was a favorite activity of the locals. Anderson often loaned the musicians for the island's events.[2]

Anderson commanded Company G, Third US Artillery, stationed at Fort Moultrie. It was one of three companies on Sullivan's Island. Among those nearly hundred officers and men that made up Fort Moultrie's garrison were Lieutenants William T. Sherman and George Thomas. The Ohioan and Virginian were frequent visitors to the Andersons' home outside the fort.

Anderson and his men would spend just under a year in South Carolina. The army was rotating the companies of the Third Artillery in and out of Florida. Anderson and Company G went to Fort Marion in St. Augustine, Florida. Built by the Spanish in 1672, the former Castillo de San Marcos was the oldest active fortification in the US Army. He was not in St. Augustine very long. Anderson and the eighty-six men of Company G were soon transferred to Fort Brook, located on Tampa Bay.

While Anderson and his men were stationed at the location of the country's last war, nine hundred miles almost exactly due west, another war broke out. On April 24, 1846, Mexican cavalry under the command of General Mariano Arista splashed across the Rio Grande River. They clashed with a small force of American dragoons from the army of Brevet Brigadier General Zachary Taylor. The dragoons got the worst of the fight. Several were killed, and most of the others were wounded. These were the first shots of the US-Mexican War that had perhaps been inevitable since Texas had gained its independence, if not earlier.

This first skirmish was quickly followed by two American victories, Palo Alto and Resaca de la Palma. Fought before Congress declared war, both were one-sided victories. American artillery played a decisive role. The first combat test of America's "flying artillery" using the tactics from Anderson's book carried out by West Point graduates was a complete success.

By September, Taylor had marched his force of US Army regulars, volunteers, and Texas Rangers into Mexico. After a bloody assault, Taylor captured the city of Monterrey. Although still a hero to the nation, the general was falling into severe disfavor with President James K. Polk. Not only did General Taylor belong to the wrong political party, but the Whigs were already openly planning his 1848 presidential run.

Taylor realized that Polk's plan for Mexico was problematic. Although American forces had won quick victories in Texas and California and the US Navy was the unchallenged master of both Mexican coasts, the Mexican government did not back down. Polk had hoped that he could pressure the Mexicans to negotiate. Polk did not understand that the political situation would not allow negotiations with the United States, regardless of how obvious it became that Mexico could not defeat its northern neighbor.

The Polk administration attempted to use political intrigue to solve the impasse. Antonio de Padua María Severino López de Santa Anna y Pérez de Lebrón was in exile in Cuba. Through intermediaries, Santa Anna led Polk to believe that if the United States helped him return to power, he would negotiate an end to the conflict that would benefit the United States. All he needed was passage to Mexico and a sizeable war chest. If successful, it was a small price to pay for a victorious end to the war. Santa Anna kept half his word. He did seize power, but then he marshaled that power to fight the United States more effectively than any other Mexican leader could have. Polk had put Mexico's best military leader back in command, a poor decision that cost many American lives.

The president, who entered the war without a clear plan for victory, now only had one option. He must capture the Mexican capital. The task went to Winfield Scott. Not only was the president concerned about Taylor's political ambitions, but he had doubts about his ability to carry out the necessary campaign. Polk was no friend of Scott, but he believed Scott was his best option, a superior general to Taylor and not nearly the political threat. Scott's strategy was to take the most direct route to his target, a seaborne invasion on the coast.

Scott's first task was building a large enough force to do the job. The Third Artillery would be part of this force. Anderson began writing to the War Department as soon as war broke out. His company was ready to do its duty and be transferred to Taylor's army.[3] Anderson's request was partially granted. Captain Anderson and Company G at Fort Brook were ordered to Mexico but not to Taylor's force. Anderson would once again be joining Scott. When his orders arrived, Anderson sent his wife and daughter to his father-in-law's plantation near Mariana, Florida. It was two weeks before Anderson's ship arrived. The government-owned bark *John Potter* was sent to carry Anderson and his men across the Gulf.

The eighty-six men of Company G were a diverse group. There were old veterans and men whose entire army careers had involved the voyage from the recruiting station in New York to Florida. There were men with military experience in Europe, and some were experienced sailors who helped man the ship since the *John Potter* was shorthanded.[4]

The ten-day voyage across the Gulf of Mexico was relatively quiet. There was a little excitement: one of the recruits, a man named Hogg from Northern Ireland, was placed under guard since he had been acting unusual. The company's doctor had assumed he was only acting insane to get a discharge. During the voyage, he climbed into the forechains, stripped naked, and jumped into the shark-infested water. He almost drowned. If he was only acting crazy to leave the army, it worked. He was granted his discharge.[5] That story did not make it into any of Anderson's many letters to his wife. He told her little about the voyage. He wrote that they passed through a few storms and that he suffered from seasickness.[6]

The *John Potter* arrived off the coast of Tampico on January 12, 1847. Tampico was the first of two staging areas for the eventual landing at Vera Cruz. The navy had captured the city without a fight over a year earlier. The Mexican garrison had abandoned Tampico two weeks before the navy and the marines landed.

Tampico sat five miles up the Panuco River, and the sandbar at the entrance of that river was usually covered with less than eight feet of water. Ships that had to wait to cross the bar sat in completely unprotected water. As the *John Potter* waited, she was struck by one of the common storms that blew in from the north. After fighting the storm for three days, it took nearly a week to make it back to Tampico. Not until January 26 did Anderson land his men in the city. While many of the men of his company credited the skill of the crew of the *John Potter* for their safe arrival, the religious Anderson thanked "the only Power which could save us."[7]

As men and baggage went ashore, Anderson learned what was happening in the war, or at least the rumors that were swirling around Tampico. The belief was that Vera Cruz was the next target. There were seven thousand soldiers in Tampico and more on the way. It was the largest concentration of soldiers that Anderson and most of the other officers had ever seen. For professional officers like Anderson, this was a reunion. His numerous letters home constantly mention old friends he had not seen in years. Anderson's Company G was the third company of the Third Artillery to arrive.[8]

The enlisted men stayed in tent cities in Tampico's suburbs and outlying areas. The regiment spent over a month there. Besides military duties, there were other activities to fill the soldiers' time. The camp was close enough to the river that soldiers could catch crabs in the shallow water to supplement their rations. A troupe of actors came with the army from Monterrey. Regimental bands played nightly concerts in the city's plaza, where the American flag flew over the stone base prepared for a statue of Santa Anna. The soldiers received two months' pay while at Tampico, which led to less innocent pursuits. The citizens of Mexico were forbidden to sell the soldiers alcohol, but there were enough American entrepreneurs who knew how to bypass the regulations that the men were well supplied. Gambling, of course, was always a popular pastime for soldiers with money, and there were usually professional gamblers who followed the army. A port city like Tampico would also have a thriving prostitution industry.[9] Anderson, like most officers, found quarters near the city's center. The officers felt no compunction about having much more comfortable surroundings than their men. Anderson shared a room with his commanding officer, Lieutenant Colonel William Gates. It was a stone home near where Tampico's wealthier citizens lived. Overlooking Tampico was the fortress Andonega. It had been renamed Fort Conner after Commodore David Conner, who captured the city. The US flag flew overhead, but the fort stood empty. Since the US Navy controlled the Gulf, it was not needed. Anderson saw this flag from aboard the ship on his arrival. It caused his heart to "leap with pride, . . . but that pride was soon checked when I thought of the power of the United States and the weakness of Mexico."[10]

After settling into his quarters and writing his daily letter to Eliza, Anderson paid his respects to the senior officer in Tampico, Major General Robert Patterson. A veteran of the War of 1812, he owed his current position to his political connections with Polk. The president had even considered him for the command of the Veracruz expedition instead of Scott but Congress had intervened.[11]

The recently vacated mansion of the customs collector for the city was the natural choice for Patterson's headquarters. It was one of the nicest homes in Tampico. The building was easy enough to identify, with a giant American flag suspended over the street in front of the entrance. Anderson held a dim view toward volunteer officers. They were using connections to steal opportunities from men like himself, who earned them during peacetime. He complained to his wife that some of his students who had failed out of West Point now outranked him in the volunteer service. Military protocol was sacred, and Anderson was polite and professional. He made sure to put in a good word for a friend from Charleston who was joining Patterson's staff as a clerk.[12]

The army's time at Tampico was relatively quiet. Anderson spent his time calling on old friends. He wrote his daily letter to his wife that every serious scholar of the war has referenced since they were first published in 1911. Anderson played the role of a tourist, visiting the market, sampling the local fare, and taking in the local culture. He even began collecting seeds from the fruit, perhaps with the idea of seeing what would grow on a future Anderson plantation.[13]

Anderson took advantage of the large concentration of regular army officers to push for the soldiers' retirement home. He had like-minded friends in the different camps who would help collect signatures for a petition to Congress. Anderson was also on the lookout for those general officers like Patterson with high political connections who could push the cause in Washington.[14]

As a company commander, Anderson's time in Tampico was not all reunions and social calls. He was responsible for drilling and seeing to the well-being of his company. Since part of Company G, like other units, were new recruits who arrived only days before the company sailed from Florida, the drills at

Tampico were the first artillery training many of them had received. Because ammunition was at a premium with the upcoming attack on Vera Cruz, most drills did not involve firing the guns. The strength of American artillery and, thus, the army itself was its mobility. Dubbed flying artillery, the guns could be moved to where they were needed, while Mexican batteries were mostly stationary once the action had begun. The drills carried out at Tampico involved the quick deployment of the guns, firing at a target about three-quarters of a mile away (when ammunition was available) and, as fast as possible, harnessing the cannon and moving to the next spot. This could be done within a minute. As the author of the US Army's manual on field and horse artillery, Anderson must have been thrilled to see his technical writings played out on such a large scale.[15]

Every officer had to take his turn as officer of the day. In this position, Anderson was responsible for "good order and cleanliness" of the areas occupied by US troops. Anderson adopted the wise policy of preventing trouble. With an armed guard, bayonets fixed, he moved through the restaurants, bars, theaters, and other houses of entertainment to keep things "moderately quiet." Anderson and the officers who took their turn at this duty filled the nondescript one-story building on the main plaza that served as the guardhouse with men whose crimes ranged from leaving camp without a pass and missing roll call, to direct disobedience of orders and drunken brawls.[16]

The honor of leading fifty men from the Third Artillery in the ceremony to welcome General Scott fell to Anderson. This ceremony had to be rehearsed. Scott was expected any day and attached great importance to those types of formalities.

Anderson and his fellow West Pointers in Tampico were anxious about Scott's arrival. Until then, they would not know where or when the army would move. Rumors swirled through the camp, and most everyone was confident that Vera Cruz was the target, but they did not know for sure. The biggest concern for the officers was who would go. It was obvious that a force would be left behind to garrison Tampico. There would be no glory in remaining behind. Anderson heard that his company had been chosen for this thankless task. He rushed to General Patterson's headquarters to protest, only to be told by his adjutant general that the decision had yet to be made.[17]

On the morning of February 19, General Winfield Scott arrived in Tampico. He was gone by the next day. Scott was on a schedule and had been forced to spend much more time than he wished in New Orleans, arranging for supplies and reinforcements and handling other administrative issues. He also spent too much time in northern Mexico trying to arrange a transfer of men from Taylor's command. Scott was in a rush. He wanted to take Vera Cruz and move his army into the interior of Mexico before summer. If his army was still in the tropical lowlands near Vera Cruz, yellow fever and other tropical diseases could destroy his army more effectively than Santa Anna.[18]

Anderson had a brief, friendly conversation with the commanding general. They discussed family and mutual friends. Anderson wrote to his wife that he had intentionally avoided Scott since the general would be preparing for the invasion. He also did not want to appear to be using their friendship to get a staff position.[19]

Lobos Island, about a hundred miles north of Vera Cruz, was Scott's next stop. The tiny island, only about one and a half square miles, was the staging area for the landing at Vera Cruz. Once the men arrived at the little island, all doubt about Scott's final target was gone. As more soldiers arrived at Camp Winfield, the island became a tent city. Supply ships, warships, and transports lay at anchor off the coast. The surfboats that Scott had built for the landing at Vera Cruz were tested with good results. Scott did not waste any time at Lobos, and by March 2, around fifty ships filled with soldiers and supplies began the last leg of the voyage to Vera Cruz.[20]

It was more than a week after Scott sailed from Tampico that Anderson followed. As the army left Tampico, his unit was one of the last. This was rather fortunate as the men who were loaded first had to wait until the last was loaded before the convoy headed south. He served as the officer of the day and had to visit the sentry posts in the driving rain that came with one of the seasonal storms. While he waited for his turn to board, Anderson was named judge advocate of a military commission named to try a Mexican citizen accused of espionage. Anderson was not pleased with this duty. He considered the prosecutor's case extremely flimsy if for no other reason than this: so many Mexican civilians crossed the lines to do business, there would be no reason for Santa Anna to send a spy. He only had to quiz the local merchants. Anderson slipped the duty by pointing out to General Patterson that according to General Scott's orders dealing with the treatment of civilians, the commission could not try a Mexican for spying. Anderson was relieved that this man's fate fell into someone else's hands.[21]

A regiment of volunteers from Louisiana and a company of regulars would remain to occupy the city. General Scott ordered Colonel Gates of the Third Artillery to stay in Tampico with one company. On the day Scott left for Lobos, Anderson was informed that Gates had chosen Anderson and Company G. Anderson rushed to see Gates. In the polite manner of the nineteenth-century officer corps, he informed his superior that he would be appealing the decision and that he hoped Gates would not take offense. Anderson argued that as the senior company commander in the Third, he was "entitled to be first sent on armed service."[22]

Anderson had not yet written his appeal when Colonel James Bankhead, the chief of artillery, sent word for Anderson to come to his headquarters. Bankhead told Anderson that Gates had misunderstood him and that the decision would be Bankhead's. He did not want bad feelings between Gates and his officer corps that would naturally ensue from his choosing an officer to remain behind. Anderson later learned that Scott had informed Bankhead that he wanted Anderson at Vera Cruz.[23]

Anderson had once again been disappointed to be informed he was being left behind, only to learn that he was the victim of misinformation. As he told his wife, he was a little embarrassed about these incidents. He did not want to be seen as a man who used friends and influence to further his career.[24]

His company sailed to Vera Cruz on a different ship than Anderson. His luggage went with the men, which caused some inconvenience. The ship had been forced to wait for several days due to weather. Anderson went ashore during this period to visit some friends in the medical department. Anderson had picked up a cough, and after a dose of magnesia, his friends insisted that he could not travel to Vera Cruz without medical supervision. This was a stroke of luck as Anderson traveled on the much faster and more comfortable *Alabama* along with General Patterson and his staff.[25]

The *Alabama* left Tampico on March 1 and arrived at Lobos Island the next day. No one disembarked as orders were waiting for the ship to continue south to Vera Cruz. They next went to Anton Lizardo, a small fishing village about eighteen miles south of Vera Cruz. The *Alabama* was one of about a hundred ships. Except for the most senior, the men and officers aboard did not know the plan. The rumor was that the army would land at Anton Lizardo and march north to Vera Cruz. They would have to cross the Jamapa River, making the journey more difficult.[26]

Anderson was worried that the landing would happen at Anton Lizardo. Not for fear of defeat or high casualties: it was unlikely that the Mexicans would resist a landing that far south of Vera Cruz. If a Mexican force did move to Anton Lizardo, they could have easily been cut off by American troops landing between them and Vera Cruz. Anderson hoped the invasion would be put off simply because his company had not yet arrived. He did not want his "Germans" to miss out on any chance of distinction.[27]

Vera Cruz was Mexico's principal city on the east coast, with a population over fifteen thousand. Its strategic importance was obvious. It had been the starting point of every major invasion of the country since Hernán Cortés and his conquistadors. The city was well prepared for an attack. At the center of the city's defense was the Castillo de San Juan de Ulua. Although nearly three hundred years old, the fortress was still a formidable obstacle. Sitting on a reef, it commanded the entrance to the harbor in all directions.[28]

Vera Cruz also had the small stone bastion, Baluarte de Santiago, at the southeasternmost end of the city's defenses. It was connected to the Baluarte de Concepcion on the northernmost end by a seawall. Forming the third point of the triangle was Baluarte de Santa Barbara and connecting it to Santiago and Concepcion was a sixteen-foot granite wall. There were nine small bastions in between. The Spanish built these defenses in 1635, and in many places they were starting to fall into disrepair. Between these positions, there were over one thousand men and 135 guns.[29]

The night before the landing, Anderson wrote his wife that this would be his last campaign. To him, there was "no more absurd scheme for settling national difficulties than . . . killing each other to find out who is in the right!"[30] Considering the effort he put into making sure he and his men would see action in this war, this should be viewed as a bit of nervousness on the eve of what might be a great battle. He also missed his family and did not want to spend this much time away from them again.

General Scott's strategy was to land south of the city and envelope it. By doing this, he would bypass the Castillo de San Juan de Ulua, the key to Vera Cruz's defense. The landing occurred on March 9, 1847, the thirtieth anniversary of Scott's promotion to brigadier general.[31] Anderson and his fellow officers on this expedition believed that the next few days would secure his place among the great generals of history.

Off the small island of Sacrificios, the men were loaded onto sixty-seven surf boats built specifically for this landing. Each one carried between eighty and ninety men. A naval petty officer or midshipman commanded the landing craft, and a lieutenant commanded each grouping of ten craft. The soldiers were naturally expected to lend a hand if there were not enough sailors to row the craft to shore. General Worth commanded the first wave of the assault. Anderson would have his wish. His company would be among the first to land. For this first stage of the Vera Cruz operation, Anderson's Company G would serve as infantry. Each man carried with him only his weapon, ammunition, and enough food for four days. All noncombat equipment was left on the ships.[32]

It was late afternoon before the invasion force began rowing away from the Isla Sacrificios toward Collado Beach. A signal gun from the *Massachusetts*, Scott's floating headquarters, began the invasion. The men in the boats and those watching from the more than a hundred ships of the invasion fleet had no idea what would happen. Behind the beach were high sand hills ranging from thirty

The US Army landing at Vera Cruz. Courtesy of the Library of Congress, LC-DIG-pga-09268.

feet to a hundred feet tall. If the Mexican Army were behind those hills, ready to resist the landing, the American forces would not know until the trap was sprung. American gunboats had approached the shore and fired into the woods behind the beach to lure Mexican batteries into firing and revealing themselves. There was only silence in reply. The gun crews of the American fleet stood by to offer supporting fire as the regimental bands played patriotic music.[33]

As the forty-foot-long boats were rowed ashore, the men fixed their bayonets as they expected shot and shell from Mexican artillery to fall among them at any moment. Some men jumped into the surf before the wooden hulls scraped sand and waded to shore. The sailors and the men waiting for their turns to be ferried ashore exploded into cheers. The lines were formed, and regimental colors unfurled. The soldiers charged forward, led by officers with swords drawn, up the sand hills, expecting the Mexican Army to open up a murderous fire as soon as the first men were silhouetted against the sky when they reached the top of the hill. Nothing but empty woods faced the invaders.[34] The Mexican Army had decided to make their defense within the city's walls.

Anderson and most of the American force were surprised that there was no resistance. To many, General Juan Morales, the commander of the defenses of Vera Cruz, had missed a great opportunity. Once the American Army was on the beach, it would have been difficult for the fleet's big guns to fire without hitting their own men. Even a small force could have caused chaos among the invaders. General Morales has not left us his reasoning behind his choice not to resist the landing. He was a professional with a great deal of experience. As a teenager, he first saw action in his country's war of independence. He led the assault against David Crockett's position at the Alamo and led armies during the Federalist Wars of the early 1840s.

Scott planned to lay careful siege to Vera Cruz. There were mixed feelings in his army about this strategy. Anderson and the other West Point–trained officers appreciated the skill necessary to carry out this operation with so little cost to American lives. They saw an assault on Vera Cruz as a foolhardy waste of lives. There were, however, those in his command who were disappointed. General Worth and many officers who had served under Taylor at Monterrey wanted an immediate assault. To them and many observers in the United States, glory lay in assaults, not in careful strategy. There was also the fear that a prolonged siege would leave them on the coast during the dreaded yellow fever season. The sooner Vera Cruz fell and they could move into the dry highland areas, the better.[35]

Anderson and the entire landing force spent the night on the sandy beach. There were no fires, and most of the command was wet from the landing. Throughout the night, musket fire could be heard on the beach as nervous pickets fired at shadows. The defenders of Vera Cruz would occasionally fire their cannons, which only served to annoy the American soldiers trying to sleep. The landing craft began ferrying supplies as soon as the soldiers were ashore. This was rushed for fear that storms might disrupt the process, a wise choice since the area was hit by a series of storms three days after the initial invasion.

About two and a half miles south of the city, the beach turned into a giant supply depot about a mile wide. The men from the quartermaster corps set up their tents, and supplies began to cover the beach with provisions for an army of nearly ten thousand: tents, blankets, the personal baggage of the officers and soldiers, and munitions.[36]

The initial landing of men and supplies was well organized. In an era of sometimes crippling interservice rivalry, the successful landing of eighty-six hundred men in five hours and supplying that force during a two-week siege with no recent precedent to follow was one of the underappreciated achievements of the war.

On March 10, Scott transferred his headquarters to Mexican soil. The city's encirclement was painfully slow because of a lack of wagons and draft animals. Worth's Division had the southeastern section of the line. The entire line would be nearly three miles long. Anderson and his men did not have far to travel to their assigned position. Since their artillery had not yet been landed and it would be three days before the last division reached the beach on the north side of the city, completing the encirclement, Anderson had time to settle into the routines of camp life. The camp of the Third Artillery sat two and a half miles south of Vera Cruz behind a high sand hill that kept it safe from the sporadic cannon fire from the city. In his tent, he could resume the letters to his wife. He complained to her about the officers trying to get their names in the newspapers or otherwise jockeying for glory.[37]

A heavy storm hit the coast. They had rain and heavy wind from March 12 to 17, cutting the army off from communication with the fleet. Only when the storm ended were the first heavy guns landed on the beach. This feat could not have been easy, considering that the weight of some of these guns could be as much as ten tons. Luckily for Anderson and his men, that job fell to the navy.

On the evening of March 19, a staff officer arrived at the camp of the Third Artillery requesting that two hundred men report to Colonel Joseph Totten on the beach. The fifty-nine-year-old War of 1812 veteran was Scott's chief engineer and directed the technical aspects of the Siege of Vera Cruz. With muskets slung and half a dozen cartridges in their pockets, Anderson marched his company along with US Marines and the Fifth US Infantry under the command of Colonel Francis Belton to the beach. Waiting for them was a young engineer named George McClellan. Under orders from Totten, Lieutenant McClellan had laid out shovels, picks, and axes for the soldiers. He then led the men single file through the darkness. There was a slight rain as they silently weaved through the sand hills surrounding Vera Cruz.[38]

McClellan lost his way in the dark and led the column within five hundred yards of the city. Anderson and the rest of the column waited in silence as McClellan and two other men searched for the assigned position. After an hour's absence, he returned, having found the route.[39]

McClellan brought Belton's men to where one of the four American batteries would be placed. Working in shifts, they began clearing brush and digging the emplacements. They threw the earth on the hill separating the emplacement from the city's walls, a half mile away. They did not attract fire from the city's defenders. Anderson claimed the honor of throwing the first shovel full of dirt in the Siege of Vera Cruz.[40]

A relief force arrived at about three-thirty in the morning, and Anderson's men quietly retraced their steps back to their camp. The Mexicans observed the battery in progress at around eleven, but by the time Anderson and his men left, enough work had been completed that the next shift could work in relative safety. As Anderson settled into his camp after the night's work, he could hear the Mexican artillery trying unsuccessfully to disrupt the building of the batteries.[41]

It took almost a week to complete the work. Anderson and his company took their turns on picket duty. They were posted between their lines and Vera Cruz's defense to give a warning if General Morales tried to launch a surprise attack against the American works. This was an unpleasant and stressful duty. The nights were cold and wet. The sand was filled with biting insects. There was the constant but ineffectual firing overhead as the Mexican guns tried to prevent the placing of the batteries. The army had only ten mortars and four howitzers, less than a fourth of what the War Department had promised General Scott. Scott grudgingly accepted the offer made by the new naval commander on the scene, Matthew C. Perry, to land some of the navy's heavy guns and their crews to take part in the siege. Of course, naval guns came with naval officers who were ready to share the glory of the conquest of Vera Cruz, and Scott did not like to share credit. However, he needed to capture Vera Cruz and move inland before the unhealthy season.[42] Blockade duty could be tedious. For the sake of morale, Commodore Perry ordered the guns worked in shifts so that the largest number of men could have their opportunity to serve on the battle line.

Once the five batteries were in place, Scott, following military tradition, allowed the opposing commander a chance to surrender. When Morales politely refused, Scott gave the order to fire. Anderson had mixed feelings about the deafening noise of his artillery battery in action. He was distressed "that every shot either injures or distress the poor inoffensive women and children, who have neither part nor lot in the war."[43] But at the same time, this was his profession. He had spent the last twenty years studying, writing, teaching, and arguing about artillery tactics. In all the combat he had seen thus far, he had always been "red-legged infantry." This was his first action as an officer of artillery. Watching his men load, fire, and reload in the carefully choreographed way, the attempt to reduce an enemy with only artillery, the walled city he faced must have thrilled him, in the manner of an artist with a fresh canvas.

Anderson's battery contained three mortars. His men worked the mortars almost constantly in twenty-four-hour shifts. They fired a ten-inch shell weighing over ninety pounds, including several pounds of gunpowder. The shell was designed to explode over its target, raining metal fragments in all directions. To set off the explosion, each one had a short fuse lit by the explosive charge that sent it flying. At night, those in the siege line and inside the city could trace the path of the shells by the streak of light made by the burning fuse.

Anderson's men worked proficiently at their mortars, throwing more than a thousand shells into the city during the four days of firing. At one point, his battery was firing a shot a minute. As the ring of fire poured destruction into Vera Cruz, Anderson ordered one of his mortars to fire into the Fortress San Juan de Ulua "to see if I could wake the Castle."[44]

The city's defenders kept up a steady return fire, but they did little damage. Casualties were "trifling." The soldiers quickly learned when to lay low and when it was safe to work their guns. A Mexican mortar claimed the life of the Third Artillery's Captain John Vinton. The only casualty in Anderson's company was a Sergeant Foster, who was grazed by a shell fragment. He was excused from duty for a couple of days Morale was high even as the men worked long shifts at the mortars.[45]

By March 26, Vera Cruz had had enough. The destruction inside the city had been horrific. Public buildings and homes alike were destroyed. Although those citizens who survived the bombardment were unlikely to complement Scott for his humanity, the death and destruction resulting from an assault would have been much worse. The defenders were frustrated that there had been no attempt to relieve them and that they could do little in response to the American bombardment. The Mexican regulars, fearing the city would be surrendered, contemplated a breakout. It was probably a strategy that would have worked. There were more than four thousand soldiers inside Vera Cruz. If they had struck the American line at one spot, they could have escaped. They could not have won a battle, but if their goal had been simply to fight another day, it would have been doubtful that Scott would have ordered a pursuit. General Morales quickly nixed the idea. He believed the defenders should stand together. At midnight, General Morales called a council of war. He handed command of the city to his second, General José Juan Landero y Coss. During the night, Morales escaped from the city by boat.[46]

On March 27, Landero surrendered to General Scott and the American Army. Besides massive damage to the buildings, more than two hundred civilians and soldiers were dead, including the teenage daughter of the British ambassador. Scott lost thirteen men killed and fifty-five wounded. Compared to Taylor's battles in northern Mexico, these were light casualties. In the tradition of early-eighteenth-century warfare, a delegation from both armies met to negotiate a surrender. The Mexican representatives asked that their army be allowed to leave the city with flags and arms. Scott would allow them to go but with a promise not to fight again in the current conflict. The Mexican delegation also asked that personal property and religious rights be respected. This was an unnecessary request, as that was Scott's plan from the start. If the Mexican people could be convinced the United States was not their enemy, the upcoming campaign would be greatly simplified.

After paroling the prisoners, as agreed in the surrender terms, the army issued food to civilians and hired work crews to clear the streets of debris. Scott gave strict orders to protect Mexicans and their property. These were not empty words. Three soldiers were imprisoned, and one was executed for crimes against civilians. Scott ordered priests and church property to be respected. One of Scott's first acts upon entering the city was to attend Mass with his senior officers. Even though the Catholic nation of Mexico had been invaded by the majority-Protestant country to the north, Scott wanted the people to know this was not a religious war. He knew there were more Mexicans who would fight for the Church than would fight for the government of Santa Anna.

Anderson was unable to attend. His Company G was one of the three companies assigned to garrison the Fortress of San Juan de Ulloa. Scott, Anderson, and the rest of the army were pleasantly surprised when the island fortress surrendered with the rest of the city. Between a bombardment from the captured city and the US fleet, it could not have held out long, but they had expected the fort's commander to at least have tried. The surrender allowed Scott to move his timeline forward.

On entering the fort, Anderson learned of the horrible conditions the Mexican troops had spent the siege in and perhaps why they were not motivated to hold out longer. The men's quarters were so filthy that building new ones was more efficient than cleaning the old ones. Anderson also learned that there had been one death at the fortress. The "unauthorized shell" he ordered was the cause of the man's death.[47] Although he felt guilty about what may have been an unnecessary death, the few shots Anderson sent into the fortress may have convinced them to surrender earlier than they might have otherwise.

Anderson was concerned that being assigned garrison duty at the fort would mean he would be left behind when the army moved inland. He need not have worried. By April 5, he and his company were back with the main body, and by April 12 were on the road west.

While waiting for the army to decamp, Anderson continued to write daily letters to his wife. Besides describing the events to her, he also complained about the volunteer soldiers and their officers. The men were undisciplined, and the officers were overly concerned with getting their names in their hometown newspapers and using their political connections to get promotions. He also gave her instructions on the family's finances. While in Mexico, he had her sell one of their horses, a thoroughbred he kept at his father-in-law's plantation. The sale was made not because of a lack of funds but because it was the proper time to sell to maximize profit. One theme that constantly runs through his letters is his desire for more letters from home. He even offers his young wife practical tips on how to write more.[48]

The Third Artillery was in Worth's Division and was among the last to leave Vera Cruz. The availability of mules and wagons dictated the speed the army would travel. Worth's Division had to wait for more to arrive before advancing. Each company was allowed one wagon for their baggage. Besides small tents, mosquito netting, and a camp bed, Anderson had his campaign trunk, a heavy coat, and three books: two religious and one volume of tactics.[49]

The target was the city of Jalapa,[50] about seventy miles west of Vera Cruz. Besides being closer to the final objective, it sits about four thousand feet above sea level, safe from the tropical diseases that could ravage an invading army. The National Highway, which Scott planned to follow to the capital, passed through Jalapa.

Anderson had not yet left Vera Cruz when the lead elements of the army encountered a sizeable Mexican force twenty miles from Jalapa under the direct command of Santa Anna. He had been extremely active since returning from exile. After assuming the presidency, he pulled together a force of twenty-five thousand. The question was where best to deliver the fatal blow to the American Army.

Scouts from Santa Anna's army intercepted a letter from Scott to Taylor. This intelligence coup informed him of the American strategy and the relative size of the two armies. Santa Anna decided to march his army north to confront the weakened Taylor. He believed the walled city of Vera Cruz and its garrison would hold out long enough for him to crush Taylor's army and then march south to meet the threat of Scott. Unfortunately for the generalissimo and Mexico, neither of those predictions came true.

Santa Anna met Taylor in the dry mountain country about four hundred miles north of the capital. The Battle of Buena Vista was a brutal fight. Both sides suffered heavily, and the Mexicans had come close to dislodging the Americans from their formidable position. Santa Anna slipped away with the remnants of his army to meet the threat of Scott in the south. The battle helped ensure Taylor's presidential victory in 1848. It also launched the political career of Jefferson Davis, colonel of the First Mississippi Volunteers.

Santa Anna was recruiting and training more men for his depleted force and reorganizing the panicked government in the capital when he learned that General Morales had surrendered Vera Cruz. He raced east to defend the road to Mexico City. Although Jalapa was a natural place to defend, it was a walled city, and its solidly built church buildings could be used as fortresses; Santa Anna decided to make his stand twenty-one miles to the southeast at Cerro Gordo. Just east of the little town was Cerro Gordo Pass, also known as Devil's Jaws. It was only four miles wide and flanked by high hills. It was a perfect place to make a stand. If the Americans did not or could not push through this impossible position, they would be trapped in the low coastal region, vulnerable to yellow fever and malaria.

Two months after his defeat at Buena Vista, five hundred miles away, Santa Anna had his twelve-thousand-man army positioned at the Cerro Gordo Pass.

Unfortunately for Mexico, within two days, Winfield Scott was in Jalapa writing his report of the battle to President Polk. The Mexican position at Devil's Jaws was not as dangerous to the Americans as the name implied. With effective scouting, hard fighting, and a great deal of luck, the battle turned into a rout. Mexican troops fled farther inland. In the hasty retreat, Santa Anna lost his personal baggage to a company of Illinois volunteers, including a spare artificial leg, one of the great wartime souvenirs of American military history.

The battle ended so quickly that Anderson, at the rear of the army, saw none of it, only the dead and dying Mexican troops and abandoned equipment that littered the road to Jalapa. There were so many abandoned muskets that American soldiers used the broken stocks as firewood.

Anderson and many other Americans were impressed with the town of Jalapa. Not only was the weather cooler and the threat of disease much lessened, but the beauty of the place struck them. A Boston reporter described its buildings as "substantially built of brick or stone, covered with plaster; the people had an air of neatness and intelligence."[51] Jalapa was a retreat for the wealthy of Vera Cruz. Anderson viewed the region through the eyes of the gentlemen farmer he strived to be. He wrote his wife about the beauty of the soil, the exotic crops that grew there, and how well the old staples did.[52]

Anderson, his men, and all of Worth's Division did not have long to appreciate the beauty. Scott wisely wanted to keep the pressure on the retreating Mexicans. The division followed the National Highway to Perote. The town and its fortress would have been another good place for the Mexican Army to make a stand. They, however, were still in a panicky retreat from Cerro Gordo. Anderson's men moved into the town without a shot fired. Scott's strategy of protecting civilians and their property was already proving advantageous to the army. The partisan attacks they faced were only minor, and the local farmers sold fresh food to the army. Fresh fruit and vegetables made their existence much more pleasant.

Anderson wholeheartedly agreed with Scott's strategy, both for its practicality and because it was morally correct. Fellow officers who sowed their wild oats while they were so far from home might get a talk from Captain Anderson on being Godly men and officers.[53]

On May 7, Worth's Division started to move toward Puebla as the rest of Scott's force began moving out of Jalapa. The army was spread in a thin line over sixty miles long. Scott believed Santa Anna could not field an effective force so soon after Cerro Gordo. He was correct. Santa Anna could only put a small irregular cavalry force in the field, which Worth easily swept aside.

Puebla was the second-largest city in Mexico. Its eighty thousand people lived in a healthy climate seven thousand feet above sea level. They were unhappy with the presence of the American Army but caused no problems. Anderson and the majority of the army would spend the summer in Puebla. By the time the army was on the road to Puebla, it was the first anniversary of Palo Alto. The terms of the one-year volunteers were over. In that era, it would have been a political impossibility to keep the men longer than their term of enlistment, even in a war zone. Plus, Winfield Scott had little respect for the volunteers and was not sad to see them go. General Patterson, who Scott was also not sorry to see go, led them back to the United States to be discharged. The rest of the army would stay where it was until reinforcements arrived.

For the next three months, the only fighting for Santa Anna and Winfield Scott was with their own governments. In Mexico City, the Congress was divided over whether to negotiate or fight, but all could agree they wanted to keep Santa Anna out of power. President Polk sent Nicholas Trist of the State Department to negotiate with the Mexican government, a responsibility and honor that Scott felt should have been his. That Polk was actively trying to take credit away from Scott did not help the working relationship between Trist and Scott.

As for the soldiers and junior officers like Anderson, they only heard rumors of what was happening in the two capitals and their commanding generals' headquarters. Not a day went by without the story swirling through the camp that Santa Anna's army was preparing to attack Puebla at any moment, that the Mexican government had collapsed and peace was at hand, or that the Americans were mobilizing and would be on the road to Mexico City any day.

Besides judging the validity of rumors, there were the other everyday activities of an army. Patrols were constantly kept in the field. Training and drills were held. Although they were combat veterans, most of the them had been civilians a year ago, and most officers still had little experience in maneuvering more than a company. Equipment had to be maintained and repaired. Men and animals had to be fed.

Anderson shared a room with a fellow officer in one of the barracks in the city. By rank, he could have claimed a private room, but he did not do so to make life easier for the junior officers. The officers joined small groups or messes to share the cost and routine of meals. Each man took his turn shopping in the local market. Anderson often complained to Eliza about the prices. However, he overlooked that adding thousands of more men to the local population would naturally affect prices, whether they were gouging or not. Anderson did more than grocery shopping. He shopped for souvenirs for his wife and family. He also did some book collecting, including a Catholic Bible over a hundred years older than his country. He promised his wife, however, that he would not fall into the bad habit of his bachelor days of spending too much money on books and art.[54] His friend Erasmus Keys was wrong when he wrote that Anderson had no vices.

While in Puebla, Anderson occasionally suffered the chills that are a common symptom of malaria. He caught it while fighting Seminoles in the Everglades, and the conditions in Mexico were causing his symptoms to flare up.

For all the routine activities, there were reminders that they were in a war zone. Men who wandered off in too small a group were ambushed, and men who had too much to drink would disappear. Anderson was shocked that men still drank to access under those conditions. There were also attempts to lure American soldiers to desert.[55]

By August, the hope of negotiating an end to the war was gone, at least until another major victory. After the arrival of General Franklin Pierce and twenty-five hundred men, Scott realized that no more men were coming, and he had to act with what he had while he still had them. Although the army was safe from tropical diseases in the Puebla area, there was a growing problem of dysentery and other illnesses caused by poor sanitation, tainted food, and general uncleanliness. It was starting to take its toll on the American Army in Puebla.

The two rival generals had not ignored military matters over the summer. Santa Anna decided to make his stand at the capital and had spent the time since Cerro Gordo building up Mexico City's defenses. He had twenty thousand men to defend the city. Santa Anna reasonably hoped that fighting behind city walls and other prepared defenses would erase his raw troops' disadvantage against the American veterans. Scott, for his part, had spent this time developing a battle plan. His engineer, Captain Robert E. Lee, and his chief topographical engineer, Major William Turnbull, had secretly traveled the roads between Puebla and Mexico City, discovering the best routes and the locations of the strongest enemy positions. By the time Scott marched his army out of Puebla amid flags waving and the regimental bands playing martial music, he had a plan to conquer Mexico City.[56]

In a move often compared to Hernán Cortés and his advance against the Aztecs, Scott abandoned his supply line and line of retreat to maximize his numbers. It was a risky move that many contemporaries predicted would fail miserably. British prime minister, the Duke of Wellington, wrote that the American Army would be destroyed in the interior of Mexico. The conqueror of Napoleon, however, added that if Scott were to emerge victorious, he would be the greatest living general.

On Sunday, August 8, Worth's Division, including Anderson's Company G of the Third Artillery, marched out of Puebla. Except for a detachment left behind to protect the twenty-five hundred sick and injured, they were the last to leave Puebla. The drummers beat the reveille at 3 a.m. for the force to be on the move by six, which Anderson felt was an unnecessarily long time for the soldiers to prepare. They covered eleven miles of rugged, dusty road that first day. The scenery impressed Anderson, and he wrote Eliza that since he was a poor artist, he wished he had had a "daguerreotype apparatus" like he saw in Niagara to share the beautiful mountain scenery of central Mexico.[57]

The army continued for three days through the rich cornfields of the valley. Then the road began to rise toward the mountain range that separated them from their target. Rain and dropping temperatures added to the discomfort of the march. They passed abandoned defensive positions constructed along the road, a constant reminder of what might have been and what still faced them at their destination.

The cold and wet conditions worsened Anderson's malaria, or his old "Florida condition," as he called it. Anderson's friends and the regimental surgeon ensured that Anderson had warm and dry shelter when possible. If he had wished, Anderson's experience in Mexico could have been over without harming his reputation. He was, however, eager to do his duty. He took advantage of the drier, warmer quarters offered to him because of his condition but always fought any effort to send him home.

Anderson gave no hint of being superstitious when he first laid eyes on the Valley of Mexico on Friday the thirteenth. As Worth's Division marched into the valley, Anderson and his company at the rear had a view of the valley spread out in front of them and the several thousand blue-clad men and white-topped wagons covering the road ahead of him. It "was the most beautiful panoramic" he "ever saw." While Anderson was struck by the natural beauty, he described the man-made structures as dirty little villages surrounded by slime-covered water.[58]

When the lead elements of the army reached within twenty miles of Mexico City, Scott had a serious decision to make. There were two practical approaches to the city. The most direct route was to continue along the National Highway. The road skirted the southernmost tip of Lake Texcoco, even crossing a small finger of the lake by a causeway. Unfortunately, this route was dominated by El Peñon. This hill was four hundred feet high and a thousand yards long. Santa Anna had fortified this position with seven thousand men and more than thirty artillery pieces. He was so confident that the Americans would use this route that he placed his headquarters on El Peñon. The other way followed an abandoned road south of Lake Chalco and Lake Xochimilco. Santa Anna believed this route to be too impractical for an army, especially after his men felled trees and rolled rocks into the road. However, Scott's scouts assured him that this route to the southern entrance of the city was usable, although difficult.[59]

Before leaving Puebla, General Scott decided he would use the southern approach. He planned to convince Santa Anna that he would fight through El Peñon. At the crossroads, the leading two divisions continued along the National Highway while Worth's Division turned south. This had the dual benefit of further misleading Santa Anna and keeping his army in position to take either route up to the last minute if the strategic situation changed.

When Worth's Division reached the crossroads, it turned south and took the lead in the march toward the Mexican capital. At this point, Captain Anderson of Company G Third Artillery guessed Scott's strategy. He also correctly understood that the southern approach would mean facing the Castle of Chapultepec. Anderson overestimated the old Spanish fortress, which was currently the National Military Academy. It looked much more formidable than it was. However, it might have been a different story if Santa Anna had fortified Chapultepec as heavily as El Peñon.

Worth's Division paused at the strip of land that separated Lake Chalco and Lake Xochimilco. Patrols were sent out to scout the possible roads along this route. Worth considered ferrying his force across the lakes with small boats as Cortés had done. Boats were gathered, and company commanders were ordered to report the number of men with boatbuilding experience. The plan was never taken very seriously and was soon abandoned. There were too many approaches to the capital for Santa Anna to guard them all in force. Some historians have suggested this was only a ploy to force the Mexicans to defend even more ground.[60]

As Worth's men cleared the road of rocks and fallen trees, Santa Anna rushed troops west to counter the threat. The Mexicans built a two-mile-long line of breastworks and gun emplacements. This formidable line ran from Lake Xochimilco southwest to the Pedregal. The Pedregal was a geographical feature, unlike anything the men of the American Army had seen. It was a field of jagged black volcanic rock that men could cross with great difficulty, and horses and wagons not at all.

On Sunday, August 15, Worth's Division went north toward the undiscovered and newly constructed Mexican line. They moved in short marches in driving rain. The skirmishers drove back the small number of Mexican soldiers who harassed Worth's men. It was slow-going, and they did not encounter the Mexican forces' main body until the morning of the eighteenth. Anderson was in the lead brigade. Their objective, the town of San Antonio, was still a mile away when the skirmishers emerged from a cornfield to discover the Mexican line. Anderson's Company G and the others were ordered forward. Anderson was "expecting and anxious for a fight."[61] Before they reached the line, they were halted. Dragoons had been shot up trying to find the weakness of the line. Worth ordered his men to withdraw almost a mile while he examined the situation.

The division discovered a conveniently located dairy farm. The Mexican artillery fired an occasional shot toward the hacienda to keep the Americans from becoming too comfortable. The rain continued to fall, and the men had to camp on the wet ground. The men helped themselves to fresh milk and, most likely, valuables left behind by the owners who fled ahead of the approaching Americans.[62]

As Worth's Division searched for a way to push through, the other two divisions passed behind him to move around the other side of El Pedregal. They encountered a Mexican blocking force. The subsequent engagement, the Battle of Contreras, was a decided American victory, ending with a Mexican Army under the command of general and former president Gabriel Valencia in full retreat. Valencia had fought in the battle against orders. An enraged Santa Anna demanded that Valencia be shot on sight. The order was never carried out; an American bullet claimed General Valencia.

When the Battle of Contreras first started to go his way, Scott ordered Worth's Division to retrace their line of march and join the battle. As it became a complete victory, the division was turned again toward San Antonio, with the plan of catching Santa Anna's main army between Worth's Division and the victorious force marching from the other side of El Pedregal. Santa Anna knew that his line anchored at San Antonio was now untenable. He ordered his men to withdraw to a new position in the town of Churubusco.

The new line ran from the bridge over the Churubusco River to the San Mateo convent. The convent was the strongest point of the 450-yard line. It had twelve-foot-high stone walls that were four feet thick. Inside were eighteen hundred men and seven cannons. The rest of the line was well-constructed earthen fieldworks. All Mexican forces were moving here, as were Scott's three divisions. What came to be known as the Battle of Churubusco was shaping up to be the decisive battle of the war. Twenty thousand Mexicans faced Scott's eight thousand.

General David Twiggs's Division began the battle at about ten-thirty in the morning. His reconnaissance force misidentified the San Mateo convent and walked into heavy fire. Worth's Division was delayed as Mexican soldiers conducted a fighting retreat from San Antonio. When Worth's men arrived at Churubusco, the rest of the army had been engaged for nearly half an hour. Worth, who felt his division had been slighted in their opportunities for glory, threw his men directly into action. He attacked directly up the road into what Anderson described as "a galling fire of grape and musketry."[63] Most of Worth's officers felt it was a rash attack launched more for glory than based on sound strategic thinking. Lieutenant Nathanial Lyon, of future Civil War fame in Missouri, put it most harshly when he described it as a "butt head attack" launched by a "stupid officer."[64] Anderson was a little more restrained, stating it was a decision that "can hardly be sustained before military men and caused the loss of many of our best soldiers."[65]

Anderson, the obedient soldier, ordered his company forward against the field fortification at the foot of the bridge. If captured, it would prevent a retreat across the Churubusco. There were five cannons and twenty-five hundred men in what Anderson described as the best position he had ever seen. Anderson, his company, and most of Lieutenant Colonel Francis Belton's battalion were trapped in the ditches and cornfields in front of the Mexican line. After two days of rain, the ground was too wet and soft for the artillery to be brought up to support them. They continued to push forward under these brutal conditions, and Belton's battalion, after hours of hard fighting, was able to take the fortification. One of the advantages of using artillerymen as infantry was that when the men of the Third Artillery took their target, they were able to accurately fire the captured cannons into the monastery, causing the Mexican line to collapse. The Mexicans who were gathered at Churubusco fought harder than any that Scott's army had faced, but in the end, their line was broken, and they had to fall back closer to Mexico City.[66]

The price of this victory was great, with 137 men killed and 877 wounded. Santa Anna's army suffered over 4,000 dead and wounded, and more than 2,700 were captured. Scott had only won the ability to push forward to the next fight. Anderson had emerged without a scratch, although the rains and physical exertion had made his Florida condition worse. Company G, according to Anderson, lost more men "in proportion to my strength than any other company."[67] Although a veteran of several conflicts, the death and destruction at Churubusco were like nothing he had seen before. Bodies mangled by canister and musket fire littered the battlefield from the Churubusco River to San Antonio and on both sides of El Pedregal. Anderson's letter to his wife is filled with the names of officers they had socialized with in Florida and South Carolina who would not be coming home or men like Phil Kearney who left limbs on the battlefield. Anderson's "heart bled" for the newly created widows and their children.[68]

As after every battle, the army paused to reorganize, treat its wounded, and bury its dead. The men of Company G were buried in the cornfield where they fell. Anderson and countless other men wrote letters to wives or other loved ones. Senior officers had to write and submit their official reports. These reports never ceased to cause anger and contention among the officer corps. Promotions were extremely slow in the US Army. They only came when new positions were created, which was rare, or when positions above opened, which was just as rare. Since there was no retirement from the army and no maximum age, most officers kept their positions long after they were too old or infirm to do their jobs. Anderson's immediate superior in the Third Artillery did not make the voyage to Mexico. Major William McClintock would spend the war at his home in Massachusetts. He was too old and unhealthy for an active field command. McClintock enlisted in the Third Artillery on July 1, 1812, and by the time he was promoted to major in 1843, he was too infirm to walk. War increased the opportunities for advancement. Not just because of the opening caused by enemy bullets, it also allowed officers to stand out and earn better postwar positions or bypass officers slightly ahead of them in seniority. This was more likely to happen if an officer received favorable mention in the official reports.[69]

Anderson was annoyed that neither his company nor his regiment received special mention in the official report. What was worse, according to Anderson, was that Colonel Belton filled his original report with praise for the Third Artillery, and it was sent back by his superior with instructions to be more straightforward. If Belton's original after-action report was anything like the letter he wrote his wife and son, it was indeed a loss to Anderson and the other officers of the Third Artillery that it did not become part of the official record.[70]

During the pause after the battle, Santa Anna reached out to Scott with a proposal for a truce while the two sides negotiated an end to the war. Scott accepted. He and Trist began working on the terms of the truce and the treaty. The truce angered many in the army. They felt they were on the verge of victory, and Scott was giving the Mexicans time to catch their breath and reorganize. Mounted dragoons had been at the gates of the capital. To many, it was the worst possible timing. Scott's three division commanders all felt Scott should push into the capital and dictate peace terms. There was also the legitimate concern that Santa Anna had no intention of agreeing to peace and would violate the terms of the truce to improve his strategic situation. In retrospect, Scott's critics were correct. Santa Anna was not negotiating in good faith. He was using the time to prepare for the next battle. Mexico City would have to be captured and occupied.

Although his critics may have been right, Scott had instructions from the president that fit his own strategic thinking. President Polk wanted a negotiated end to the war. He had hoped it would come after every victory. That there was a senior State Department official on hand showed how serious Polk was. If the Mexican government surrendered, Scott could avoid another battle and the numerous problems involved with an occupation.[71]

Although he did not have all the information Scott had, Anderson agreed with his commander. He believed the final battle for Mexico had been fought and thanked God for that. Anderson had seen enough. "What a sacrifice of life!

God grant that Victory may be crowned with Peace. We cannot stand many such victories." He promised his wife to "never, no, never, to leave my beloved land to fight again in foreign lands."[72]

Within sight of the city, the American Army settled into camp. Supply problems had to be solved along with typical camp life issues. Anderson was appointed judge advocate to deal with crimes committed against Mexican civilians. The commission met in one of the old Spanish mansions in Tacubaya. Anderson took time between cases to examine the home's vast art collection. There were six rooms full of paintings, which Anderson described to his wife in detail. He was even slightly tempted to take an expensive souvenir. After all, the owner "is said to be the richest man in Mexico; his heirs would not miss the picture, were he to give it to me."[73]

On September 6, Santa Anna began reinforcing Castle Chapultepec. This was a clear violation of the truce. The war would continue. Anderson and his men prepared to move at a moment's notice. They had to wait more than a week as Scott and his staff developed a plan of attack. Scott sent patrols out to find the best approaches to the city and any possible weakness in the Mexican position. From these reports, Scott gained the unwelcome knowledge that the southernmost route past the formidable Castle Chapultepec was the only feasible one. He also received what turned out to be the spurious intelligence that, as part of their defensive preparations, the Mexicans were removing church bells and turning them into cannons. This was being carried out at a flour mill called Molino del Rey, the King's Mill. Although the reports proved false, there was plenty of evidence to convince Scott of their validity. Considering the amount of artillery captured, it made sense that Santa Anna would take drastic steps to replenish his supplies. Santa Anna's shifting of troops to defend this group of stone buildings strengthened the argument that something important was happening there.[74]

Besides the information he received that Molino del Rey was a cannon foundry, other things played into Scott's decision. After Santa Anna's betrayal over the peace negotiations, Scott was likely impatient to strike at something. Foundry or not, Molino del Rey was the next natural target on the road to Mexico City. Leaving a fortified position on his flank and his rear as he attacked the capital was potentially fatal. General Gideon Pillow argued vehemently against the operation. Scott gave the job of capturing Molino del Rey to Worth. Worth believed he could easily carry Molino del Rey. Although Worth and Scott had serious personal difficulties with one another, Worth was a professional. His opinion counted more than that of the political appointee Pillow, especially when it was the same as Scott's.

Scott left the attack entirely to Worth, perhaps evidence that Scott did not believe this would be a serious battle. Scott did suggest to his subordinate that it be carried out at night. Worth did not feel this was necessary. A sunrise attack would still give them the element of surprise without all the difficulties and dangers of a night operation.[75]

At about 2 a.m., the officers of Worth's Division began waking their men. By two-thirty, they were on the road north. They moved as quietly as possible. When they arrived a few hundred yards from their target, they were moved into position and ordered to lie down to avoid attracting attention. More than thirty-four hundred men lay in the grass alone with their thoughts, waiting for the sun to rise.

Molino del Rey was a group of stone buildings in a line about three hundred yards long, connected by a wall. The line ran north to south and was about one thousand yards west of Castle Chapultepec, which sat on a hill overlooking the buildings. The flat Mexican-style building and the sandbags stacked on the roof made each little building a fortress. Directly to the northwest was a larger stone building called the Casa Mata. The Mexican line formed a ninety-degree angle. A drainage ditch and patches of the prickly Magua plant ran in front of the wall. Between the American and the Mexican positions was an open field sloping gently upward.

Worth's strategy was to strike the center of Molino del Rey with five hundred men under Major George Wright. These men were hand-chosen from units throughout the division. To Wright's left, Colonel James McIntosh would lead his brigade against Casa Mata, the northwest end of the Mexican position. On the far right of the American line was Colonel John Garland, whose brigade included Anderson and the rest of the Third Artillery. They were tasked with striking the southernmost end of the Mexican position. There was a reserve force, including mounted dragoons. The dragoons were tasked with preventing the Mexican cavalry and other reinforcements from entering the battle. An artillery battery supported each of the three striking forces.

Just before the sun rose, Captain Benjamin Huger, Anderson's friend and West Point classmate, opened the battle by firing his twenty-four-pound siege guns over the heads of Wright's men into the walls of Molino del Rey. The Mexicans showed great discipline that morning and did not return fire. This would cost the Americans greatly. After a few shots from the big guns and no Mexican response, Worth sent two engineers halfway across the field to assess the situation. Seeing no reaction from the Mexican position, they decided Molino del Rey had been abandoned during the night. Wright's five hundred stormed the enemy's center.

When Wright's men arrived within two hundred yards of the buildings, they learned that Molino del Rey was not abandoned and was much better defended than anyone had initially thought. Two full brigades were inside, in front of, and on top of the stone buildings, with more on the way from Castle Chapultepec. Mexican cannons fired canister shot into the Americans. The musket balls and pieces of metal loaded into the guns devastated the attacking column. Mangled bodies fell on the gently sloping field. Wright ordered his men to rush the cannons before they could fire again. As they closed the distance, musket fire cut down even more men. The closer they drew, the more effective the fire from the Mexican infantry became. Wright's men were driven back over their own dead and wounded. Three-fourths of the column's officers had been killed or wounded, including Wright, who was among the seriously injured.

After Wright launched his assault, but before the results could be known, the two wings of the assault were launched. Neither took advantage of their artillery. As in the center, the infantry was ordered in after only a few shots by the artillery. Perhaps they hoped to overrun the Mexican positions before the arrival of the Mexican force at Chapultepec. The failure to let the artillery do its work before sending the infantry proved an unnecessary waste of life.

McIntosh's brigade got within thirty yards of Casa Marta before being driven back. Colonel Garland's brigade had the first success of the day. They drove north against the flank of the Mexican position. Like everyone else, they received brutal Mexican fire once they were within two hundred yards of the enemy. Because of their line of approach, Garland's men were able to get partial cover where the wall angled away from the Mexican front.

Anderson and Company G were at the angle in relative safety when Anderson saw the men of Captain Simon Drum's two-gun battery pushing and dragging their cannons into position. They were moving slowly on the soft, wet ground. Anderson jumped from his safe position to help haul the big gun into place. Once done, he returned to his men. On Anderson's way back to his men, he "felt a severe blow against my right shoulder," and a few moments later, "a tingling pricking sensation in my left arm." Once back in his concealed position, he told a fellow officer that a ricochet had touched him. It was more than that, the officer replied. Anderson was bleeding. As Anderson had suggested, one of the hits had been a spent ball, leaving him with only a bruise. The other shot, probably fired from the rooftop due to the angle of entry, buried a half-inch lead ball in his chest just below his shoulder. With the adrenaline flowing, Anderson carried on with a severe wound. Drum's guns did their job, and Anderson and the rest of Garland's command could push through the gates

BATTLE OF MOLINO DEL REY, FOUGHT SEP.T 8.TH 1847.
Blowing up the Foundry by the Victorious American Army under Gen.l Worth.

The Battle of Molino Del Rey, fought on the outskirts of Mexico City, where Anderson was seriously wounded. Courtesy of the Library of Congress, LC-USZ62-62219.

and into the labyrinth of small buildings. Anderson was shot a third time, this one grazing the bone just below his knee.

With the help of artillery, McIntosh was able to take Casa Marta. The wings began pushing toward the center. The Mexican position collapsed, and the soldiers retreated to Chapultepec. There were pockets of resistance, and it was two hours before the guns fell silent. Once again, many in Scott's army were disappointed that they were not allowed to pursue a defeated enemy.

Once the battle was over and the adrenaline rush began to wear off, the wounded Anderson began to feel the pain. "A drink of spirits from a soldier's canteen revived me, but in a few minutes, I fell."[76]

Anderson's war was over. He would only be a distant spectator to the capture of Chapultepec and Mexico City. As the Battle of Molino del Rey still raged, Anderson and other wounded men were carried back to Tacubaya. He was placed in a hospital that was the converted home of a senior Mexican general. Among his fellow patients was Huger.

By the end of the month, while still not well enough for duty, Anderson was up and walking, even playing tourist in Mexico City. He bought some engravings for his wife. He was accompanied by his new orderly, Peter Hart, a German immigrant from New York. His original aide had also been wounded at Molino del Rey. In October, Anderson was invited to move to General Scott's headquarters, a space he shared with Scott and Trist.

Scott gave Anderson the odd and interesting job of examining and researching the Aztec Calendar stone, then residing next to the Cathedral of the Assumption of the Most Blessed Virgin Mary in the central plaza. Scott considered taking the ancient artifact as a war trophy if the Mexican government did not sign a treaty soon. Scott, of course, left the artifact where it stood. His decision was probably influenced by the fact that it weighed fifty-four thousand pounds.[77]

On October 24, 1847, Anderson was ordered back to the United States. He carried with him a report from the surgeon that he would be unfit for duty for the next three months and the new rank of brevet major for his "gallant and meritorious service" at Molino del Rey. After the trip overland to Vera Cruz and then by ship to Savannah via New Orleans, Anderson would have as much as two months to spend with Eliza at her father's estate before the two traveled to his next duty station. The war had been hard on Company G. Of the eighty-six men Anderson had brought with him from Florida, fewer than thirty men remained available for duty.[78]

During this time, Trist and Scott negotiated the Treaty of Guadalupe Hidalgo with a new Mexican government. The treaty added a half million square miles of new territory to the United States. Polk got what he wanted. However, the addition of this new territory set in motion the chain of events that led to the American Civil War and cemented Anderson's place in history.

CHAPTER 8

THE INTERWAR YEARS

To say that the thirteen years that followed the firing of the last gun in America's war with Mexico were difficult is a vast understatement. A brutal, bloody civil war was coming. The causes of that conflict were wide and varied. The events that brought about the war were political. For the most part, professional soldiers like Robert Anderson did not take part. He spent the tumultuous 1850s, as most Americans would, growing his young family and earning a living.

Eliza Anderson was described as sickly and often too ill to accompany her husband to frontier posts; instead she lived with her father in Georgia or in New York City to be close to the doctors under whose care she always seemed to be. Regardless of her poor health, she gave birth to five children. Maria, their second child, was born in 1849. Sophia was born three years later. Duncan was born in 1857, and the baby, Robert Jr., was born seven years later, in 1859.

Anderson's post–Mexican War career was nothing like the danger and excitement he saw in Florida and Mexico. In 1848, the army assigned him to Fort Preble. Its whitewashed brick walls defended the harbor and city of Portland, Maine. The fort was forty years old. It was built to enforce President Jefferson's 1807 embargo. During the 1830s and early 1840s, when the possibility of a war with Britain loomed, Fort Preble faced the prospect of fighting the British fleet. In the mid- to late 1850s, Portland would grow into a major port, a winter destination for goods on their way to Canada. However, Anderson's four years at Fort Preble were uneventful.

Major Anderson was able to have his family with him. Initially, they lived in the fort's officers' quarters, but Anderson rented a house in Portland as soon as one was available. In the fort, they were isolated from local society. The Andersons wanted little Eliza to be able to play with the neighbor children. The family needed more space as well. Sophia joined the family in 1852, and Anderson hired a nurse to care for the children, as his sickly wife often could not.

In 1849, Anderson's father-in-law, Duncan Clinch, passed away. Born in 1787 in North Carolina to a relatively well-to-do farm family, Clinch had become a wealthy and politically important man. The Georgia Legislature passed a resolution honoring him for his service to the nation. "Honor, gallantry, and faithful discharge of every trust were his shining virtues."[1] He was only eighteen years older than his son-in-law. Clinch could easily have been one of Richard Clough Anderson's sons.

Clinch was survived by his wife, three daughters, and five sons. His estate was worth nearly two million dollars. He owned land throughout Georgia and Florida, including a plantation in both states. Clinch's wife was given the use of his Georgia plantation for the rest of her life. On her death, the plantation went to his oldest son. Except for the plantation his wife would live on, the rest of his property was divided between the rest of the general's children. Two hundred slaves and parcels of land were sold, and the proceeds were divided among the children.

Eliza Anderson inherited two slaves directly, Willis and Charlotte. Neither of the Andersons opposed slavery. Although Robert Anderson's brothers had come to question the institution, his personal experiences differed from those of his family, who stayed in the Kentucky and Ohio areas. Regardless of their beliefs about slavery, they were not in a position to keep slaves. Not only was it illegal in Maine, but their Portland neighbors would surely have shunned them.

Duncan Clinch Jr., the executor of his father's will, sold his sister's bondsmen for her. Unfortunately for Anderson's finances, sickness broke out among the slaves, and their sales were rushed. Anderson got much less than fair market value. Fortunately for Clinch Jr., he did not have the same problem with the slaves he sold. Anderson was too polite to say it directly but believed his brother-in-law was cheating him. His time with the Army bureaucracy had taught him how to keep a careful eye on money. He politely suggested to his brother-in-law that Eliza was not getting her fair share of her father's estate. Clinch Jr. responded that if Eliza was destitute, all they would have to do was ask, and the family would be charitable. This was a serious insult to a proud man like Anderson. He could do little from Maine and did not want to wage a family war over money. Anderson invested the family's new wealth in a Paducah, Kentucky, bank and bought stock in a small railroad in Ohio. It was the first time Anderson had more "money at my command than was necessary for my annual expenses."[2]

Except for his wife's constant illness, these were good years for Anderson. His daughters were healthy and happy. He was financially secure, and his career trajectory was still moving upward. Even his dream of a retirement home for soldiers was moving forward.

Anderson had done all he could to bring about the soldiers' home. It was now in the hands of others. He had collected the data required to argue for the need and costs to Congress. He proposed to collect the disciplinary fines of soldiers to offset the cost of the facilities. According to Anderson, that amounted to around forty-two thousand dollars a year. The self-destructive behavior of the soldiers would fund their retirement. Anderson researched the only comparable homes in the United States to arrive at a cost: mental institutions. Most of them were spending about $43 per inmate. The home would be self-sufficient with around a thousand old soldiers.[3]

Anderson appeared before several congressional committees, arguing for the need and presenting technical details. He used the opportunity of the Mexican War to collect a petition signed by almost every officer in the army. He won General Scott over to the cause as well as General Clinch.

A friend from the Black Hawk War days finally brought Anderson victory. Senator Jefferson Davis of Mississippi pushed through Senate Bill 392, and the House of Representatives quickly followed suit. President Millard Fillmore added his signature the same day it passed the House.[4]

Congress authorized the building of homes in four cities: Washington, DC; New Orleans; East Pascagoula, Mississippi; and Harrodsburg, Kentucky. The law also created a board of directors to oversee them. They chose Brevet Major Robert Anderson to be the first head of the Harrodsburg home, a fitting reward for a man who had worked so hard for its creation. Brevet Captain Abraham Buford of the First Dragoons, also from Kentucky, was chosen as Anderson's secretary-treasurer.

The two Kentuckians did not get along. Anderson felt Buford was not doing his job and was abusing his position as treasurer to sell the home things it did not need. Anderson pushed to remove him, and Buford countercharged that Anderson was acting out a personal grudge against him. Anderson asked Senator Davis to come to his aid. At Davis's behest, the board investigated the situation. Buford was allowed to resign, and the board told Anderson that he could have handled the situation better.[5]

Anderson's work kept him extremely busy. He had to hire staff, organize supplies, manage construction, accept residents, and even negotiate railroad contracts. Regardless of his hectic work schedule, he spent more time with his brothers and sisters than at any time since before joining the army. Harrodsburg was only seventy miles from Louisville and just over one hundred miles to Cincinnati. His four brothers lived in the Cincinnati area. Larz was a successful businessman, and Charles and William were successful lawyers. John Roy served as deputy postmaster for the Cincinnati area. His brothers would all eventually join the newly created Republican Party. Although they all grew up with slaves, or because they did, they were all antislavery men. The year he spent in central Kentucky with his brothers and sisters, as opposed to his in-laws and Southern officer friends, surely affected his outlook on the growing political crisis.

Even though the board of directors of the Soldiers' Home was ecstatic with his work and unanimously voted to keep him on as director of the Harrodsburg home, his tenure lasted less than a year. In early 1854, Secretary of War Jefferson Davis issued a directive ending detached duty for all captains. Since Anderson was only a brevet major, thus still technically a captain, he would have to return to his company.

Anderson's company was in San Francisco. In 1853, the US Army Corps of Engineers began work on Fort Point, considered the key to the bay's defense. Anderson's Company G of the Third Artillery would occupy the site and aid construction. Anderson wrote the secretary of war and asked for a different assignment. Eliza's health was once again failing. Her doctor claimed the voyage to California would kill her. Anderson requested either a station in the Northeast or a leave of absence. Davis, himself a widower, was sympathetic to his friend's plight. Anderson's promotion to major went through soon after Davis received Anderson's letter. The rule about detached duty no longer applied. Instead of boarding a ship to Panama, followed by a trip across the isthmus and another ship voyage up the coast, Anderson and his family boarded a train to Trenton, New Jersey. The promotion to major required a transfer to the First Artillery. He had been in the Third his entire army career.

Anderson's new post was the Trenton Iron Works. As the army's representative, he inspected the artillery and other equipment the company provided to the army. He would do the same job for two employers. He was also reporting to the Treasury Department's Office of Construction and was paid by both. Had he gone to San Francisco, he most likely would have spent the next decade there. His company would remain at Fort Point through the Civil War. A San Francisco–based Anderson would have been unavailable for the Fort Moultrie assignment. Like the officer who took his place in San Francisco, Anderson would have been just another obscure antebellum officer.

Anderson enrolled his three daughters in Clement's Boarding School in Beverly, New Jersey. Even though the headmistress, Mrs. Macauley, gave the family a deal—three for the price of two—having all the girls in one school was still more expensive. He must have remembered his loneliness as a fourteen-year-old from a big family alone at Buck Pond Academy.[6]

Mrs. Anderson lived in a New York City hotel to be closer to quality medical care. This became even more important when she became pregnant with their fourth child. Duncan Lamont Clinch Anderson was born in August 1854.

Named after his maternal grandfather, Duncan was a sickly child and barely lived past his fifteenth month.[7] This tragedy and her health issues did not prevent the Andersons from continuing to grow their family. Robert Anderson Jr., the last of the Anderson children, was born in 1859.

The inspector position in Trenton proved good for Anderson's career. The actual work did not take up nearly as much of his time as did the Soldiers' Home or even a regular company command. This allowed Anderson to continue revisions on his field artillery tactics manual and serve on an army committee examining coastal fortifications. He was able to take detached duty from his detached duty.

In November 1859, he was ordered to Fortress Monroe as the second in command at the Artillery School of Practice. The school had been closed in 1834 but was now being revived. He would serve under Colonel Justin Dimick. Before he began to prepare for the move, Anderson was sent to New York to oversee the publication of his *Evolutions of Field Batteries of Artillery, tr. from the French and Arranged for the Army and Militia of the United States*. The War Department paid for a thousand copies to be published by the D. Van Nostrand Company and wanted it put into the hands of every artillery officer in the army.[8] Many more would be published as volunteer officers tried to learn their craft in the upcoming Civil War.

With the publication of his book complete, Anderson was once again ordered to Fortress Monroe, Virginia. Along with two captains, he was to arrange a program of instruction for the newly formed artillery school. Anderson wrote Samuel Cooper, the adjutant general, and asked for leave. He had been promised time before he had gone to New York. He told Cooper that he would not be idle during this time. He wanted to reach out to other artillery officers and solicit their opinions about the program. Cooper granted his request. Anderson was true to his word; over the next five months, letters from artillery officers flooded into his New York apartment.[9]

In May 1860, Anderson was in Fortress Monroe preparing for his wife and son's move to Virginia and beginning work on the new program when he was called upon to serve on a congressional committee investigating the West Point curriculum. It was another great career opportunity. The commission's president was the former secretary of war and, once again, senator from Mississippi, Jefferson Davis. On the committee was Senator Solomon Foot of Vermont, soon to be president pro tempore of the Senate, and Congressmen John Cochrane of New York and Henry Winter Davis of Maryland. The two military men on the committee were Major Anderson and fifty-year-old Captain A. A. Humphreys, who had a respectable career in the Corps of Engineers.

In 1852, Colonel Robert E. Lee was named superintendent of West Point. He graduated second in the class of 1829, four years after Anderson. Lee was a favorite of Scott's, and the old general shepherded Lee's career even more than he did Anderson's. Both men were serious professionals in a small force. They would have known each other, especially since both men had a close relationship with Scott. Neither man's papers suggest that theirs was anything but a professional acquaintance.

Superintendent Lee instituted many reforms to West Point and its curriculum. Although the Mexican War was a great success, critics claimed West Point had not prepared its graduates for that war. Much of this criticism was from the officers themselves. Lee wanted to add more field instruction, classes on military law, and Spanish. Considering that most of the Western Hemisphere spoke that language, adding Spanish seemed common sense. The new additions would make West Point a five-year program instead of four. Lee was able to convince Congress to allow the change.

The cadets were not happy with this change for obvious reasons. Although they were surely not the only students displeased with decisions made at their institution, West Point cadets had some political influence. They did, after all, need a congressional recommendation to be admitted. The political pressure worked, and Secretary of War John B. Floyd ordered the Academy to return to the four-year curriculum. Lee was no longer the superintendent, and his replacement did not resist as Lee might have.[10]

Congress created a commission to investigate the West Point situation. The report the committee produced was thorough. In his popular history of the Academy, Stephen Ambrose called it "the best description of pre–Civil War West Point available."[11] Throughout the summer of 1860, the committee interviewed cadets and faculty. They reviewed records. In the evenings, they dined and socialized with faculty, army officers, and other visitors who came up the Hudson River. The army band gave concerts, and the famous French Zouaves, then touring the country, performed at West Point while General Scott was visiting. Anderson even traveled with Scott to meet the future king of Great Britain, Edward VII, when he visited New York.

Anderson enjoyed this pleasant atmosphere alone. His daughters remained in school, and his wife and Robert Jr., still a toddler, were with family in North Carolina. The mail service was much more dependable between New York and North Carolina than between Florida and Mexico. He wrote to her daily. He admitted to his wife the only example of himself acting in a nonbusiness-like manner. While a professor was testifying on a point of not great interest, Anderson was writing a personal letter.[12]

The summer at West Point and the memory of his faculty days in the 1830s convinced Anderson to apply for the soon-to-be-open superintendent position. He spoke to Senator Davis about it. Davis agreed to put forward Anderson's name, along with ten others, but it was doubtful he would be chosen. As Davis explained, the superintendent had always come from the engineers. Eliza wanted him to use his influence with Senator Davis and the commanding general to secure the post. Anderson refused. Although he had done just that to stay out of California, that was for the sake of his family, not his career. He would not "depart from the rule of my life and ask friends to try and get the appointment for me."[13]

If West Point was not an option, there were other similar, if not as prestigious, positions. Many states had military academies. In the last couple of years, several states had founded military schools. Louisiana hired the former artilleryman William T. Sherman to head their new school. North Carolina hired another artilleryman, D. H. Hill, as commandant of their new military academy. The North Carolina academy had an open position for an engineering drawing instructor at two thousand dollars a year. He and his wife discussed it but passed on the opportunity. At almost fifty-five, and with a wife and four dependent children, he must have felt it was not the right time for a career change. Major Anderson had been in uniform his entire adult life. It would have been hard to leave

Over coffee in the mess or wine with dinner, the growing political crisis was a common topic of conversation. The army had tried to police the recent trouble in Kansas. With a detachment of marines, Colonel Lee ended John Brown's failed slave revolt in Virginia. Senator Preston Brooks had severely beaten Senator Charles Sumner on the Senate floor. The regional antislavery Republican Party had reached national prominence and would likely win the presidency in the election only a few months away. The Democratic Party had split, producing three candidates for president.

After more than a century and a half of hindsight, it is easy to wonder why more people did not see the great storm coming. While visiting his daughters, Anderson attended a speech by John J. Crittenden. A fellow Kentucky Whig, Senator Crittenden did not believe the crisis threatened the country's future. Both men had lived through the bitter politics of the Jackson era. Like Jackson Fever, this too would pass. He was so confident in that belief that he invested a thousand dollars in the Pensacola and Georgia Railroad, an investment his friend "Cump" Sherman would destroy in a few short years.

With the report's completion, Anderson returned to Fortress Monroe to begin work on the Artillery School's curriculum. It was a position arguably as satisfying as commandant of West Point, a job that went to his former student P. G. T. Beauregard. Anderson would spend only four months at Fortress Monroe. In December 1860, the secretary of war needed a calm, professional officer he could trust in Charleston. Major Anderson was soon on his way to the center of the political crisis that would tear the nation in two, and his name would forever be linked with the still-unfinished fortress in Charleston Harbor.

CHAPTER 9

CHARLESTON HARBOR I

On November 18, 1860, Major Robert Anderson received Special Order 189 from the office of Adjutant General Samuel Cooper. Anderson was to report without unnecessary delay to Fort Moultrie. With the election of Abraham Lincoln on November 6, it was likely that South Carolina and other states of the Deep South would attempt to leave the Union. President James Buchanan was in a complicated situation. The president was no friend of secession and even told southern senators that he would oppose it with all the power at his disposal. That, of course, was the problem.[1]

It was the opinion of Buchanan and his attorney general, fellow Pennsylvanian Jeremiah Black—after a careful study of the US Constitution, federal law, and the nation's history—that the president had no real power to act. This position has led to much derision of the president. If a state could not leave the Union, but the federal government did not have the power to stop it—that was the perfect recipe for a weak president looking for a reason not to act. This assessment is unfair to Buchanan, for there was, in fact, little he could do. The existing laws were not adequate for the current crisis. Buchanan adopted a policy of patience. He believed that if everyone stayed calm until the Lincoln administration took office, the South, especially the border states, would see that a Republican president with a Democratic-controlled Congress posed little danger to them. For this strategy to be successful, he needed the Republicans to refrain from any bold or outrageous statements, and he would avoid taking any action that would drive southerners to start a revolution.[2]

It was to carry out this strategy that Buchanan sent Anderson to take command of the garrison at Fort Moultrie. Anderson replaced Colonel John Gardner, a professional officer whose resume was not that different from Anderson's, having fought in Florida and Mexico, and marched with Scott to Mexico City. A native of Massachusetts, Gardner had rubbed the South Carolina authorities the wrong way when he attempted to strengthen Fort Moultrie by transferring arms stored at the federal arsenal in Charleston to the fort. For this, he was banished to Texas.

Anderson was also given a second order from Cooper to report to Secretary of War John B. Floyd in Washington, DC. Anderson had been the personal choice of Secretary Floyd. At the height of the coming crisis, he would say, "Major Anderson is a man of honor, and truth, and courage. I selected him myself, not only from that but other services that were high and honorable."[3] Floyd was the former governor of Virginia, and his loyalties were with the South. Indeed, he would later join the Confederacy and serve as a general in its armies. Whether his loyalties were with the secessionists at this point has been much debated. He most likely felt that Anderson, as a Kentuckian and a man married into a respectable southern family, would be sympathetic to the southern cause, or at least would show extreme discretion in dealing with South Carolina officials.

Anderson knew he was going into a complicated and sensitive situation. The first thing he did on receiving his new orders was to see Winfield Scott. No fan of politics, at least since his 1852 presidential defeat, Scott made his headquarters in New York City. Although physically not what he once was—he could not even rise when Anderson entered—General Scott was still mentally sharp. After the November election, he warned President James Buchanan that "there is some danger of an early act of rashness." He pointed out southern forts that were either totally unmanned or severely undermanned. New Orleans, Mobile, Pensacola, Savannah, Charleston, and the Chesapeake made Scott's list. He wrote that "all these works should be immediately so garrisoned as to make any attempt to take any one of them, by surprise or coup de main, ridiculous."[4] This was an extremely wise suggestion on Scott's part, which he should have made months earlier. It was probably already too late to do so without causing a violent reaction from South Carolina.

General Scott did not offer his protégé any clearer instructions than what had come from the official orders from the secretary of war. Floyd had not consulted Scott on either the relief of Gardner or the appointment of Anderson. Since Scott had advised Buchanan that it was best to allow southern states to leave peacefully, he had been sidelined.[5] Scott could offer Anderson no clues as to what Floyd expected of him. Scott requested that Anderson make a full report of the situation and send it as directly to him as possible.

Unsatisfied with the results of his meeting with Scott, Anderson paid a visit to a trusted friend, George W. Cullum. A native New Yorker and career army officer, Captain Cullum was stationed at Fort Hamilton in New York, but he had spent the previous five years in Charleston overseeing the construction of Fort Sumter. If Anderson had any doubts that his new posting would be the most challenging of his long career, they were erased as Cullum briefed him on the troubling situation in Charleston, South Carolina.

Cullum reported to Anderson that the people of Charleston were beyond agitated; they were at the point of violence. They saw the election of Abraham Lincoln as a direct attack on their way of life. It was a "triumph of Northern sectionalism over Southern Rights."[6] "That South Carolina will arm, and take action for her safety and independence in the event of Lincoln's election, is as certain as his election is certain."[7]

To South Carolina planters, Lincoln represented the abolitionist movement, and that movement was more than an attack on their way of life; it was a threat to their lives. In areas of South Carolina, Mississippi, and Louisiana, where slaves and freedmen outnumbered whites, sometimes as much as nine to one, abolitionism meant only one thing: savage and bloody servile insurrection. When New England abolitionists professed pacifism to southern planters, it appeared to them as a blatant lie. In their eyes, the only possible result of the abolitionist message was a violent revolt, as had happened in the French colony of San Domingo. Slave owners believed the abolitionists were putting the "torch and poison" into the hands of their slaves.[8]

South Carolinians had been in constant fear and anger since John Brown's failed Harper's Ferry raid. If any doubt remained in South Carolina and the other southern states that abolitionists and their political party meant to destroy the southern way of life in blood and fire, Brown ended it. South Carolina's leaders were now convinced that they were no longer safe in a union with northerners, especially if the new Republican Party were to seize control of the federal government in the upcoming presidential and congressional elections.

None of that information would have been unknown to Anderson. What Cullum could tell him was what the newspapers could not. How universal were these passions? Was it just the words of the angry fire-eaters that were printed, or was most of the population as stirred up? Cullum, the professional military engineer, could also enlighten Anderson about the military situation of his new command. How grimly Cullum portrayed the picture in Charleston, we do not know, but he assured Anderson that South Carolina would secede.

With a clearer picture of the situation, Anderson left Eliza and Robert Jr. in New York and traveled by train to the nation's capital. He met with Secretary Floyd in the old two-story War Department building next door to the White House. Floyd stressed the political sensitivity of the situation and that it must be handled delicately. He did not tell Anderson that no reinforcements would be sent to his hopelessly undermanned garrison.

In what was a harbinger of the problems faced by the South in the next four years, it took Anderson five days by train to reach Charleston. Three days before he arrived, the aptly named *Charleston Mercury* ran a brief biography of the new commander of the harbor forts. He was a Kentuckian and southern in "his views, principles, and interests."[9] He was obviously an improvement over Massachusetts-born Gardner. Fort Moultrie was not the only command change. Colonel Benjamin Huger, a native of Charleston and friend of Anderson's, was sent by the army to take command of the US Arsenal.

The fifty-six-year-old Anderson quietly arrived on November 20, 1860. His graying hair was about to become much grayer. He took the midafternoon boat from Charleston to travel the four miles to Fort Moultrie. The quintessential professional, Anderson went to work immediately. The first obligation of a new commander is to examine his command, men, officers, and facilities.

Anderson knew none of the officers now under his command. He had served his entire career with the Third Artillery, and although he had been with the First for a few years, it had all been detached duty. Even though none of the officers had served with Anderson or knew him personally, they knew him by reputation and respected him. One of his senior officers, the New Yorker Abner Doubleday, described Anderson "as a gentleman; courteous, honest, intelligent, and thoroughly versed in his profession."[10]

Anderson had two companies under his command. Although in numbers, there were barely enough men to form one company. Captain Truman Seymour commanded Company H. The thirty-six-year-old Vermonter was a West Point graduate and veteran of the Mexican War. Seymour was also a talented artist who would sell sketches of the upcoming crisis to newspapers. Under Seymour was Lieutenant Theodore Talbot. The thirty-five-year-old Talbot was from a wealthy Kentucky family but had grown up in Washington, DC. He had served on John C. Frémont's famous western expeditions. Also in Company H was Second Lieutenant Norman Hall. He was from Michigan and a recent West Point graduate. Hall was the youngest officer at Fort Moultrie and served as the adjutant and quartermaster for the small command.

Captain Abner Doubleday commanded Company E. He was from a politically connected family. Doubleday was an unapologetic abolitionist, a position that had made him unpopular as a West Point cadet. Under Doubleday was Lieutenant Jefferson C. Davis. A rarity in the US Army, Davis rose from the enlisted ranks. He had joined an Indiana volunteer regiment and was awarded a commission in the regular army for his service at the Battle of Buena Vista.

The Corps of Engineers had two officers overseeing the construction of Fort Sumter. Captain John Foster was a West Point graduate from New Hampshire. Like Anderson, the thirty-eight-year-old Foster had served as a West Point instructor and had been wounded at the Battle of Molina Del Rey. His assistant was Lieutenant George W. Snyder. The New Yorker had graduated first in the

Robert Anderson and his officers. The photograph reproduced in newspapers across the country was taken during the siege of Fort Sumter. Standing left to right, Truman Seymour, George W. Snyder, Jefferson C. Davis, Richard Meade. Sitting left to right, Abner Doubleday, Anderson, Samuel Crawford, and John Foster. Courtesy of the Library of Congress, LC-DIG-ppmsca-35459.

West Point class of 1856. Anderson also had a surgeon attached to his command, Wiley Crawford. However, when push came to shove, Anderson could count on the thirty-one-year-old Pennsylvanian as a fighting officer.

The seventy-one enlisted men, as were most soldiers of the antebellum army, were primarily northern men with a fair number of immigrants. These men would remain loyal to the American flag. Assuming they were mere mercenaries, South Carolina officials tried to win the men over with feasts and free drinks. Anderson's friend Captain Edward Ord warned him that the same tactic was being used against his men at Fortress Monroe. An unknown man was recruiting foreign-born soldiers for a "southern army." The soldiers enjoyed the parties, got drunk, and behaved badly but obeyed their officers in the end and often went above and beyond the call of duty. Anderson was not happy with the lack of discipline he found. But that was a problem he believed began at the top. With Gardner gone and with West Point–trained officers, he was confident he could bring the command up to his exacting standards. Other problems were not as easily fixed.[11]

The defenses of Charleston Harbor, now under Anderson's command, consisted of four structures. There was Castle Pinckney. Located on a small island less than a mile from Charleston, the small round masonry fort was started in 1797 to defend Charleston from the French during the Quasi-War. Instead of an entire garrison, the castle was manned by Ordinance Sergeant James Skillen, his wife, and their fifteen-year-old daughter. Skillen's job was to maintain the installation and its equipment. Fort Johnson on James Island was nearly two miles south of Castle Pinckney. Dating from before the revolution, it had all but been abandoned by 1860.

Just over three miles from Castle Pinckney was Fort Moultrie on Sullivan's Island. Most of Anderson's men were there—in a poor defensive position. Ongoing repair work left significant gaps in the walls. The work was carried out by local men. Officers of the state militia strolled through the fort taking notes. Sandhills near the walls allowed perfect cover and concealment for infantry to fire into the fort. Blowing sand had created ramps against the wall of such slight grade that sentries often found cows roaming the ramparts. It would have been only a slightly better situation if Fort Moultrie had been fully manned and in perfect condition. It was a sea battery designed to stop enemy vessels from approaching Charleston; it was highly vulnerable to a hostile land force on the island.[12]

One mile from Fort Moultrie and two and a half miles from Castle Pinckney was the massive Fort Sumter, or at least the shell of Fort Sumter. Construction had been authorized in 1829 as part of a series of forts along the Atlantic, Pacific, and Gulf coasts and had continued for over thirty years. When international tensions were high, the pace of construction increased, and when the country faced economic woes, the work would come to a standstill. When it was finished, and its garrison of 650 men manned its 146 heavy guns, no ship could enter or leave Charleston Harbor without the consent of Fort Sumter's commander. In December 1860, it was occupied by construction workers, and none of its powerful guns were in place.

Per his orders, Anderson carefully examined the situation and submitted a full report to the secretary of war through Adjutant General Cooper. As an experienced military professional, Anderson made several unarguably accurate observations to his superiors. The local population was openly hostile to the federal government and the presence of the US Army. South Carolina forces planned to seize all federal installations in and around Charleston. His current location could not be held unless Fort Sumter was garrisoned. Anderson recommended in his report that at least two companies should occupy Fort Sumter and Castle Pinckney. If Fort Sumter fell into enemy hands, the other positions would be cut off from reinforcement or resupply. Castle Pinckney had lost value as a defense against incoming ships. However, a garrison so close to downtown Charleston would be a serious deterrent to any attack by South Carolinians. Not only did reinforcements need to be sent quickly, but quietly. If South Carolina believed reinforcements were coming, they would occupy Fort Sumter and Castle Pinckney before Anderson could act. Anderson accurately pointed out that this was not a purely military situation but a political one as well, and he needed instructions from his civilian leadership.[13] Anderson was not telling his superiors anything they did not know, but if anyone was paying attention, he was telling his superiors where his loyalties lay. His suggestion of aiming the guns of Castle Pickney at downtown Charleston sounded more like Andrew Jackson than a man of supposed southern sympathies.

Anderson took what action he could while awaiting further instructions. He reorganized guard duty, with H Company watching the western wall and E Company the eastern wall. The officer of the watch would be stationed on the southern wall facing the water, and a guard would stand at the gate watching the street that ran right in front of the fort. The garrison was so shorthanded that officers' wives took turns on sentry duty.[14]

Captain Foster was not directly under Anderson's command; he was junior to Anderson, and as the engineer assigned to a position, he gave deference to its commander. That Foster had respect for Anderson and that they generally agreed on the needed course of action made what could have been a problematic working relationship run smoothly. Foster, at the head of 120 civilian workers, rushed repairs to Fort Moultrie, while his second, Lieutenant Snyder, moved to Fort Sumter to oversee the 109 workers there.

Anderson received a reply from Adjutant General Cooper on December 4, three days after it was sent. Cooper made it clear in the letter that all orders, information, and opinions were directly from the secretary of war. Based on information "thought to be reliable," an attack was highly unlikely. If an attack did happen, Anderson's actions "must be such as to be free from the charge of initiating a collision. If attacked, you are, of course, expected to defend the trust committed to you to the best of your ability." The reinforcements Anderson had requested would not be sent as it would add to the "excitement and might lead to serious results."[15] Anderson had been in the army long enough to know when officials were preparing the paper trail to blame someone else for failure.

Although Anderson had been warned that defensive preparations might stir up the local population, people from Charleston were not overly bothered by the work being carried out to strengthen the defenses of Fort Moultrie and finish Fort Sumter. Captain Doubleday understood why. He could see the noose around their position already tightening. South Carolina was moving artillery to Sullivan's Island to close off federal access to Forts Moultrie and Sumter. He heard rumors that ladders were being stored nearby so that the militia starting to arrive could storm the walls. Secretary of War Floyd was spending money on the improvements to the two forts, but as Doubleday understood, "forts constructed in an enemy's country, and left unguarded, are built for the enemy."[16]

That Anderson and his garrison were in a dangerous position was no secret. Northern newspapers wrote in early December that Anderson's "force was wholly insufficient to resist an organized assault from the land side." Also, the government was "well informed, for no concealment has been practiced, that it is designed to take Fort Moultrie by a *coup de main,* as soon as the ordinance of secession is passed."[17]

As much as Washington was trying to place the blame for the surrender of the Charleston forts on him, Anderson knew his duty. His responsibility was to hold the positions assigned to him until he was relieved. He was to resist with all his strength if an attempt to take any of the works was made. In the meantime, it was a dereliction of duty if he did not make all possible preparations for their defense. Anderson wrote a former comrade in the Third Artillery "that it is not worthwhile for me to say anything about our force or the weakness of our little fort. I am doing all I can to make it less weak than it was and think that it may cost more to take it than it will be worth to the state."[18] That his orders stated that he was to make no moves that might anger the locals complicated his position. Anderson prayed that a political solution could be worked out before he had to kill his fellow countrymen in defense of Fort Moultrie or shed his own blood in defense of federal property, especially considering the end result would be fratricidal war. Attempts at compromise were being made in the nation's capital, but that would be impossible if there was fighting at Fort Moultrie.

On December 5, Anderson crossed the harbor to meet with local leaders. Charleston's mayor and others promised to do all they could to prevent an angry mob from attacking Fort Moultrie. However, everyone Anderson met stressed the importance of the forts being handed over to them the moment the state seceded from the Union.[19] Their meaning was clear: if they were not handed over, they would be attacked not by a drunken mob but by state forces.

Anderson wrote again to the secretary of war to stress the dangerous position he and his garrison were in. Anderson wanted Floyd to clarify his somewhat contradictory orders. He desired to know how far he could go with his defensive preparations before it would be considered inflaming the locals. Anderson wanted to level the dunes and burn down the buildings near the fort. Anderson was beginning to think beyond a wild charge by militia but about an organized siege. He was starting to see positions all around him that could shield batteries or where riflemen could keep his men from working the fort's guns.[20]

Anderson submitted a requisition to his friend Colonel Huger at the Charleston Arsenal for rifles and ammunition, the same request that had Gardner relieved. Huger wrote to Secretary Floyd for permission. The need to consult the secretary of war had as much to do with the awkwardly organized antebellum army as it did with the crisis in Charleston. There were no secrets in the War Department, and Anderson's requests were soon in the nation's newspapers.

On December 7, Floyd sent Major Don Carlos Buell of Colonel Cooper's staff to deliver instructions to Anderson and report on the situation. Buell was also a West Pointer and a veteran of the Mexican War. The Ohio-born major traveled to Charleston by train. Although he was ordered to commit all the instructions to memory, they were not that different from what Floyd had already sent Anderson through the mail.

Buell got a much better sense of the temperament in Charleston than anyone in the Buchanan administration. He traveled across the harbor to Fort Moultrie, where he had a long conference with Anderson. As two long-serving army officers, both men believed that orders should be in writing whenever possible. They sat in Anderson's office as Buell wrote out what he titled "A Memorandum of Verbal Instructions." His instructions were "to hold possession of the forts in this harbor, and if attacked, you are to defend yourself to the last extremity." And "carefully to avoid every act which would needlessly tend to provoke aggression." In the two pages of written instruction was the line permitting Anderson to "put your command into either of the forts, "which you may deem most proper."[21] That line would draw the most scrutiny in the months to come.

Although not in writing, Buell advised Anderson to move the garrison to a more defensible position, Fort Sumter. Buell was not the only one who made this suggestion. When they met in New York, Cullum advised Anderson to move the command to Fort Sumter. Captain Doubleday made a pest of himself with the constant suggestion to move. Even the aged General Scott had suggested the move. In the letter Anderson received from his friend Ord, he had assumed Anderson had already relocated.[22]

It was not only Anderson's comrades who appreciated the superior position of Fort Sumter. South Carolina newspapers spelled out the strategic situation of Charleston Harbor. Each stressed the danger to South Carolina's cause if federal forces garrisoned Fort Sumter. They preferred all federal troops to evacuate the state, but to have them all in the vulnerable Fort Moultrie was almost as good. The *Charleston Mercury* fumed on December 7 that relocation to Fort Sumter "will lead to bloodshed and rupture."[23] South Carolina's new governor, Francis Pickens, also appreciated the weakness of Anderson's position and the danger if Anderson garrisoned Fort Sumter. Francis Pickens had only become governor on December 16, 1860. The fifty-five-year-old was the grandson of Revolutionary War general Andrew Pickens and had been active in politics since his early twenties. Most recently, Pickens had been the US ambassador to Russia. The state legislature chose the governor in antebellum South Carolina, and they had been wise to select a professional diplomat for the post at this sensitive moment. Unfortunately for them, they chose the wrong diplomat. Pickens proved to be rash in the coming months when patience would have served his cause better.

Traditionally, the position of governor in South Carolina had been that of a figurehead. The state legislature wielded the real power. This relationship, however, changed when the state tried to leave the Union. Governor Pickens's command of the militia took on real significance in the next several months. The governor ordered Captain Charles H. Simonton of the South Carolina militia to patrol the channel between Forts Moultrie and Sumter to prevent Anderson from changing positions. If Anderson attempted to move his men to Fort Sumter, Simonton's orders were to order them back if they refused, to sink them, and then to occupy Fort Sumter. To carry out this task, Simonton commandeered two small steamers, the *Nina* and the *General Clinch,* ironically named after Anderson's mentor and father-in-law.

The presence of the two ships greatly complicated the situation for Anderson. The move itself was now dangerous, not just the potential outcome. However, Fort Moultrie was untenable if an attack came, and every day, it looked more and more like that attack was inevitable. The two ships could just as easily have been used to ferry South Carolina troops to Fort Sumter or Fort Moultrie's vulnerable beach.

The decision to stay at Fort Moultrie or risk the crossing of the harbor was Anderson's alone. He had written the secretary of war several times, asking for more clarification or direct orders. There was no answer. Anderson would have to make the decision that might not only cost him and his men their lives but also could plunge the nation into a destructive civil war. Regardless of its outcome, the country he had served his entire life and that his father had fought to create would never exist again in the same form. The stress affected Anderson's health, which was already weakened by injury and illness acquired in service to the nation.

He received numerous letters from friends and family from Kentucky concerned about his predicament and worried that the army was not doing enough to support him. His brother Larz in Cincinnati wrote to offer the family's sympathy and prayers for the difficult position the army had placed him in.[24] He also received letters from strangers or acquaintances throughout the

Midwest and Northeast. These were letters of support, thanking Anderson for his service to the nation. Much to the surprise of Anderson's admirers, he responded to each. He even received a few offers for fighting men willing to join him in Charleston.[25]

On December 20, 1860, South Carolina's secession convention voted to "dissolve the union now subsisting between South Carolina and other states, under the name of the United States of America."[26] This declaration of South Carolina independence was celebrated well into the night in Charleston. Militia companies paraded, military bands played throughout the city, fireworks exploded, bonfires burned, and the Palmetto flag waved everywhere in place of the Stars and Stripes. The outspoken Unionist judge James Petigru visited Anderson and his officers soon afterward. He was confident the South Carolina government would soon try to drive them out. With tears in his eyes, Petigru gave Anderson his apologies and farewell.[27] As Charleston celebrated, it was a sleepless night for Anderson and his men.

The actions of South Carolina did not surprise Anderson. In his short time in the state, he had already written it off as a lost cause to the Union. He feared that the "malady" would not be "confined to her," and "other states may follow her example, and our glorious confederacy will disappear from the galaxy of nations."[28]

The attack on Fort Moultrie that Anderson feared did not occur. Whether this was due to the South Carolina government being able to control the people or the defensive preparations of Anderson and his officers, we can only guess. From his arrival in South Carolina, civilians and government officials had told Anderson that once South Carolina left the Union, they would expect Anderson's position to be immediately handed over, or it would mean war. Now that South Carolina had left the Union, Anderson and his men were running out of time.[29]

By this point, Anderson had concluded that not only was the move to Fort Sumter necessary but it was within his orders. The only problem was the phrase in his orders that he could transfer his men if there were "tangible evidence of a design to proceed to a hostile act." He was confident that a hostile act was coming, but what would be considered tangible evidence, and would what he saw as real evidence be considered such afterward by a board of review? If he waited for unquestionable evidence, would it be too late to act?

On December 22, Buchanan and his cabinet met to discuss the Charleston situation. Only at this late date did Buchanan inquire to what Anderson's exact orders were. Floyd had to send an aide back to his office for his files. The written orders that Buell had delivered to Anderson were read aloud. Buchanan agreed with the order except for one line. He believed the phrase "defend yourself to the last extremity" might lead to the useless loss of life. New instructions were written excluding this phrase and replacing it with a much softer order to avoid "a vain and useless sacrifice . . . upon a mere point of honor." Buchanan signed the new version, which required that Anderson keep these orders strictly confidential, even from his officers. Indeed, Anderson kept these orders secret for the remainder of his life, to the detriment of his reputation, or so his family believed.[30] Considering that one of his senior officers, Captain Doubleday, had influential relatives in Massachusetts and his letters were finding their way into Republican newspapers, the confidentiality order does not seem unreasonable. The new orders were sent by courier to Fort Moultrie.

The orders convinced Anderson of the conclusion that Doubleday and many northerners had reached months earlier. Anderson and his little command were pawns in a much bigger game. They were being hung out to dry. If their lives and honor were to be spared, Anderson must act. He would move his command to the safety of Fort Sumter. He had to hope it was not too late.

Relocation would not be an easy task. Moving his officers, men, and their families and supplies across Charleston Harbor was a massive undertaking. To do it all secretly, not even telling his officers until the last minute, was nearly impossible. If South Carolina officials got even a hint that Anderson was planning on "throwing" his command into Fort Sumter, they would have instantly occupied it. Nothing was stopping South Carolina from doing just that whenever they pleased.

On December 24, 1860, South Carolina sent a three-man delegation to Washington, DC, to negotiate with what they saw as a foreign nation on the question of the forts and numerous issues regarding what they believed would be the peaceful withdrawal from the United States. James L. Orr, James H. Adams, and Robert W. Barnwell, three long-serving South Carolina public officials, boarded the train to Washington. Anderson knew the departure of the delegation set into motion a strict timeline. He correctly assumed they would meet the president on December 26. If the trio failed to convince the president to hand over the forts, they would probably send a telegram the same day to Governor Pickens, who was likely to launch an assault immediately.

Richard Clough Anderson had been on Anderson's mind a great deal since he arrived in Charleston. His late father had defended Charleston against the British during the Revolution. Robert Anderson could not have helped to think that he might have been standing in the same spot as his father. However, as Colonel Anderson had looked out to sea for the incoming enemy, Major Anderson's enemy came from his own country. It also could not have

escaped his attention where his father had been exactly eighty-four years earlier—also preparing a surprise boat trip. The Colonel had been with George
Washington when, with a blizzard as cover, the general crossed the Delaware
River, catching the British and Hessian troops by surprise. A blizzard was
unlikely in Charleston Harbor, but just like his father, he would cross a body
of water in the darkness, praying that he could maintain the element of
surprise.[31]

Anderson decided to move his command to Fort Sumter without consulting or informing his officers or his superiors. Not only did he not tell his men,
but he did all he could to convince them that he planned to make a stand at
Fort Moultrie. This caused much frustration among his officers, who saw Fort
Moultrie as more untenable every day. It was not that Anderson did not trust
his officers, but if they did not know, they could not accidentally betray the
secret.

There was a rainstorm on Christmas Day, so Anderson postponed his move
one day. Anderson attempted to spend the holiday as normally as possible. He
mailed a letter to his wife, regretting he had not bought her or the children
Christmas presents. That he was apart from his family at Christmas made the
whole situation worse for Anderson. He and several of his officers, those not
on duty, attended a Christmas party hosted by Captain Foster and his wife
at the cottage they rented near Fort Moultrie. It must have been an awkward
party. There were a few locals, and everyone's mind must have been on the
crisis. Anderson and Foster had enough in common to make small talk. Both
had been wounded at Molina del Rey, were married to southern women from
influential families, and had fathers who fought in critical battles of American
history. Foster's father had been with Perry on Lake Erie. However, one of
Anderson's officers was there to have a good time. Davis spent the party flirting
with Mrs. Foster's unmarried younger sister.[32]

Doubleday could not keep his mind off his duty. He asked Anderson if
he could purchase wire to improve Fort Moultrie's defenses. Anderson gave
Doubleday a quizzical look and told him, "You shall have a mile of wire if you
require it." As Doubleday prepared to leave immediately to take care of this
task, Anderson stopped him. It could wait. To Doubleday, this was evidence
that something was about to happen, or at least that is what Doubleday wrote
years later.[33] What South Carolina merchant was going to sell the US Army
wire on Christmas Day, Doubleday does not say.

On the morning of December 26, Anderson formed his entire command
on the parade ground and began to give orders. He was not yet giving anything away, and his men still believed he was preparing to make a stand. The

command's two boats, small flat-bottomed sailing craft, would be used to carry wives and children of the men to the nearly abandoned Fort Johnson. Anderson placed Lieutenant Hall in command of the two boats. Anderson told Hall that the move to Fort Sumter was happening and gave him further secret instructions. Everyone else believed Anderson planned to fight it out at Fort Moultrie and that the noncombatants were being moved to safety.

Along with the seventeen women and twenty-three children, Hall was to load six months' worth of supplies and some of the soldiers' personal possessions. As Hall was overseeing the work, two locals approached him and demanded to know what he was doing. The answer Anderson had prepared—that the wives were being sent north—seemed to satisfy the two men, who no doubt reported the movement to the growing state forces in Charleston. By noon, Hall's little flotilla was on its way to Fort Johnson. His orders were to wait at Fort Johnson in the boats until he heard the signal, the firing of two guns, and then hurry to Fort Sumter. If the civilian pilots of the boats got suspicious, he was to pretend to inspect the barracks before letting the women move in.[34]

Anderson also confided in Captain Foster. Foster quickly and quietly procured eight large boats to transfer the garrison of seven officers and sixty-five men. They were hidden on the beach near the fort. It was not too difficult a task, considering that he had been moving construction equipment to Fort Sumter. Except for those few who had been let in on the secret, no one suspected Anderson's move. He had ordered the rest of the men to strengthen the defenses on the landward side of Fort Moultrie. This work would have convinced anyone watching that Anderson was staying on Sullivan's Island. Mary Doubleday, the wife of Captain Doubleday, sent her husband to invite Anderson to evening tea. Although her husband grew frustrated by Anderson's inaction, she would not forget her manners or social responsibilities. When Doubleday approached, Anderson was in conversation with a group of officers. It was obvious something was happening. Before he could pass on his wife's polite invitation, Anderson began giving him orders. Doubleday had twenty minutes to form his men and ready them for the trip across the channel to Fort Sumter. It was almost 5 p.m., and the sun would set soon. There was a short period between sunset and when the patrol boats took up their station, and Anderson hoped to be gone before they arrived.

Doubleday was probably relieved to discover that instead of spending another awkward evening with his commanding officer, they would be taking action, something he had long advocated. Doubleday and his men were given the honor of being the first men across. It was risky. If South Carolina had already placed guards or their forces were alert, they might respond before the rest of the US forces could arrive. Doubleday's task had the potential to be a dangerous mission.[35]

Doubleday ordered his men to form up with muskets and packs. Once he was sure they were ready, he hurried back to his wife to tell her the news and that fighting would soon break out. He told her to leave the fort and stay with friends. If the cannon began firing, she was to take shelter behind the sand dunes. She quickly packed a few belongings and went to the home of the Reverend Matthias Harris, the fort's chaplain.

Once his wife was out of the fort, Doubleday strapped on his 1860 Model Colt revolver and reported to Anderson that his men were ready. Anderson waited inside the main gate with the garrison's massive twenty-by-thirty-five-foot flag rolled up under his arm. The men quietly marched the quarter-mile to the shore. They passed several houses whose residents either did not notice them or did not understand the importance of what they saw. Lieutenants Mead and Snyder had carried out their jobs and waited on the beach directly across from Fort Sumter with three boats. They and their men were behind the remains of the old sea wall, more to stay out of the cold wind than to avoid detection. The men were loaded into the boats. They set off in three directions to improve their odds of remaining undetected. Doubleday's boat would take the most direct path so that it would arrive first.

Once Anderson decided to move the garrison, he was prepared to do what he had to, even if that meant opening the hostilities himself. At Fort Moultrie, the garrison surgeon Samuel Crawford, Captain Foster, and five enlisted men manned five preloaded heavy cannons. Their orders were to fire on the patrol boats if they attempted to stop the crossing. Firing on a state militia inside Charleston Harbor would have definitely started hostilities. Doubleday's boat came the closest to being detected by the guard boats. The steam-powered ship came within a hundred yards of Doubleday and slowed significantly. The quick-thinking Doubleday ordered his men to remove their uniform hats, tall black wool shakos, and army coats with their bright buttons, giving them the appearance of ordinary workmen. The patrol boat passed by, oblivious of the danger it had faced from the possibility of being destroyed by the heavy guns of Fort Moultrie.[36] The *General Clinch* was still at the docks in Charleston. Perhaps the spirit of the old general was looking after his son-in-law.

As planned, Doubleday and his twenty men reached Fort Sumter first. They advanced through the main gate with weapons ready. The civilian workers in the fort outnumbered Doubleday's small force. He placed them under guard. Although a number cheered at the arrival of US troops, he assumed most had southern sympathies. The other two boats soon arrived. After unloading, they returned to Fort Moultrie to pick up the rest of the command. It took three

trips, but by eight o'clock, the entire command, with the exception of Lieutenant Hall with the families and the rear guard under Foster and Crawford, was
at Fort Sumter. Anderson ordered a cannon to be fired. It was answered by Fort
Moultrie. This was the two-gun signal for Hall to come to Fort Sumter. Anderson had caught everyone completely by surprise. The pilots of Hall's boats did
not catch on until the signal guns were fired, and Hall gave him the order to
proceed to Fort Sumter. One pilot, who obviously thought he was aiding in the
first step of the complete evacuation of the forts, had to be restrained for the
trip to Fort Sumter. His treatment at the hands of the young West Pointer and
his sergeant surely got worse with each retelling.

When the rear guard at Moultrie received the signal, they went to work carrying out Anderson's orders. All of Fort Moultrie's cannons were spiked. Musket ramrods were hammered into the touch holes and broken off. The wooden
carriages of the guns that faced Fort Sumter were burned, and the actual guns
were pushed off the walls. They then chopped down the flagpole and threw it
in a ditch, a symbolic act that made it more difficult for South Carolina forces
to fly the Palmetto flag that the garrison had come to despise. They were able
to carry away all of the hospital supplies and most of the small arms. They
could not bring the remaining supply of food or any of the garrison's fuel oil,
two things that would be sorely missed in the coming months. Most of the
officers' personal effects were also left behind. Anderson had brought only the
bare minimum to Charleston and lost very little. The Doubledays, too, had left
most of their more valuable possessions in their New York home.

As they waited for the rear guard to arrive at Fort Sumter, Anderson retired
to what would be his office for the next four months. It was 8 p.m. He wrote
two letters. As he had done on a regular basis since their marriage, he wrote
his wife, Eliza, in New York that he was safely inside Fort Sumter and that "the
whole force of South Carolina would not venture to attack us."[37] There is a sense
of great relief in his letter. He had made a decision and taken action, and at least
momentarily, the stress of the question of what he should do was removed. He
next wrote to the adjutant of the army, Samuel Cooper, to report his situation.
"By the blessing of God," he had removed his garrison. He had four months'
supply of food and a year's worth of hospital stores, and except for a handful
of men carrying out the destruction of Fort Moultrie, his entire command was
safely inside the walls. He informed Cooper that he had taken this action "to
prevent the effusion of blood."[38]

Lieutenant Davis and his men of the rear guard were the last to arrive.
Anderson and the other officers cheerfully greeted him. The mission had gone
as planned with as little trouble as they would experience crossing the West
Point campus. Anderson joked that he would serve as Davis's counsel if he

were court-martialed for the destruction of army property at Fort Moultrie. Davis responded by producing a small flask of brandy. Anderson proposed a toast "to the success of the garrison," and the flask was passed around.[39] For the first time in more than a month, they were not under the threat of an attack at any moment. Feeling joy and relief that night, Anderson and his officers would have to wait until the next day to learn how their enemies and friends would react to their bold move.

CHAPTER 10

CHARLESTON HARBOR II

Few men of the garrison had been able to sleep the night of the crossing— partly because there was work, including guarding the 115 workmen, but mostly the excitement and relief they felt made sleep difficult. The move to Fort Sumter felt like a great victory, and it came without the cost of any lives. When the sun rose, the men stood on the ramparts, looking toward Charleston. It may have been an unreasonable expectation that the soldiers would see an instant reaction when Charleston learned of their nighttime subterfuge. However, their morning vigil was rewarded when the steamboat filled with South Carolina militia, the same one that passed Captain Doubleday's boat in the dark, passed near Sumter on its way back to the Charleston docks. The *Emma* may not have been close enough for Anderson's men to see the shock and anger on the militiamen's faces, but they surely could have sensed it.

Anderson had spent the last few weeks thinking about the possible reaction of a sudden move to Fort Sumter, not only South Carolina's but of his superiors as well. Now it was time to work. The fort could dominate the harbor, and his command could be safe inside its thick stone walls. However, much was to be done before they were secure. The first issue to deal with was the civilian workers. A few volunteered to remain on the job and share the upcoming hardships with the garrison. Most refused, either from loyalty to the southern cause, for fear that the fort would become a battleground, or a combination of the two. These men were sent back to Charleston in the boats that had carried the garrison to Fort Sumter.

The people of Charleston awoke on December 27 to the news that the US Army had occupied Fort Sumter. The news was carried by the militia from the *Emma* and the dismissed laborers. It spread quickly through Charleston and the surrounding area. Telegraph wires were soon buzzing in all directions. Secessionist allies in the other southern states and Washington, DC, were informed officially and unofficially. Newspapers across the country would soon have the story. The morning papers of December 27 only had rumors to print on the Charleston situation, most predicting the Buchanan administration would surrender the forts. This would make the shock of the news even greater. Anderson had no idea the firestorm he had caused.

Anderson's initial strategy was to continue day-to-day operations as if nothing out of the ordinary had occurred. Moultrie, Pinckney, Johnson, and Sumter were all federal property under his command. If he decided to move his men, it was no different than if he had moved his office from one side of Fort Moultrie to the other. Anderson sent Captain Foster to Charleston to take care of routine business. He posted the garrison's mail, including Anderson's letters to his wife and Secretary Floyd. He also went to the bank to make arrangements to pay his former workers. It quickly became apparent to Foster that the people of Charleston were not prepared to accept the business-as-usual approach, and it was not safe for a US soldier to travel alone in Charleston.

Governor Pickens was furious when he learned the news. Anderson's move was predictable. Pickens expected it and had made preparations for it. Anderson had made him look foolish. Pickens had assured everyone that such a move was impossible. He took his anger out on Colonel James Pettigrew who commanded the militia onboard the patrol boats. The colonel and his aid, Major Ellison Capers of the South Carolina militia, were dispatched to Fort Sumter to determine the true state of affairs.

The two men were rowed the three miles out to Fort Sumter. Colonel Pettigrew presented his calling card to the sentry at the gate. With military formality, the officer of the watch escorted the two men in their full-dress uniforms to Anderson's office, which was on the second floor of the building that comprised the officers' quarters. Most of Anderson's officers were present for the meeting. Pettigrew asked if he could speak before these officers. Anderson answered in a friendly affirmative. He had no secrets from his officers. Pettigrew, who had refused the chair politely offered him, informed Anderson that the governor was quite dismayed that he had chosen to "reinforce" Fort Sumter. Anderson had spent a career serving on military courts and writing and following orders. He understood the importance of a single word. He interrupted Pettigrew. "I have not reinforced the fort. I have simply moved my command here."[1] Pettigrew had to concede that point. But the angry militia officer explained to Anderson that President Buchanan had pledged that he would maintain the status quo inside the harbor. Anderson's move had broken this pledge, and "bloodshed might now be avoided no longer."[2]

Anderson claimed that he knew of no such pledge. This statement was probably only partially true. He had been paying close attention to the political situation in Charleston, and it is unfathomable that he had not heard of the agreement. However, he had not been officially informed of this by his superiors, and that was all that mattered in Anderson's world. He could not act or refuse to act based on rumors. In this, he was correct, as the "pledge" itself was the mushy creation of politicians that could be taken many ways. On December 10, before South Carolina's secession, the state's congressmen met with the president. According to Buchanan, they told him that although they could not speak officially, Anderson and his command were in no danger of being attacked "provided that no reinforcements shall be sent into those forts, and their relative military status shall remain as at present." Buchanan did not like being tied to an agreement. He told the congressmen that his policy was to maintain the status quo. He reserved the right to change his mind; he would make no pledge. Nothing was put in writing. The South Carolina delegation, however, walked away from the meeting believing a promise had been made.[3]

What's more, Governor Pickens believed such a pledge had been made, and his two representatives were there to demand that Anderson honor it and return to Fort Moultrie. Anderson refused. His position had been threatened at Fort Moultrie by the patrol boats filled with armed men. He had moved his command to Fort Sumter for their own safety. Perhaps sensing the meeting was becoming too heated, Anderson spoke the words that would unfairly color his actions over the next four months and for later generations. "In this controversy between the North and the South, my sympathies are entirely with the South. These gentlemen," referring to his officers, "know it perfectly well."[4] During the heat of war and the political turmoil that followed its conclusion, this statement sounded significantly different than it did in 1860. When the words were spoken, many men north of the Mason-Dixon Line, especially westerners, agreed with Anderson's take. Radical abolitionists were driving the nation to war. Many felt that the end of slavery could come without a war if it were not for men like John Brown and other radicals. But he added that his duty as an army officer came first. Although Anderson was no Republican or abolitionist, his southern sympathies ended with secession.

To Anderson, the officer and gentleman, both the behavior of abolitionists and southern fire eaters was undignified. As during the Nullification Crisis of 1832, it would take cooler heads to prevent war. Anderson still hoped to buy time for the government to solve this crisis peacefully. His statement was meant to calm the situation and the two South Carolina soldiers. Arguing about the importance of preserving the Union or who was at fault for the current crisis would serve no purpose.

Anderson refused to leave Fort Sumter, whatever his stated sympathies might be, and Pettigrew and Capers left unsatisfied. Anderson's next act would better reflect what he believed than what he had said to those two men.

THE PRAYER AT SUMTER, DECEMBER 27, 1860.

The flag-raising ceremony and prayer on the first day the garrison was at Fort Sumter. Courtesy of the Library of Congress, LC-USZ62-126966.

Anderson ordered his command and the workmen to the parade ground. The regimental band was on the ramparts. The soldiers came to attention as Anderson walked onto the parade ground with the US flag he had carried from Fort Moultrie. The men were ordered to parade rest. The men and officers bowed their heads and removed their hats as the chaplain began to pray. Anderson kneeled. He had sent for the chaplain, who arrived in time for the ceremony. A strong Unionist, Chaplain Harris thanked God for their safe and successful transfer to Fort Sumter and asked for the flag to fly again over a united country. When Harris finished, Anderson rose with great dignity and raised the flag. The band played "Hail Columbia." When Old Glory reached the top of the staff and unfurled in the harbor's cold, strong breeze, the men and officers broke into cheers. It was an extremely emotional moment for all who were there.[5]

Even before the emotional flag raising over Fort Sumter, Major Robert Anderson and his small garrison began to prepare the fort for an attack. Anderson did not know how South Carolina would react to his movements. His garrison could have been in a fight before the day was over. Anderson and his officers expected a direct assault. If men landed on the island, they might be able to overwhelm the small garrison. Fort Sumter was built to fight an enemy at long range. Fully manned with all its cannons blazing, an enemy force could not reach the fort. It was not designed for a few men to defend against an infantry attack. The old veteran Anderson would set about to change this.

The first obvious danger was the embrasures. Since he only had about eighty men, including musicians, this was an untenable position. They could not stop an assaulting force from climbing through these openings. The embrasures in the most strategic places and most necessary for the use of cannon were identified, and the rest were bricked shut. The fort was designed to have three tiers of guns. The second level was unfinished, and the brick and flagstones needed to complete it were stacked all over the parade ground. Each gun emplacement, or casemate, was its own small room with an open side facing the fort's interior. Anderson had the men stack the bricks and stones to form the casemates' fourth wall. This served two purposes. Unlike an attacking naval force, which Fort Sumter was designed to fight, the South Carolina forces could fire mortar shells over the walls of the fort. If the stones and bricks had been left, their fragments would have been turned into deadly projectiles. Now the stones would protect the men as they worked the guns.

When they first arrived, the soldiers had trouble navigating the parade grounds with sixty-six unmounted guns, almost six thousand projectiles, stacks of bricks, and the sand needed to make mortar in the way. Only fourteen guns had been mounted, but they all faced the sea. Among the living quarters, only the officer's quarters were finished. These were designed with small porches that opened on the outside of the fort. This was a nice addition for the comfort of the officers but a serious weakness in the event of an assault.

If a determined storming party of a hundred men equipped with a few ladders attacked the fort in these early days, it would have easily been taken. What saved the garrison during this period was the mistaken belief in Charleston that Fort Sumter was much more powerful than it actually was. The *Charleston Courier* proclaimed the fort could hold out against all of Charleston and easily level Fort Moultrie.[6]

To put the fort in a defensible position took several weeks of hard labor. Mounting the guns was the most challenging job. Some of them weighed as much as fifteen thousand pounds. The priority was mounting the guns on the bottom tier; these would be the most useful against a landing party. The main gate also had to be secured. The huge gate faced toward Morris Island, where South Carolina would most probably build an artillery battery. The fort had been made to engage an enemy arriving from the Atlantic. All of Fort Sumter's weaknesses, including the gate, now faced the direction of the new enemy.[7]

The outside gate had two heavy iron doors. Once a visitor passed through those doors, he entered a wide tunnel and came to a heavy wooden door raised by ropes and pulleys. Both sets of doors were highly vulnerable to artillery fire from Morris Island. If the doors were destroyed, Fort Sumter would be open to an assault. To counter this, a large brick wall was built behind the innermost door. It had an opening large enough for one man to step through at a time. The visitor passing through that opening would face an eight-inch howitzer loaded with canister shot. An attacking force attempting to rush through the main gate would be cut to pieces by nails, musket balls, metal fragments, or anything else the garrison could find to stuff in the barrel.

Anderson also wanted the massive ten-inch Columbiads on the upper tier. Their massive presence would be a serious deterrent. Raising the fifteen-thousand-pound gun fifty feet into the air was no easy task. The first Columbiad was put into place without incident, but the second snapped its ropes and fell to the ground. Amazingly, no one was killed. Once they were in place, the ammunition still needed to be moved. Each projectile weighed 128 pounds. One evening, a couple of sergeants challenged the men's ability to lift and carry the heavy shot. After this contest, more than sixty iron balls had been moved to the top parapet. This became a nightly event for the remainder of the siege.[8]

The other Columbiads were buried breach down in the parade as mortars aimed toward the city. This was an unorthodox tactic, so the obvious decision was made to test-fire it. The big gun was loaded with two pounds of gunpowder, the standard charge being eighteen. The artillerymen predicted that the

128-pound ball would travel less than a thousand yards. As it turned out, the Columbiad made a very efficient mortar. The officers and soldiers watched nervously as the shot streaked across the sky, falling just short of the city. The gun was not tested again, and a delegation from Charleston was sent out to learn why they had been fired upon.[9]

The most likely spot for an enemy landing was the stone wharf. It faced the main gate and was built to unload men and equipment. Two five-gallon bottles filled with gunpowder were placed under the wharf. Each one had two fuses, guaranteeing the structure would be destroyed if an enemy attempted to land. Also on the south wall was a paved area where an attacking enemy could stand and be safe from the fort's guns. To counter this, a pile of rocks was pushed against the wall, giving the impression of unfinished construction but not giving any hint of the explosives hidden underneath that would rain stone down upon any attacking force.

Unlike the star-shaped fortress of an earlier generation, a man could stand close to the wall and be out of the field of fire. Fort Sumter's defenders adopted a medieval solution to this problem. Wooden boxes, securely fastened, hung over the top of the walls. They were lined with iron plates to make them bulletproof. And holes in the bottom allowed a soldier to fire straight down. Hand grenades were improvised as well to drop through. Large stones that could have been used as stepping stones into the embrasures were rolled into the water.

Anderson allowed his officers wide latitude to develop unorthodox solutions to the fort's security shortcomings. Captain Seymour developed a simple but highly effective weapon. A barrel was filled with broken stones, and a charge of gunpowder was placed in its center. The device was detonated by a friction primer attached to a long cord. The barrel would be rolled down the wall and would explode at the end of the cord, measured for maximum effect. When Seymour's device was tested for the first time, most of the garrison went to watch. This attracted the attention of the ships in the harbor and the South Carolina militia on Johnson Island, who watched through field glasses. A description of the test also appeared in several Charleston newspapers. This and the other defensive improvements had a deterrent effect on South Carolina. A landing and infantry attack on Fort Sumter would cost many lives.

The brutally hard work of preparing Fort Sumter not only had to be done, but it also served the secondary purpose of distracting the minds of the men and officers from their dire situation. Anderson had to wait and wonder how the rest of the country would view his move. The delegation that had visited the fort made the official reaction of South Carolina obvious. Still, as for the rest of the nation and the his chain of command, he could not know. An attack from South Carolina could come at any moment.

Governor Pickens believed that Buchanan's pledge had created a truce that Anderson had violated. This belief caused Pickens to commit the first actual hostile act of the conflict. Colonel Pettigrew and as many men as he could fit on the patrol boat *Nina* steamed to Castle Pinckney. At the castle were thirty workmen, Lieutenant Richard Meade, Sergeant Skillen, and his small family. As Pettigrew's men scrambled down the *Nina*'s gangplank onto the island, Meade ordered the gate closed and barred. Still angry about what they saw as Anderson's betrayal, Charleston's residents strained to watch the action from the city's shoreline.

After following the landing with curiosity, the thirty workers retreated to their quarters, some going as far as hiding under their beds. Meade and, we can assume, Sgt. Skillen would have resisted if they had any means of doing so. Pettigrew and his South Carolina men used the ladders they had brought to scale the walls. Colonel Pettigrew informed the lieutenant that he was taking the fort by the governor's authority and would give Meade all the proper receipts for the public property under his command. The defiant Meade refused any paperwork from Pettigrew as he did not recognize the governor's authority. He would not offer his parole, a promise not to fight in exchange for not being held captive, or acknowledge his status as a prisoner of war. Meade did ask that Skillen and his family be treated with courtesy.

Pettigrew had not thought to bring a flag with him, so when the US flag was lowered, he replaced it with the *Nina*'s flag, a red field with a lone star. Kate Skillen, the fifteen-year-old daughter of the ordnance sergeant, watched the proceedings with tears. One of the militia officers reassuringly told her that she and her family would be safe. She snapped back that she was "not crying because I am afraid! I am crying because you put that miserable rag up there."[10] She then taunted the officer for bringing so many men to capture a position held by two soldiers and a teenage girl. One can only imagine that had Lieutenant Meade the ability to resist, Kate Skillen would have been another Molly Pitcher, working the cannons in defense of her country.

The abandoned Fort Moultrie was seized soon afterward. Fear of land mines and other booby traps made this a much slower process. South Carolina had now taken US government installations by force of arms. The battle lines had been drawn. The capture of these two forts hardened Buchanan's shaky resolve and ensured that he would not order Anderson and his garrison back to Fort Moultrie.

Anderson's relocation to Fort Sumter made the mission of South Carolina's agents in Washington much more difficult. The three commissioners arrived in Washington on December 26 to negotiate the surrender of Fort Moultrie. They were greeted at the train station by William Trescot, a thirty-eight-year-old native of Charleston. A Harvard-trained lawyer, Trescot had a successful career in the diplomatic service, rising to the rank of assistant secretary of state under Buchanan. He had resigned the moment South Carolina left the Union, but in the months leading up to secession, he passed confidential information to the government of South Carolina. Now he acted as South Carolina's unofficial representative and had arranged the commissioners' meeting with the president.

The meeting was set for the next day, December 27. Buchanan refused to recognize them as representatives of the independent nation of South Carolina. He would, however, see them as private citizens, a symbolic distinction that would have made little difference. Buchanan had agreed to pass their proposals to Congress. Their prepared proposal was straightforward. The land that the forts sat on had been given to the federal government in 1805 for the express purpose of defending South Carolina. The agreement no longer stood now that South Carolina was out of the Union. South Carolina was prepared to be reasonable, at least in her mind, and reimburse the federal government for all the cost of building the fort and other improvements on the land.[11]

As the four discussed strategy for the upcoming meeting with President Buchanan, Texas senator Louis Wigfall burst into the house with the shocking news from Charleston that Anderson had moved his command to Fort Sumter. Although he lived in Texas, the Charleston-born Wigfall was a South Carolina man at heart. He was one of the more radical secessionists, even suggesting to Secretary of War Floyd that they kidnap the president. Wigfall had only heard rumors of Anderson's movements and had come to see if they were true. This news, delivered by the highly excitable Wigfall, put the other four men into a highly agitated state. Secretary of War Floyd arrived as the five men discussed the implications of Anderson's actions. They demanded answers from the secretary, who was as shocked as they were. He insisted that they must be misinformed. He insisted that he had given clear and direct orders to Anderson to take no action.[12]

Trescot, in the meantime, had received telegrams from Charleston confirming the news. Floyd returned to the War Department to fire off a message to Anderson. Trescot, along with the commissioners, traveled to the White House. Along the way, they collected two of South Carolina's strongest supporters in the Senate, future Confederate president Jefferson Davis of Mississippi and future Confederate secretary of state Robert Hunter of Virginia. The six men met the president in his study. Although Buchanan attempted to open the meeting with pleasant small talk, Davis interrupted him in order to get straight to the point. On learning that the president had not yet been informed of Anderson's move and was perhaps the last person in Washington, DC, to know, Davis told the president of the "great calamity" that had befallen them.[13]

A visibly distressed Buchanan assured the gathered southerners that Anderson's movement had not been ordered and was against his policy. Buchanan sent for Floyd to verify the report. He arrived shortly, obviously already on his way with the telegraph he had sent Anderson: "There is a report here that you have abandoned Fort Moultrie, burned your carriages, and gone to Fort Sumter. It is not believed, as you had no orders to justify it. Say at once what could have given rise to such a story."[14] It was an odd telegram for the secretary of war to send. The message did not ask for verification, nor did it send instructions as one would expect in a message from the secretary of war to a subordinate in a politically problematic situation. Floyd clearly intended this message to distance himself from Anderson's actions. Floyd was concerned about his reputation, not just over the issue with the Charleston forts, but also his involvement in a complicated and illegal financial ploy involving government contracts. Floyd had not profited personally from the transactions, but that did not change the illegality of his actions or the cost to American taxpayers.[15]

Floyd had been asked to resign by Vice President John Breckenridge since Buchanan wanted to avoid the confrontation. Floyd was taking his time in resigning, and Buchanan was not pressuring him to act quickly. The president allowed him to pick the opportune time to quit to save face. This would have been a nice gesture had the country not been in the midst of a great crisis. In the meantime, however, he allowed Floyd to act as secretary of war.[16]

Floyd's strategy was to make it appear as if he had resigned not because he was forced to but because he was making a protest against what he viewed as the administration's immoral handling of the Fort Sumter affair. The telegram he sent Anderson was the start of Floyd's exit strategy.

> The telegram is correct. I abandoned Fort Moultrie because I was certain that if attacked, my men must have been sacrificed, and the command of the harbor lost. I spiked the guns and destroyed the carriages to keep the guns from being used against us.
> If attacked, the garrison would never have surrendered without a fight.[17]

Anderson quickly replied to Floyd's telegram.

Included in the mail delivery that brought the telegram from Floyd was a letter from Anderson's brother, Larz. Writing from Cincinnati before his brother transferred his command to Fort Sumter, Larz stated that if the government ordered him to surrender, he would be justified in questioning "the authority of a subordinate officer, however high."[18] Anderson did not consider his actions as insubordinate. He had been given the discretion to move his command if threatened. Buchanan and Floyd had overlooked or forgotten about that part of his orders.

The president called an emergency cabinet meeting on the afternoon of the twenty-seventh. Major Don Carlos Buell was summoned to the White House in case the cabinet wanted clarification about his conversation with Anderson. Before he entered the meeting, an agitated Floyd told Buell that Anderson's actions had "made war inevitable." Slightly shocked, Buell replied, "I do not think so, sir. On the contrary, I think it will tend to avert war if war can be averted." His response to Buell showed that he was so caught up in his own view of events that he was surprised to learn that others thought differently. "But it has compromised the President!" was Floyd's weak response.[19]

Floyd angrily denounced Anderson. He argued that because of the major's rash actions, the only possible option to avoid war was to give in to all of South Carolina's demands. Secretary of State Jeremiah Black had heard enough. Like the president, Black was from Pennsylvania, and the two men were longtime friends. He approved of Anderson's move and stated that his actions were in accordance with his orders. If Black had meant this as a trap, Floyd stepped directly into it. Floyd angrily repeated that Anderson had violated the direct orders from the War Department. Black summoned Major Buell.

Don Carlos Buell looked after the best interests of his fellow Mexican War veteran and brother officer. Not only had Buell provided a written record of Floyd's verbal orders to Anderson, but he also made a second copy that he submitted to the War Department and thus had to be endorsed by Floyd and the president. Buell may have simply been a creature of army bureaucracy who dictated that everything was to be recorded, or he may have correctly predicted that Anderson would have been sacrificed for the political benefit of others. With the order in front of them, there was no way to argue that Anderson was in the wrong.

Of course, the question was what action to take now. To Floyd, the solution was simple: the US Army had to be withdrawn from South Carolina. Secretary of State Black, Attorney General Edwin Stanton, and the Kentucky-born postmaster general Joseph Holt vehemently disagreed. Black compared abandoning Fort Sumter to Benedict Arnold's attempt to hand over the American fortress at West Point to the British and added, "A president of the United States who would make such an order would be guilty of treason."[20]

"Oh no! Not so bad as that, my friend. Not so bad as that!"[21] the president answered. Black's point had struck home. Floyd's influence with the administration was over.

Buchanan is usually portrayed as having a change of heart, shifting from his southern-leaning advisers to men like Black, Seward, and Holt. Buchanan had not changed. From the beginning, his strategy had been to do nothing. When Anderson and his garrison were in the indefensible position at Fort Moultrie, the do-nothing strategy benefited South Carolina and was championed by

Floyd. Now that Anderson was in Fort Sumter, Buchanan's strategy of taking no action seemed to be Buchanan taking decisive action in defense of the Union and was strongly supported by part of his cabinet. Buchanan had not changed. Anderson had changed the situation.

On December 28, 1860, Robert Anderson was perhaps the most famous man in the United States. The states were not so united over their opinion of him, but they all talked about him that December Thursday. Northern newspapers, even solid Democratic papers, celebrated Anderson's move. According to the *Chicago Tribune,* "Old Kentucky had saved the Union," and "a general feeling of joy prevails in this city."[22] After decades of retreat and giving in to the threats of southern politicians, someone finally said no. Not in words or newsprint, those things had proven worthless. Unsupported by Washington, Anderson had denied the Great Slave Power the control of Charleston Harbor. "A mighty throb of relief and exaltation went through all the land." This "brave and true officer" finally stood up to the bully. Although not his intention, Anderson had become the hero Unionists had been seeking for years.[23]

While newspapers across the North celebrated Anderson's bold defiance, there was also pessimism that "the miserable imbecile" in the White House would order Anderson back to the indefensible Fort Moultrie or, worse yet, out of Charleston completely. If the president took this action, numerous newspapers called for nothing short of indictment for treason or impeachment.[24]

To southern newspaper editors, Anderson had violated his orders and the sacred trust between the president and South Carolina. Most southern newspapers attempted to separate Buchanan from Anderson's actions. Anderson had moved contrary to orders. To one South Carolina newspaper, it was "a gross breach of faith, and very derogatory to him as a man of honor.[25]

Northern Unionists saw this as their nation finally awakening to the dangers they faced, and southerners were optimistically hoping that was not the case. In their optimism, southerners attempted to distance Buchanan from Anderson's actions. If it was, however, "the first step of the government toward coercion," it would "be met in that spirit."[26]

Anderson's move was more shocking, and its effects on the public mind greater, because only the day before, rumors had been published in papers across the country that Anderson had been ordered to hand Fort Moultrie to South Carolina. This was speculation published as fact, and although he technically handed Fort Moultrie over to South Carolina, it was obviously not what anyone expected. The public reaction to Anderson's move in the North stiffened the resolve of some of Buchanan's cabinet.

The president still had to answer the South Carolina commissioners. Even had he not intended to give the pledge that the situation would not change in South Carolina, they believed he had, and Buchanan had done nothing to dissuade them of this belief. The president wanted to find a way to preserve his honor in the face of what seemed like going back on his word. Black broke the spell that had Buchanan thinking only of the issue of his honor. Black threatened to resign if Buchanan did not take a firm stance with the commissioners. When Buchanan protested that "my personal honor as a gentleman is involved," Black shot back that as president, his honor must be secondary to the laws of the nation and his oath of office. Buchanan relented and asked Black to draft recommendations for a response to the commissioners.

Black and Attorney General Stanton did more than recommend a response. They wrote it for the president. The document the two men produced was direct and unyielding. The United States did not recognize South Carolina's independence; thus, South Carolina did not have the right to be represented by diplomats. The United States would not enter negotiations over its own property. Fort Sumter would be held, and Major Anderson was "a gallant and meritorious officer." The document concluded with the powerful statement "I am urged immediately to withdraw the troops from the harbor of Charleston. . . . This I cannot do. This I will not do." Had these been Buchanan's own words and had he led his cabinet to this position instead of following, and had he said it months earlier, this might have been the defining statement of his presidency.

When the statement was presented to the entire cabinet, the northern members were relieved that Buchanan had finally seen the light. Floyd and Secretary of the Interior Jacob Thompson were angry and frustrated. Floyd publicly resigned as a matter of honor, an opportunity he had been waiting for. He would soon return to Virginia to work toward convincing the people of Virginia to leave the Union as well.

Before the statement became public, Georgia senator Robert Toombs visited the president to inquire if he had made a decision. Buchanan asked the senator why a fort at Charleston would matter to Georgia. "Sir, the cause of Charleston is the cause of the South," Toombs responded.

"Good God, Mr. Toombs, do you mean that I am in the midst of a revolution?" was the president's shocked reply.

"Yes sir—more than that, you have been there for a year and have not yet found it out."[27]

Anderson had the unenviable honor of being the first in the battle line of that revolution.

CHAPTER 11

ON THE BRINK OF WAR

South Carolina had voted to leave the United States of America, had seized Fort Moultrie and the US Arsenal at Charleston, and closed the federal court. With only two exceptions, the US government did not exist in South Carolina. Major Anderson flew the American flag over Fort Sumter. Its thirty-three stars were visible to the people of Charleston and a constant reminder that not everyone respected their right of secession. Anderson and his men were pleased to have the other representative of the federal government in the state, the US Postal Service. Like any soldier, Anderson always longed for letters and news from home. The isolation and stress of his current command made this desire even stronger.

Anderson received more than the usual mail from family and friends. He got letters from old friends and acquaintances he had not spoken to in decades. Anderson also received messages from total strangers. He was now a national celebrity. In one letter, Anderson was told, "You can have no idea how much you have endeared yourself to the people." "We never heard of you six weeks ago," but now there is "not a farmhouse where your name is not affectionately spoken."[1] A New Yorker wrote that Anderson "made us feel as we had a country yet, and as if some did not fear to take a little responsibility for its defense."[2] Adam W. Spies, the New York arms manufacturer who would do extremely well financially in the coming years, wrote, "You know your duty to God and country and dare perform it." In a prophetic line, Spies added, "If you are attacked by the people of Charleston," "the entire North would be delighted to know that Charleston was bombarded and every house in it burnt." He added, "This one act of yours may save the country."[3] Others offered to fight alongside him.

Anderson received a more somber letter of support from a West Point classmate whom he had not heard from in many years. Alfred Beckley graduated in 1823, and as a fellow member of the Third Artillery, the two men's paths crossed in Florida and at Fortress Monroe. He left the army in 1838 and was writing Anderson from his home in western Virginia. "All who know you will be aware that the Star and the Stripes 'The Star-Spangled Banner' will not ingloriously give place to the Palmetto Flag." He despaired the coming of a "military monarchy" or a "Southern Empire" in the name of "King Cotton." The nation, he wrote, had "fallen on hard times." He reminded Anderson that the border states were watching "and awaiting events." The events in Charleston Harbor would determine the fate of the nation. Although he remembered "when disunion was a forbidden word," when war came, he followed Virginia into the Confederacy as a general of militia.[4]

Full newspapers and clippings were mailed to the officers and men. They were overwhelmingly patriotic and supportive of Anderson and his move to Fort Sumter, a move that would allow "the country to breathe freer in the assurance that the stars and stripes are not to be disgraced by a surrender which would be shameful to the union."[5] The newspapers and letters from their families cemented the loyalty of Anderson's men. They were following a hero.

The *Baltimore Sun*'s editor wrote on January 1, 1861, "The people of the United States will enter upon the perilous and undeveloped future of the ensuing year with the most sensitive concern and anxiety as to what its course may evolve. All is uncertain. . . . Yet, with all the evils that fanaticism and folly may possibly challenge, we have confidence."[6] Anderson felt more concern and anxiety than he did confidence. As he sat in his office, Anderson contemplated his career and where he had been on other New Year's Days, from his service in Tampa Bay in 1847 to Trenton only the year before. He took notes on the back of an envelope. *Harper's Weekly* and other newspapers asked him to write his life story. He was producing a bullet-point list of where he had been stationed. Anderson was an army man.[7]

The wives of Doubleday, Seymour, and Foster had been left to fend for themselves when the garrison had transferred to Fort Sumter. This was the unhappy fate of officers' wives in the nineteenth century. Mrs. Foster was granted permission to travel to Fort Sumter to visit her husband. Mary Doubleday refused to seek permission and boldly dared anyone to stop her. Louisa Seymour was denied approval and had to sneak across the harbor to visit her husband. The women stayed only a few days before reluctantly returning to the North and leaving their men to their uncertain fates.[8]

Eliza Anderson waited for news along with her children in their New York City hotel room. She was undoubtedly pleased that New York City considered her husband a hero. The city fired a hundred-gun salute in his honor, and she had a constant stream of callers wishing to tell her how great her husband was. She was too unwell to see most of them, but two-year-old Robert Anderson Jr., in a blue artillery officer's uniform, did greet many of the callers. Eliza

Anderson was angry at how her native South treated her husband.[9] That the armed boat that watched her husband and might be used in an attack against him was named after her father was a further insult.

Eliza Clinch Anderson had always been a sickly woman. Because of this, she had been spared many of the hardships of the life of an officer's wife. She allowed her older husband to care for her as her father had. The current crisis would change her. She would shake off her weakness and go to her husband's aid. When John A. Kennedy, the New York City superintendent of police and family friend, learned of her trip, he insisted she be escorted by one of his men. By January 3, Mrs. Anderson was on a southbound train accompanied by a policeman and former artilleryman, Peter Hart. He had been her husband's aid in Mexico after Anderson had been wounded at Molino del Rey. She had most likely met Hart when he escorted her injured husband home and would have taken a special liking to the man. Since Mexico, Hart had left the army and was a patrolman in New York's Twentieth Precinct. Hart's father had been a policeman in Germany. Hart's mother had brought the family to America after he had been killed in an attempt to apprehend smugglers. Hart was also most likely one of the hundreds who had come to pay their respects. Whether she requested Hart or if it was Kennedy's or Hart's idea is not known. It was unlikely Hart had to be convinced to go to Charleston, and he had probably already decided he would stay with Major Anderson before he left New York. Anderson received many letters from men in the North who wanted to join him at Fort Sumter; an old soldier who had served with Anderson would have jumped at the opportunity.[10]

When Hart and Mrs. Anderson arrived in Charleston, they were met by her brother and her brother-in-law. Bayard Clinch had grown wealthy from the plantations he inherited from their father and strongly supported disunion. He had come to Charleston because it was the center of the action, but perhaps he also had the wild hope that he could persuade his brother-in-law to change sides and hand Fort Sumter to South Carolina. Larz Anderson was there for a different reason. He wanted to brief his brother on public opinion in the North, add strength to his resolve, and see if he could do anything to aid him.

Governor Pickens knew and respected General Clinch and assented to Mrs. Anderson's trip to the fort. He initially balked at the presence of Hart, who had requested to remain. Although he was only one man, he was technically a reinforcement, which was the question at the center of tension with the federal government. Pickens allowed Hart to go to Fort Sumter on the condition that he joined the workers, not the garrison, an agreement that would make little difference once the fighting began.

Anderson was shocked and overjoyed to see his wife. "My glorious wife!" he said. She and Larz brought the most welcoming news that the northern public was behind him to such a degree that President Buchanan could not repudiate Anderson's move to Fort Sumter. That would have been a humiliating defeat for Anderson. More importantly, they delivered the news that his family supported him. That his wife brought him a trained artilleryman of unquestionable loyalty was the surest sign of her support.

Anderson was less happy to see his other two visitors. Besides his brother-in-law, an unapologetic secessionist, was Robert Gourdin, a local merchant with business connections to the Clinch family and who was highly active in secessionist politics. In a series of letters over the next two months, Gourdin would try to convince Anderson to surrender his position. They only stayed an hour. Charlestonians offered their homes to the daughter of General Clinch. Perhaps they assumed having the wife of Major Anderson in your home would prevent its destruction once the firing started. She refused and returned to New York.

Throughout the visit, the fort was a hive of activity as Anderson's men continued to ready the fort for an attack. As Anderson prepared, so did South Carolina. The damage done to Fort Moultrie had to be repaired. Major Walter Gwynn of the South Carolina militia was placed in charge. The Virginia-born Gwynn was a West Point–educated artilleryman and a retired railroad engineer. He was initially given command of the workers who refused to stay at Fort Sumter. As it turned out, they were no more interested in working at Fort Moultrie than at Fort Sumter, as most did not return from their first lunch break. The issue had been more a desire to stay out of the line of fire than loyalty to the Union or southern causes. To replace them, Gwynn was loaned forty slaves by the South Carolina Railroad. The gun carriages that Anderson's men had destroyed needed to be rebuilt, and he wanted the wall strengthened. The dunes, which Anderson had so complained about, were now sorely needed back against the walls as they would absorb the shock of Fort Sumter's heavy guns.

Forty cadets from the Citadel, South Carolina's military academy, were sent to Morris Island along with ninety militiamen. Under the command of the school's superintendent, they were to construct a battery directly south of Fort Sumter. This battery could fire on any ship attempting to relieve Fort Sumter. Men on both sides worked feverishly to prepare for the fight. When the soldiers looked up from their work, they saw men on the other side working just as hard. Every day that passed made resupplying or reinforcing Anderson and his garrison more difficult.[11]

In Washington, Buchanan's strategy had evolved into supporting Anderson. The major, however, needed practical support, not just political. General Winfield Scott, who had been kept away from Washington by his own ill health and the hostility of former secretary of war Floyd, approached the president with the request to reinforce Fort Sumter. The president assented, and Scott began putting a plan into action. Initially, the old general wanted to take two hundred men from Fortress Monroe in Virginia, the closest body of US troops to Charleston, and send them with supplies to Fort Sumter aboard the US sloop of war *Brooklyn,* the most modern ship in the navy.

Buchanan's newly found strong will and the old general's burst of energy were short-lived. Scott's suggested move started to seem to the president like aggressive action, and he began to moderate. Buchanan felt that sending the *Brooklyn* before the South Carolina commissioners could read and respond to Black and Stanton's letter would be impolite. Of course, this was absurd as the letter stated that South Carolina did not have the right to be represented by diplomats, yet Buchanan was postponing the government's actions to be polite to those same diplomats. Also, the presence of the *Brooklyn* and several hundred soldiers would have affected the response of South Carolina. Buchanan considered sending an officer to Charleston to meet with Anderson and determine if he needed reinforcements. This would further delay action.

Winfield Scott also began to back away from his earlier aggressive decisions. He worried about removing so many men from Fortress Monroe during a crisis. Instead he decided to send men from the recruit depot in New York. He chose to send the men and supplies aboard an unarmed civilian steamer. He believed that a merchant ship would be able to reach Fort Sumter and unload its cargo before the government in South Carolina realized what was happening. Whether the general was being naïve or if this was just wishful thinking is anyone's guess. There was no way a civilian ship could be hired, loaded with locally purchased supplies, and soldiers could board without anyone in a city filled with southern sympathizers noticing and sending a telegram to Charleston. The Buchanan administration could not even keep it out of the newspapers. The *Brooklyn* sailing from a military installation like Fortress Monroe would have had a better chance of operating secretly. William Walker, the *Brooklyn*'s commander, would be a dedicated officer during the Civil War. He would have been priceless in the crisis.

The army hired the *Star of the West,* a paddle-wheel steamer built by Cornelius Vanderbilt for his Panama line. At 228 feet long, the *Star of the West* could comfortably carry the men and supplies to Charleston. A price of $1,250 a day had been negotiated, which included the crew and her captain, a naval veteran from the Mexican War. Traditionally, a ship hires a local pilot to steer her into the harbor. Since this was not an option, a New York pilot was hired who, although he had never been to Charleston, was confident he could pilot the *Star of the West* to Fort Sumter's wharf.

The *Star of the West* slipped away from her pier seemingly unnoticed on the evening of January 5, 1361. She picked up the two hundred soldiers under the command of First Lieutenant Charles Woods from Governor's Island, the recruit depot in New York Harbor.

Before the *Star of the West* and its cargo arrived, rumors that a relief ship was in transit spread through Charleston. These were not general rumors but were extremely specific, including the name of the ship, its time of departure, and the exact nature of its cargo. Washington, DC, and New York City could not keep a secret. When these rumors reached Fort Sumter, they were dismissed by Major Anderson. He assumed that General Scott knew better than to send reinforcements in anything but a US Navy vessel. He also assumed that he would have been informed if the government planned to take any action in the harbor. They had, but the letter was still in the mail when the *Star of the West* reached Charleston.

The *Star of the West* arrived at 1:30 a.m. on January 9, 1861. With the channel markers removed and the standard navigation lights extinguished, the ship's captain and her pilot decided to wait until dawn to enter the harbor. This would make it easier for them to see but also to be seen. When Captain John McGowan ordered his ship into the channel, he had no idea he was expected. Everyone involved in the planning had assumed that confusion and indecision among the South Carolina batteries would buy enough time to complete the mission. The *Star of the West* encountered one of the city's patrol boats waiting at the harbor's entrance. She signaled, but when the *Star of the West* made no reply, the little ship raced back to Charleston, firing signal rockets. Everyone now knew what was happening except the officers and men of Fort Sumter.

The alarm was raised on Morris Island, and the Citadel cadets rushed to their posts. The camp was hidden behind the dunes so that all that could be seen from the water was the small red Palmetto flag flying over the batteries. When the *Star of the West* was still two miles away from Fort Sumter but only a thousand yards from Morris Island, Colonel Peter Stevens gave the order to fire. Senior Cadet George Edward Haynesworth pulled the lanyard that sent a twenty-four-pound iron ball high over the *Star of the West*. The first shot of the war had been fired.

Captain Abner Doubleday was the officer on watch that morning. He ordered the drummer to beat the garrison to quarters while he reported to Major Anderson that a ship bearing the US flag had been fired upon. Most of Fort Sumter's guns were manned before the second shot from Morris Island fired.

Captain John McGowan had been given a large US flag to raise in case of trouble. The flag would be dipped and raised again as a prearranged signal to Fort Sumter. This, of course, was all in the letter that Anderson had yet to receive. To the gunners at Morris Island, the wagging flag was an act of open defiance, and they continued to fire. Of the more than a dozen shots fired before the ship was out of range, only two struck her, and they did no real damage. Fort Moultrie fired a few shots when the *Star of the West* was still a half mile out of range. When Captain McGowan saw the patrol boat *Clinch* moving to perhaps cut off his escape, and with no aid coming from Fort Sumter, he decided to retreat to the open waters of the Atlantic.

The *Star of the West* incident illustrated how poor a decision not to send a warship had been. The unarmed steamer had entered and left the harbor with only minor damage. Not only would Fort Sumter have supported, without question, a US Navy ship like the *Brooklyn,* but with the *Brooklyn* returning fire at the Morris Island batteries, the cadets' accuracy would have been even worse. Charleston Harbor was far from sealed on January 9, and the administration had missed its opportunity to reinforce and resupply Anderson.

The men aboard the *Star of the West* and those men at Fort Moultrie and Morris Island were surprised that Fort Sumter had not opened fire in defense of a ship flying the flag of the United States of America. Their appearance caught Anderson by surprise. He held a quick conference with some of his officers out of sight of the men. This was the hardest decision of Anderson's professional career. Had he known it was supplies and reinforcements for his garrison, it may have affected his decision. Obviously, had he known orders were coming by mail that had yet to reach him, telling him to use force to support the *Star of the West,* his actions would have been different. Although it was too late to aid the *Star of the West*'s mission, the United States flag had been fired upon, and Anderson and the majority of his officers and men wanted to open up with the full force of Fort Sumter.

On the other hand, Lieutenant Meade urgently pointed out to Anderson that if Fort Sumter fired, it would mean war, and there would be no going back. Like many senior professional officers, Anderson had the foresight to know what a bloodbath an American civil war would be. Meade also suggested that the shots might have resulted from poor discipline among the South Carolina militia and not an official act. This was not an ungrounded belief. Only the day before, a sentry on Castle Pinckney had mistakenly killed one of his own men, and another militiaman had been shot in the leg during an accidental shooting.[12] Anderson saw sense in Meade's argument and decided to wait. Doubleday and Davis were not at the meeting and most likely would have argued forcefully for action. Most of the occupants of the fort were unhappy with the decision. Captain Foster crushed his hat as he ordered the men to stand down. One soldier's wife had to be restrained from firing one of the big guns.[13]

As the *Star of the West* steamed out to sea, Anderson called a council of all his officers. Most were upset and frustrated. As the events of the past few moments began to sink in, the stoic Anderson grew angry at this insult and attack on his flag. Anderson suggested to his officers that they use the big guns of Fort Sumter to shut down Charleston Harbor, a threat they could easily carry out. The majority of his officers agreed they should take action immediately. Again, Lieutenant Meade disagreed on the grounds he had stated earlier. It would mean war. Lieutenant Jefferson Davis, of no relation to the soon-to-be Confederate president, and Surgeon Crawford agreed with Anderson's proposed plan with the exception that the opportunity for immediate action had passed and now the governor should be informed. Anderson agreed and sent Lieutenant Hall to Charleston with a dispatch for the governor.[14]

Anderson gave the governor the opportunity to repudiate the firing on the American flag. If Pickens did not, Anderson would "not permit any vessel to pass within range of the guns." Hall was rowed ashore under a white flag. Charleston residents lined the shore, still excited about the morning's events. The rumors about town were that Hall had come to deliver the official word that the city was about to be bombarded.

On reading Anderson's letter, Pickens gave Hall a written response and a military escort back to his boat. The governor's response was direct. South Carolina was no longer part of the United States, and the *Star of the West*'s attempt to bring troops into the harbor was a hostile act against the sovereign nation of South Carolina. The message was much more diplomatic than anything Pickens had written before. This new tone was probably because the *Star of the West* had entered and successfully exited the harbor. Even though she had not unloaded her cargo, she showed that South Carolina could not yet control her most crucial port, and Anderson could carry out his threat of closing Charleston.

The governor was wise not to send a belligerent message. In the time it took to row across the harbor and back, Anderson had regained his temper. Anderson sent Lieutenant Theodor Talbot, a fellow Kentuckian, to Washington for more direct instructions. Until then, he would wait. Pickens was happy to give Talbot safe passage out to the state. The delay was to the governor's advantage, something an extremely frustrated Doubleday understood. The New York abolitionist was pushing for decisive action. Doubleday was also annoyed that Anderson allowed South Carolina to strengthen her position in the harbor. More heavy batteries were being moved to James, Morris, and Sullivan's Islands. Since men and equipment could only be moved by ferry, it was well within Anderson's power to stop them.

On January 11, two days after the *Star of the West* incident, Pickens sent two representatives to negotiate with Anderson. Andrew Magrath, a former federal judge who resigned his post when he learned Lincoln had been elected, was now the secretary of state of the Republic of South Carolina. David Jamison, the secretary of war, was part of the planter elite and had served as the presiding officer of South Carolina's secession convention. Anderson met them outside the gate and escorted them to the guard's room just inside the main gate. There was no need to show the enemy any more of the fortress than was necessary. The two senior South Carolina officials had come to ask nicely for the fort's surrender.[15]

Anderson, always the officer and gentleman, politely refused after going through the motions of consulting with his officers. He reminded them that he had sent one of his officers to Washington and would abide by whatever instructions he received. That would not be acceptable to South Carolina, as they knew that Buchanan, now under the influence of his new secretary of war, was unlikely to submit.

Magrath tried to convince Anderson and his officers that they were serving a lost cause. The old Union was disintegrating. States were leaving every day. President Buchanan was drifting into senility, and there was no way he could hold the country together. Anderson and his officers needed to look after their own best interests. That was what South Carolina was doing, and they would possess the fort even if that meant the "harbor waters would redden with blood." It would be the humanitarian thing to do to give up the fort before thousands had to die.[16]

Anderson responded that his duty was clear; he could not hand Fort Sumter over without direct orders. He appealed to Magrath to do all he could do to prevent the outbreak of violence, turning Magrath's argument back on its source. Anderson then offered that if Pickens sent a commissioner to Washington, DC, he would send one of his officers to report on the fort's status. Anderson, just like Pickens, was attempting to buy time. Every moment that passed without South Carolina attacking was an opportunity for either a peaceful settlement or aid to arrive.

When Governor Pickens received Anderson's offer, he instantly assented. Charleston was not yet in a position for an armed clash with Fort Sumter or the US Navy. The *Star of the West* had proven that. A truce, which was what Anderson had essentially offered, benefited the governor politically. Had Anderson responded with a simple no, the governor would have been called on to act, and he was not yet ready. His bluff had not been called. Instead, Pickens sent Isaac W. Hayne, South Carolina's attorney general, to negotiate once again the peaceful handover of Fort Sumter.

Anderson sent Lieutenant Norman Hall, his youngest and most junior officer, to carry his report about the *Star of the West* incident but also the entire situation at Fort Sumter. Hall also carried personal letters from some of the garrison's officers. Included was a letter from Doubleday to his wife. Doubleday was frustrated at Anderson for not taking more aggressive action, not only in response to the *Star of the West* incident, but also for allowing South Carolina to surround Fort Sumter with artillery. He questioned not only Anderson's judgment but his loyalty. An equally angry and frustrated Mary Doubleday shared the letter with her brother-in-law, Ulysses Doubleday. He sent a copy of the letter to Abraham Lincoln. Except for the young officer who swore him into militia service during the Black Hawk War, this was the president-elect's first impression of Major Robert Anderson, who in January 1861 was in command of the most important military post in the country, one that would determine the future of the country and potentially the success of his presidency. Had Lincoln been privy to the letters exchanged between Anderson and his brothers—especially Charles, who had recently been driven from Texas for his Unionist views—he would have had a very different impression.

Before Haynes could attempt to meet with the president, he was approached by Senator Clement C. Clay of Alabama. Clay represented a cabal of southern senators whose goal was a new nation comprising the southern slave states. They believed this could be carried out peacefully. In their ranks were men like Jefferson Davis of Mississippi, Howell Cobb of Georgia, and Benjamin Fitzpatrick of Alabama. These senators were using their official position to undermine the US government. What these men saw as the greatest danger to the southern cause was South Carolina taking unilateral and rash action that would start a war and end all hope of peaceful separation.[17]

Clay convinced Hayne that delivering an ultimatum to President Buchanan was not to the advantage of the South Carolina cause, which was the same as the cause of all southern states. It would be in the best interest of South Carolina if nothing happened until a southern government could be formed. Hayne took the advice and dragged out his mission for over a month. As long as he remained in the capital, the truce in Charleston Harbor remained in effect. This would allow the southern states to strengthen their position politically and for South Carolina to improve her position militarily.

Buchanan was in no rush either. He had about a month and a half left in his presidency. He welcomed every day that he did not have to make the dread decision that might plunge the nation into civil war and found him one day closer to his quiet Pennsylvania home. Buchanan still hoped that when Lincoln took office and was unable to take any type of drastic action without the support of Congress, the other southern states would realize how much South Carolina was overreacting. Without the support of the other states, South Carolina would back down just as she did during the Nullification Crisis thirty years earlier, or at least he hoped.

On February 4, 1861, the decisions that controlled the fate of Fort Sumter shifted from Washington and Charleston to the western city of Montgomery, Alabama. Five southern states joined South Carolina in leaving the Union and were now meeting to discuss a new government. After only four days of meetings at the capitol building and in the local boardinghouses, the Confederate States of America was formed. With only a few minor changes, the original Constitution of the United States was adopted for the new Union. Although the representatives of the six states present at Montgomery had not been empowered to go as far as to create a new government, they acted aggressively because time was not on their side. Abraham Lincoln was scheduled to be inaugurated as the sixteenth president of the United States in less than a month. The universal opinion of the Montgomery delegates was that their best chance of successful secession would be while James Buchanan was still in the White House.[18]

There was also, of course, the issue of Fort Sumter. Most of the delegates strongly believed that in the face of a fully formed government of several united southern states, the federal government would not only relinquish Fort Sumter but would reluctantly recognize the Confederate States of America. They feared that Governor Pickens and South Carolina would act rashly, bring about armed conflict, and maybe even galvanize northern public opinion in support of the Republicans.[19]

The representatives also took the radical step of naming themselves the first Confederate Congress instead of the time-consuming step of holding elections. They also gave themselves executive power until a president and vice president could be chosen; they settled on Jefferson Davis of Mississippi and Alexander Stephens of Georgia, respectively. Although there were backroom debates and other men who desperately desired these positions, the Confederate Congress wanted to show a united face to the outside world. Davis and Stephens were chosen because they would be the most acceptable to those states that had not yet joined the Confederacy, namely Virginia, Maryland, Kentucky, and Missouri.

Anderson was disappointed but not surprised that his old comrade and patron was now leading the movement that he described to his brother Charles as an epidemic.[20] In the 1850s, Secretary of War Davis called Anderson a close friend. Writing nearly thirty years after the events at Fort Sumter, Davis claimed Anderson had written him a letter that showed "how bright was the honor, how broad the patriotism of Major Anderson, and how fully he sympathized with me as to the evils which then lowered over the country."[21]

Davis was sworn into office on February 18, 1861. In his inaugural address, Davis called for the creation of a Confederate army and navy. On February 27, after much debate, the Confederate Congress took his suggestion and created the provisional army of the Confederacy. The military situation in Charleston Harbor was now a problem for the Confederate States Army and the first Confederate general, Pierre Gustave Toutant Beauregard.

Beauregard was a native of Louisiana and of French ancestry. He was a career army officer who graduated from West Point in 1838. His cadet years corresponded with Anderson's time as an assistant instructor of artillery. Most of Beauregard's career was with the Corps of Engineers. He worked on many of the coastal fortifications along the Gulf of Mexico. Like Anderson, he was a wounded veteran of the Mexican War, having marched with Scott to Mexico City. Beauregard's last position with the US Army was as commandant of West Point. He resigned from the position after only a month when his native Louisiana voted to leave the Union. That he had cast aside the position that Anderson had so desired and been told he could never have must have been truly galling.

The arrival of Beauregard had both negative and positive implications for the garrison. Beauregard was a professional who knew his job. The quality of their opponent had greatly increased. If it came to a fight, the opponent's artillery would be well placed, and Beauregard was less likely to make a stupid mistake than the local plantation owner playing soldier. However, with a professional officer in charge, it was much less likely he would do anything rash. That meant time—time for Washington to find a solution or to at least give him clear orders. It was much less likely that war would start before negotiations could be carried out.

Beauregard arrived in Charleston to take command on March 3, 1861. Almost instantly, he was a favorite of the city's elite. Men wanted to serve on his staff, and his neatly trimmed goatee became the fashion among the men of Charleston. Women filled his hotel room with flowers and gifts. He was the epitome of the southern gentleman with enough of the hint of the exotic with his jet-black hair, olive skin, and uniform that was just a little more European than what his contemporaries wore to set him apart.

After surveying the military situation, Beauregard decided he had two tasks. First, he needed to seal off the harbor. The *Star of the West* had shown how easy it would be for a naval expedition to reinforce and resupply Fort Sumter. Beauregard also had to make preparations to retake the position. He dismissed the idea of a direct assault. He knew Anderson was also a professional and would be prepared for an infantry attack. Beauregard had seen his share of attacks against stone fortresses in Mexico and knew that, even when successful, it carried a heavy price.

Beauregard planned to encircle Fort Sumter with heavy batteries, including as many mortars as he could procure. The mortar batteries would allow the

Confederates to fire explosive shells in a high arch into the fort. The garrison inside could not hold out very long against that kind of attack. Beauregard commanded nearly nine thousand men to put his plan into effect. Over the next three months, this force would put into place nearly fifty heavy guns in thirteen different batteries surrounding Fort Sumter. Major Anderson, his officers, and his men could only watch. Anderson described the situation as "a sheep tied watching the butcher sharpening his knife."[22]

Besides the steadily worsening strategic situation, life inside Fort Sumter continued to decline. Even before Governor Pickens took action, Charleston merchants refused to sell supplies to the garrison, either out of patriotism to the southern cause or out of fear of retaliation from their neighbors. The men would be without fresh meat or vegetables for nearly four months. Anderson, through a few friends in the city, was able to arrange for some fresh food to be smuggled into the fort, but it was just enough to keep scurvy at bay. Their diet mostly consisted of salt pork and hardtack. The pork was stored in barrels of a saltwater solution and thus would last longer than anything edible probably should. Hardtack was simply flour and water baked into a rock-hard cracker. Soldiers learned to cook the two together. The grease and fat of the salt pork made the hardtack a little more edible. Even this unappetizing fare had to be cut in half as the garrison ran dangerously low on rations.[23]

The daily coffee allotment was cut in half for the men, and the officers had to go completely without. This was a particularly difficult staple to do without during the winter. Most people think of South Carolina weather as hot summers and mild winters. Even though there was no snow on the ground or ice in the harbor, the soldiers spent a very uncomfortable winter inside Fort Sumter. The winds off the Atlantic feel colder than a dry interior wind, regardless of what the thermometer says. Dampness permeated everywhere in the fort. The fort was designed with a heating system to keep the men dry and warm, but there was never enough fuel to run it properly. The coal necessary to heat the fort quickly ran out, and firewood obtained by tearing down unnecessary buildings was also in very short supply. The walls intended to keep out enemy gunfire also prevented direct sunlight from entering the fort for all but a few hours a day. Personal supplies and extra clothes that could have made the experience more bearable were left behind during the hurried transfer to Fort Sumter. That the enemy was now enjoying the coal and extra clothes left behind only added insult to injury.

The women and children of the garrison were sent north in early February. Not only did their presence put them in danger in case hostilities broke out, but it was also more than forty more people that had to be fed and kept warm from the garrison's shrinking store of supplies. Governor Pickens allowed Anderson to make arrangements with a northern steamship company still doing business in Charleston. Pickens hoped that the removal of the women was the first step toward the removal of the entire garrison. The US Army would board the wives and children at Fort Hamilton in New York. Henry Ward Beecher, the famous abolitionist, and his congregation raised funds to supply the women and children. Anderson wrote the reverend thanking him for his kindness but assuring him that the government was taking care of the families and charity was not needed and that it would "be an act of injustice to the charitably-disposed of your flock to accept their alms."[24]

Anderson and his officers cannot be held too much to account for being caught short of food and supplies. Their assumption was that they would be resupplied or that they would have to quickly fight a battle. That they would face a lengthy siege, unaided by their superiors, seemed highly unlikely as they transferred to Fort Sumter. That was, however, the situation they found themselves in, and in a report that reached the president's desk on March 4, Major Anderson wrote that he had supplies for less than six more weeks. This was one of the last documents Buchanan read as president and one of the first for Lincoln. This was now the Republican president's problem, and the outgoing president was more than happy to let him have it.[25]

CHAPTER 12

UNDER FIRE

For Anderson, the situation at Fort Sumter was still a waiting game. His major concern was the welfare of his men. They were short of firewood and coal. He ordered the destruction of unnecessary buildings to use as firewood. In late January, he felt he had enough food to last for the foreseeable future. His concern was the lack of fresh vegetables since the people of Charleston would no longer sell to the garrison. Pork and bread alone are not a healthy diet. Anderson wrote Colonel Cooper, the adjutant general, that since South Carolina would not let him buy supplies, "it seems to me that they will not object to the government sending us provisions, groceries, and coal from New York."[1] Anderson did not appear to understand just how much of an irritant his presence in the harbor was to the South Carolinians.

Anderson still received bundles of mail from well-wishers in the North. Some men requested permission to join him at Sumter; others wrote to express their patriotic fervor or to tell him they were praying for him and his command. That all of the letters came from the Midwest and Northeast and none from the South made it obvious to Anderson what the battle lines would be if war came. As with all border-state men, he could not know on which side his home state of Kentucky would fall. It was a question many were asking in the early months of 1861. Kentucky was a slave-holding state, but it had close economic ties to the northern states. Lincoln and Jefferson Davis were both born in Kentucky. In politics, Kentucky had always been strongly Whig, the party that tended to support nationalism. Henry Clay, the father of the Whig Party, was a hero to his fellow Kentuckians. Anderson had met him many times as a young boy when the Great Compromiser had visited his father's home.

Like most of the officers of the border states, Anderson was deeply troubled by the question of loyalty to his state or his nation. Anderson was loyal to the United States and Kentucky. He would not take up arms against either. If Kentucky joined the Confederacy, he would leave the army and move to Europe to sit out the war. He would not fight his state. He had no such loyalty to the new Confederacy. If Kentucky remained in the Union, he would continue to serve. Eliza Anderson was loyal to her husband above all things and was angry at how South Carolina treated him. When a friend from South Carolina visited her in New York to ask which side her husband would join if it came to war, she told him she did not know, but for herself, she would not be on the same side as South Carolina. Eliza also asked her husband if he were forced to leave Fort Sumter to ask the United States to allow him to blow it up instead of letting South Carolina have it. To her, South Carolina was committing treason, and she was ashamed to be a Southerner. She also saved some of her anger for the government in Washington, DC. There was no excuse for reinforcements not being sent to her major.[2]

Anderson's superiors asked him to address rumors appearing in the newspapers. No, his men had not gotten drunk and attempted to desert while attending a murder trial. No, a boat carrying his men from Charleston had not been fired upon. None of his officers made public statements in Charleston supporting the new Confederacy. Anderson also kept his superiors informed about the military situation in the harbor. He wrote to Cooper about the size and strength of the Southern forces and their placements. What he described to Cooper was a situation that was continuing to worsen.[3]

On the last day of February, Anderson prepared a package for the incoming president. He wanted to put a clear report of the situation into the president's hands, not what men in Washington had interpreted his letters as saying over the last three months. Besides his appraisal, he called a council of his officers and asked them each to write their estimation of what would be required to relieve Fort Sumter. He asked them not to consult one another. Anderson and his officers came to similar conclusions. Each one wrote that to relieve the fort, the Confederate positions would all have to be captured. Every officer believed that, along with full naval support, it would take thousands of men to carry out the mission. Lieutenant Davis was the most optimistic, thinking it could be done with three thousand men. Anderson was on the higher end, with an estimate of twenty thousand regulars. Captain Seymour was the most pessimistic; he did not think it was possible with any number of men.

On Monday, March 4, 1861, Abraham Lincoln took the oath of office as president of the United States. In his inaugural address, he promised to maintain the Union and to "hold, occupy, and possess . . . all property and places belonging to the government." He promised no aggressive action except when necessary to hold the forts or reclaim coastal forts and collect the customs duties.

Although most of us have the image of Lincoln as a dignified, brilliant statesman from the black-and-white portraits, this was not how he was viewed during his lifetime. At best, he was the amiable backwoodsman; at worst, he was an ignorant gorilla whose election proved the shortcomings of the democratic system.[4] Over the next four years, Lincoln would grow into a great president, but in March 1861, he still had a great deal to learn, and he was stepping into the presidency at arguably the most challenging time any man has. The moment he sat down for the first time behind his desk in his White House office, Holt, still temporarily the secretary of war until Lincoln's own choice, Simon Cameron from Pennsylvania, could arrive, delivered the news that the situation at Fort Sumter was much worse than what Lincoln had believed when he had given his inaugural address that day. Lincoln promised to hold Fort Sumter confident that it was secure and that any change to the status quo would require action by the South. He now learned that bold, immediate action was required of him.

Holt handed the president the most recent report from Anderson in which the major included his and his officers' estimations of the necessary size of a relief force. Anderson stated that unless he were resupplied, his command would eat the last of their bread in less than thirty days. He also reported that because of the Confederate batteries being built around him, his position was fast becoming untenable. The figure of twenty thousand men to resupply, reinforce, and hold Fort Sumter shocked Lincoln.

Lincoln had not realized just how dire the situation was. Holt assured him that he was as taken aback as Lincoln. Holt informed the president that Anderson's earlier reports had not cited the dangers his command faced. Holt told the president that this report was the first that mentioned the problematic supply situation and that although he had reported the building of the Confederate batteries, he had never before stressed the danger they presented.[5] That Holt and the War Department viewed the document as of an "unexpected character" was not the fault of Anderson, nor was Holt completely to blame.

Anderson's reports and letters were not addressed to the secretary of war but to Adjutant General Samuel Cooper. Cooper had been a professional soldier since he graduated from West Point in 1815. Anderson did not need to tell Cooper that a battery placed at a certain point would endanger his command. He would have known. Cooper also would have understood the supply situation without Anderson having to spell it out. That Cooper did not correctly translate Anderson's military reports to the civilian Holt is not surprising. Cooper resigned his commission in the US Army three days after Lincoln's inauguration. He accepted the position of inspector general in the Confederacy and was the senior ranking general in the Southern service. Cooper may also have felt that it was degrading to educate politicians on professional military issues. This professional snobbishness was a problem that plagued Lincoln throughout the war with many of his generals. Holt and Lincoln took what they saw as Anderson's hiding of crucial facts as a reason to question the major's loyalty.

Anderson and his command were isolated at Fort Sumter. They had no idea what was happening in Washington, DC. What reached them were rumors from friends and newspapers or outright falsehoods from South Carolina. There was little official word from the capital. Even if Anderson had been in Washington, he would unlikely have had a clearer picture. No one in the nation's capital or Montgomery, the Confederate capital, knew exactly what was happening.

Lincoln's advisers were torn about what should be done and what could be done. Winfield Scott believed that a peaceful breakup of the Union was preferable, but that if Fort Sumter was to be held, a full-scale invasion needed to be launched. William Seward, whom Lincoln would ask to serve as secretary of state, believed that the best strategy was to do nothing that the secessionists could use to rally moderate Southerners to their cause. To Seward, this meant giving in to South Carolina and the new Confederate government.[6]

Montgomery Blair, the new postmaster general, not only strongly believed that the president's pledge to hold Fort Sumter must be honored, he had a plan to do so. Blair was a fellow Kentuckian and West Point graduate. The Blairs were a powerful political family and founding members of the Republican Party. The plan was authored by Blair's brother-in-law, Gustavus Fox. The thirty-nine-year-old Massachusetts-born Fox had served in the US Navy for fifteen years before resigning in 1853 for better opportunities in the civilian world. During the war with Mexico, Fox was in charge of the flow of supplies from New Orleans to Vera Cruz. If anyone knew how to resupply Fort Sumter in the face of a determined enemy, it was Gustavus Fox.

In late January 1861, Fox sent the outlines of a straightforward plan to Blair. When Blair approached the commanding general with his brother-in-law's plan, Scott had the political sense to give it a polite reading. He was impressed enough with Fox's plan and credentials to ask Fox to come to the capital to discuss it further.[7] Fox met with Scott, the secretary of war, and Lieutenant Norman Hall. Hall had not been idle since Major Anderson had sent him to Washington. The press and political leaders sought him out as the expert on the situation inside Fort Sumter.[8]

As a navy man, Fox seriously doubted the ability of shore batteries to stop ships. To Fox, the *Star of the West* incident had proven that. The real threat to a relief vessel would be the armed patrol boats. To counter this threat, men and supplies would be ferried from the large steamer to Fort Sumter by two powerful New York City tugboats. Two navy ships would come as close in as possible and, with the aid of Fort Sumter's guns, would keep the patrol boats away from the tugs as they landed the men and supplies.[9]

The decision of what action to take lay with the president. Lincoln wisely sought all the information he could to make this difficult choice. He also went to an unlikely source: Mary Doubleday. The displaced wife of Captain Abner Doubleday was in Washington. Lincoln went to her temporary home and asked if he might read the letters from her husband. Lincoln hoped to get an honest insider's view of the situation from these letters that were not written for public consumption. Captain Doubleday, the avowed abolitionist, believed the fort was in a much better defensive position than almost anyone else, and his letters were full of frustrations that Anderson and the government were not acting more aggressively. In one of his letters, Doubleday explained to his wife the extreme difficulty of hitting a moving ship with artillery, the same argument Fox made.[10] Partially due to Doubleday's letters, Lincoln would present Fox's plan to his cabinet as a supporter.

The president's cabinet had mixed opinions on the desirability of supplying Fort Sumter and the visibility of Fox's plan. Seward believed any attempt to supply the fort would "provoke combat and probably initiate civil war."[11] Very troubling to the president was that his secretaries of war and the navy, the two departments who would be tasked with carrying out the plan, agreed with Seward. So, too, did Caleb Smith, the secretary of the interior. Montgomery Blair, obviously, led the opposing view, arguing that a show of strength was needed for the morale of the North and to strengthen the will of Southern Unionists. He was supported by Salmon Chase, the secretary of the treasury, who believed it was highly unlikely that war would emerge from action taken at Charleston. Although the majority of the cabinet favored doing nothing, the decision ultimately rested with the president.

Those who favored taking no action, whether in his cabinet or the many so-called experts on the editorial pages, did not do so out of cowardice or disloyalty. They, for the most part, believed that the secessionists had risen to power from fear of the Republican-controlled government—and that if the Lincoln administration took no action, the radical Southern leaders would lose credibility, and the entire movement would fall apart. That had been Lincoln's original plan, as spelled out in his first inaugural address. The report from Anderson changed matters. The ball was now squarely in Lincoln's court. He had to take action: either resupply the fort or evacuate it. Abandoning Fort Sumter would be a step backward. Seward, however, under the delusion that he was the real power behind the throne, began laying the groundwork for a withdrawal.

The Confederate government, like South Carolina earlier, sent commissioners to Washington, DC. Considering separation a foregone conclusion, they were in the US capital to work out the details. The largest detail, of course, was Fort Sumter. The Confederate representatives were Martin J. Crawford of

Georgia, John Forsyth of Alabama, and Andre Roman of Louisiana. All had impressive credentials. Crawford was a former judge and a longtime member of the US Congress. Forsyth had been a newspaper editor in Mobile, Alabama, and had served as Franklin Pierce's ambassador to Mexico, which was a difficult post after the US-Mexican War. Roman was the former governor of Louisiana. Unlike the South Carolina commissioners, they were moderates. Forsyth had editorialized against secession in his newspaper, and Roman had voted against secession in Louisiana's convention. Like many Southerners, once their home states left the Union, they were completely loyal to the cause. Confederate president Jefferson Davis described them as "discreet, well-informed and distinguished citizens."[12]

Crawford was the first to arrive in DC, and through his contacts he made it public knowledge that if the government did not recognize him as the representative of the new Confederate government, there would be no way to prevent war. Seward knew that if he met with Crawford and the other representatives or communicated with them officially, it would be tantamount to recognition of the Confederacy as a foreign nation. He did not, however, want to pass up an opportunity to calm the storm and perhaps take the leadership role in the new Lincoln administration.[13]

On March 13, the commissioners sent a formal request to the US State Department for an official meeting with the secretary of state. Although they were playing for time, it was still, they thought, beneficial to keep pressure on the Lincoln administration. Without consulting the president, Seward unofficially responded. Through William Gwin, a former Mississippi representative but now a California senator and well-known friend to the Confederacy, Seward told Crawford that the government would not take any action leading to war. Even though Lincoln promised to hold Fort Sumter, Seward believed he could convince the president to take the wiser course. He also passed on his overall strategy to the Confederate diplomats. With his guidance, the Lincoln administration would save "the Border States to the Union by moderation and justice, the people of the cotton states, unwillingly led into secession, will rebel against their leader, and reconstruction will follow."[14] Seward let it be known that there would be a telegram informing Jefferson Davis of the evacuation of Fort Sumter within a week.[15]

After five days, the commissioners telegraphed General Beauregard for confirmation that Fort Sumter had been or was in the process of being evacuated. The general responded that the fort had not been evacuated and that Anderson and his command were diligently working on its defenses. When Seward was confronted with this news, he assured Davis and the Confederate representatives through his intermediaries that Fort Sumter would be evacuated. Most historians credit Seward's bizarre strategy as his attempt to control the administration and prevent it from making decisions that would lead to war.[16] Perhaps Seward's belief that he should have been president caused him to act like he actually was. Jefferson Davis viewed Seward differently. He firmly believed Seward was intentionally misleading the Confederates in order to distract them from the operation to resupply the fort.[17] One can easily understand how Davis came to believe this, especially after it became public knowledge that the Fox expedition was being planned and organized when Seward gave his word that the fort would be evacuated.

Anderson was completely unaware of the political and diplomatic intrigues of Washington and Montgomery. The garrison was getting outside information, but it was secondhand at best. The newspapers and letters from family, friends, and well-wishers they received all painted contrasting pictures of events outside their fortress island. There was frustratingly little official word from the army high command or the Lincoln administration. The fate of the nation had been placed on Anderson—a man whose military training and experience had not prepared him for such a complicated situation, although in fairness to the major, it is doubtful that anyone in the nation was equipped to do so. A poor or rash decision or even indecisiveness on his part could have plunged the nation into a bloody civil war and put the North in a position where it would be impossible or difficult to win that conflict. Instructions or at least words of support from the new administration would probably have gone a long way to relieving some of the stress he was under. It also did not help that it had been over two months since Anderson, an extremely devoted family man, had seen any of his family.

The garrison faced food shortages. US forces had always depended on local civilian sources of supply. Anderson had purchased supplies from locals for himself and his fellow officers as they marched across southern Mexico. Usually, this was not a problem, but these were not normal circumstances. Their regular supplier feared repercussions if he sold to the fort. There were friends of Anderson and the nation in Charleston who smuggled in supplies, but it was a mere trickle compared to what was needed. The men had been on half rations of coffee for the last two months, and the officers were doing without. Fresh vegetables were a scarce luxury, and they had to settle for pork packed in barrels of saltwater for longer than anyone wanted to think about. Soap and candles were also a thing of the past.[18]

The general mood in Charleston had greatly improved, thanks to the news from Seward and newspaper reports. It was generally believed that Fort Sumter would be evacuated at any moment and that the people of South Carolina were well on their way to independence. Governor Pickens sent an emissary to

Major Anderson with the news. The governor was gracious in victory. Not only would he do all he could to aid Anderson's departure, but he wanted the Major to know that he thought all of Anderson's actions had been just and right.

Over the next few days, a number of Northern visitors coming to Charleston sent a mixed message to the city. Colonel George W. Lay arrived from Washington for a long meeting with Pickens and General Beauregard. Lay had recently resigned as General Winfield Scott's assistant and probably reported to them Scott's waning support of any attempt to force aid into Fort Sumter.

The following day, Gustavus V. Fox arrived. Fox's cover was that he had come to deliver dispatches to Major Anderson and prepare for the garrison's withdrawal. Fox's push to relieve Fort Sumter had appeared in many newspapers, and Lay had obviously informed Pickens and Beauregard about the new visitor. An old navy friend of Fox's secured him an audience with the governor. Pickens was suspicious of the peaceful nature of Fox's mission. Fox was allowed to visit Fort Sumter as long as he was escorted by his friend Captain H. J. Hartstene, formally of the US Navy but now serving South Carolina. Hartstene's instructions from the governor were not to allow Fox and Anderson the opportunity to meet alone. In this, the captain failed, but the short private meeting did not have the detrimental effect on South Carolina that Pickens had feared.[19]

Fox and Anderson met alone on the fort's wall. Anderson explained to Fox his belief that the only chance of securing Fort Sumter was at least capturing Morris Island to the south of the fort. Fox was only partially listening, however. In his mind, Fox was seeing his tugboats run the gauntlet and unload their cargo on the fort's wharf. Once again, the two men were thinking about two different ends. Fox had not thought beyond putting extra men and supplies into the fort. To Anderson, without securing Morris Island, the plan was a short-term solution at best.

Fox did not share his plan with Anderson, but the major gleaned enough of the naval man's plan that he wrote a warning to the War Department that where Fox would have to land supplies would be under the hostile guns of Fort Moultrie.[20] When Captain Foster, the engineer officer, received orders on what to do if the position were abandoned, it seemed even more likely there would be no fight.

The next to arrive was Ward Lamon, a close friend of and adviser to President Lincoln. The Virginia-born US marshal was known well enough among South Carolinians as a Lincoln associate to almost have become the victim of an angry mob. Only the friendly intervention of South Carolina's representative to the Confederate Congress and passionate Southern nationalist Lawrence Keitt saved him. Having the man who had perhaps come to give South Carolina all it wanted hung or beaten to death in the streets of Charleston would not be a good development.

Lamon met with the governor and told him he was in South Carolina to make preparations to abandon the fort. Lamon also went to Fort Sumter, where he gave Anderson the same impression that the command would soon be moved. Lamon's instructions from President Lincoln were simply to observe and report. Lamon's meeting with Anderson and the governor was entirely of his own doing.[21] Lincoln's friend was not conspiring against the president. He was caught up in his own importance and assumed the fort would be evacuated. One can easily understand why Davis felt the Lincoln administration had misled them.

At their meeting, Anderson told Lamon that he had said more than once, "If attacked and overcome, not a soul would have been left alive." "I would blow up this Fort, as they entered the walls, and all who might be in it."[22] Lamon reported this conversation to General Scott on his return to the capital. The old general sent Anderson a short note with a tone of desperation. He forbids "it as your commander, being against your duty both as a soldier and a Christian ."[23] A frustrated Anderson shot back that he was "mortified at the want of confidence in me, as a "soldier and Christian." He complained, "Cut off from all intercourse with my government, I have been compelled to act according to the dictates of my own judgment." He also justifiably stated, "that responsibilities of a higher and more delicate character have been devolved upon me than was proper, and I frankly say that such is the fact at this present moment." He concluded, "Were it not for my humble but firm reliance upon God, my heart would have no spring, no hope, but I know that He will, in his own time, dispel the clouds which now hang over our country and give us light."[24]

The universal belief, strengthened by the recent visitors, in Charleston was that Fort Sumter would be evacuated. A sense of calm came over the city. Beauregard and Anderson exchanged a series of friendly letters. Rations were served regularly, and the last barrel of flour was opened on March 29.

However, Governor Pickens and the population of Charleston's collective patience began to wear thin. US officials had said that the fort would be evacuated, but the garrison sat there in the harbor, menacing as always. Anderson was also growing impatient. On April 3, he wrote Secretary of War Simon Cameron asking for instructions. His supply of bread would only last for five more days.[25]

By the time Anderson had put pen to paper, the plan to relieve Fort Sumter had already been set into motion. Unfortunately for Fox, everything that could have gone wrong did. The secretary of state launched a rival expedition to Fort Pickens in Florida in the odd belief that saving Fort Pickens at the cost of Fort

Sumter would pacify Unionists without angering Southerners and convince the border states that preserving the Union was the issue, not slavery. The competing expedition would cause confusion and delay and cost Fox the most powerful ship at his disposal. New Yorkers were slow to do business with Fox when they realized his mission. Many had Southern sympathies, and those who did not wanted to avoid a war. The entire situation frustrated the naval man. Fox wrote Montgomery Blair on March 31 that he felt "like abandoning my country, moving off somewhere, I am sick down to my heel." Fox was upset that, "in the hour of peril . . . hands and hearts that should stand by our government" were falling away in droves. Fox was "heartsick, not discouraged at the delays, obstacles and brief time allowed for a vital measure that should have had [a] month's careful preparation."[26] That Fox arrived only a day late was much to his credit.

Despite the numerous visitors from Washington, Anderson was still operating under the rules given to him by Secretary of War Floyd and President Buchanan five months earlier. This was not an oversight as much as a matter of trust. Between Anderson's Southern ties, Doubleday's letters, and the fact that Floyd had approved of Anderson for the position, Lincoln was afraid the major might sabotage any plan. It was best, Lincoln thought, not to give him any more information than was necessary. Considering the number of military men who left the service, Lincoln should be excused for mistrusting Anderson.[27]

On April 7, Governor Pickens contacted the Confederate commissioners still in the federal capital to see when the fort would be in South Carolina's hands. The commissioners responded promptly the next day with out-of-date intelligence. Fort Sumter, they reported, would be evacuated at any moment. That same day, a former member of Anderson's command and newly promoted captain Theodore Talbot returned to Charleston along with Robert L. Chew, a minor clerk from the State Department. Carrying a message from the president, Chew was granted an audience with the governor. His instructions were simple. He was to inform the governor that the US government would resupply Fort Sumter with food and fuel, but no men or munitions would be sent as long as South Carolina did not resist. Chew was not to accept a reply or communicate with any representative of the Confederate government. He was to deliver no honors or courtesies to the governor. The message was not even signed; it was just a statement of fact. Lincoln was making the powerful statement that he was the president of the United States and would resupply his soldiers. That this brusque message was delivered by an unknown and lowly clerk was an intentional slight to the governor.[28]

Pickens might not have believed this message was legitimate had the messenger not been escorted by Captain Talbot. If Pickens and Beauregard were not disturbed enough by this news, Talbot's request to rejoin the garrison was too much. The two men were escorted to the train station and sent out of the state.

On the same day, Anderson received his first official communication from the Lincoln administration. It was not what Anderson wanted to hear. He had no faith in Fox's plan and believed it would do nothing but bring about bloodshed. Anderson had borne insults to the flag, which, as a career soldier, cut him deeply. He had kept his orders from Buchanan secret from his officers and men and had thus lost their respect during the *Star of the West* incident.[29] He was not a young man, and the physical privations of his lonely vigil would cause Anderson serious health problems for the rest of his life. Now Anderson was looking at his new orders that he knew meant war, which seemed to him to make all of his sacrifices a wasted effort.

At some point during his first troubled month in the White House, Lincoln had concluded that there was no peaceful way to preserve the Union. The disunionists would accept every concession the government offered and then use those same concessions as evidence of its weakness and proof to their followers that a new government should be formed. Lincoln also held the deep conviction, as he so eloquently stated in his Gettysburg Address, that the preservation of the Union and the preservation of the Constitution were the same thing, and if they were not preserved, America's republican form of government would "perish from the Earth."[30]

Once Lincoln had reached the conclusion that the options were only war or disunion, it was as if a switch had been flipped, and he became resolute. On April 4, Lincoln met privately with John B. Baldwin, a member of the convention Virginia had called to discuss secession. Baldwin had Unionist leanings. He told Lincoln that if Fort Sumter were abandoned, Virginia would stay in the Union. Lincoln accepted. "If you will guarantee to me the State of Virginia, I shall remove the troops. A State for a fort is no bad business."[31] As Lincoln suspected, nothing came of this offer. Some historians claim that Baldwin misunderstood, but this seems unlikely. The president's offer was clear: "a state for a fort."[32] Lincoln had simply called Baldwin's and Virginia's bluff. They would leave the Union after squeezing every concession politicians like Seward would give them, and no amount of appeasement would change that. Baldwin may have honestly believed his offer, but Lincoln understood that Baldwin was promising something that could not be delivered.

Lincoln also knew what Anderson knew. Fox's attempt to resupply Fort Sumter would mean war. However, Lincoln was confident that there was no longer another option. The question, now, was how it should start. What would give the most political, moral, and international advantage to the Union cause?

Before his inauguration, Lincoln received a letter of advice from an old Illinois friend and future US senator, Orville Browning. Much earlier than Lincoln, Browning had seen the inevitability of war and suggested how it should begin. "In any conflict between the Government and the seceding States, it is very important that the traitors shall be the aggressors and that they be kept constantly and palpably in the wrong."[33]

Once Lincoln's resolve had stiffened, he took Browning's advice and turned Fort Sumter into a win-win situation. If Fox was successful, it was a sign of strength by the new administration. If South Carolina fired on unarmed ships carrying only food, they were the aggressors, which would only help the Union cause domestically and internationally.

Many influential Southerners believed that if the Confederacy acted aggressively on the Fort Sumter question, it would cement the support of the other Southern states, especially the border states like Virginia and Kentucky. To Confederate president Jefferson Davis, none of this mattered. From the beginning, he believed that his new nation would have to be born in blood and that a peaceful separation would not be possible. He also firmly believed that the North had long been the aggressor in this conflict, dating back over a decade, and that it would not matter who fired the first cannon in Charleston. After all, how could an attack on a military fortress with due notice given compare to the brutal, cowardly invasion of John Brown and his abolitionists?[34] This would not be Davis's last major political miscalculation of the war.

Beyond the official statement delivered by Chew, Beauregard and Pickens had evidence that something major was coming. Chew's notice could have easily been about another *Star of the West*–type operation, a lone unarmed ship trying to use speed and surprise to get through. The Confederates now learned that the new expedition was escorted by US Navy warships, prepared to fight their way through. Operational security was pathetic, and the Confederate commissioners were reading details of Fox's plan in the newspapers. In defense of Fox, this was a problem commanders on both sides would struggle with throughout the war, and the political shenanigans in the capital made his task even more difficult.

Much more reliable than what was in the newspapers was Anderson's own words. On receiving his orders from Simon Cameron, Major Anderson replied in a letter to the secretary of war voicing his concerns about the plan. Not only would it guarantee war, which Cameron already knew, but he was convinced that the operation would fail. The problem with the scheme—he did not dignify it by calling it a plan—was that even if Fox's supply boats were able to run the gauntlet of enemy fire, they would be sitting ducks as they unloaded. Also, as he had long maintained, resupply was useless if the surrounding Confederate works were not captured. He also complained that he had not been informed. Had he not been under the false impression that he was to be evacuated, he would have made different preparations.

Anderson had sent this message through the mail, and along with an official report from the engineer Foster describing the defensive measures of Fort Sumter, it was in the hands of General Beauregard. Instead of being sent northward, as had been done before, Fort Sumter's letters were now being forwarded to the governor's office. There Beauregard, Governor Pickens, and former federal judge Andrew Magrath each tried to pass the responsibility for opening mail not addressed to them to the others. After seizing federal property and firing on ships bearing the US flag, opening the US mail was apparently a line they were loath to cross.[35]

The debate about what to do in the Confederate president's cabinet was short and decisive. Those who feared that firing the first shot would cost them support in the North were overruled by those who believed that it was necessary to "sprinkle blood in the face of the Southern people" to guarantee their support. On April 10, Confederate secretary of war Leroy Walker sent word to General Beauregard that if he was confident there would be an attempt to resupply Fort Sumter, he was to demand the fort's surrender and "if this is refused, proceed in such a manner as you may determine, to reduce it."[36]

Since December, Fort Sumter's garrison had watched as the Confederates prepared to attack and had made counterpreparations. In the few days before war broke out, Beauregard's men revealed gun emplacements that completely changed the situation and showed that Beauregard had been paying attention to his artillery instruction at West Point. Anderson, surely, lamented his skill as a professor. On April 8, the men and officers rushed to the north wall because of an explosion on Sullivan's Island. Confederate forces had destroyed a house, and when the smoke and dust cleared, there was a well-constructed four-gun heavy battery. Their location would make it impossible to safely fire the guns on the top of the fort, or barbette-tier, without added protection, and there was not the time or supplies to add those protections.

On the morning of April 11, the garrison discovered that the Confederates had moved into place overnight another heavy battery. The floating battery, as it quickly came to be called, was constructed in Charleston's dry dock by a former US Navy officer. Built of palmetto palm logs and covered in railroad iron, it was one hundred feet long and twenty feet wide. Large enough to hold four big guns and the men necessary to work them, the battery was based on a concept the British had used against the Russians during the Crimean War. During the night, Beauregard had the massive floating battery towed to the west end of Sullivan's Island so that its big guns would bear on the fort's weakest point and the most likely spot for Fox to unload his boats. The revelation of these two new batteries further depressed the already gloomy garrison.[37]

At three-thirty in the afternoon of April 11, a small boat approached Fort Sumter, flying the white flag. Lieutenant Jefferson C. Davis met the boat at the wharf. On board were three of Beauregard's staff with an important message. Beauregard had more aides than he needed, but becoming a member of the general's staff was a must among Charleston's fashionable elite. Delivering the message was Colonel A. R. Chisholm, a prominent local plantation owner who had lent his slaves to the war effort. Also on board was Colonel James Chesnut. The South Carolina–born, Princeton-educated Chesnut had resigned his seat in the US Senate to take part in his state's secession convention. Although he played an important role in the Confederate government, he is best remembered as the husband of Mary Boykin Chesnut, whose diary is mandatory reading for anyone interested in the history of the Confederacy. The junior officer of the three was by far the most capable. Stephen Dill Lee was a graduate of West Point. He resigned his commission immediately after South Carolina left the Union and ended the war as a lieutenant general.

They were escorted into the guardroom, and Anderson was summoned. The message from Beauregard was simple and straight to the point. Fort Sumter had to be evacuated. The Confederate government would aid them in leaving and allow the flag to be saluted as it was lowered. The three South Carolinians were asked to wait while Anderson put the terms to his officers in another room. Unanimously, they rejected the offer. Even the Virginian Meade, who would later fight for the Confederacy, voted to refuse the offer.[38]

Anderson wrote a response to Beauregard politely refusing the offer. He then escorted the three men to their boat. As they walked across the wharf, Anderson asked if he would be given notice before he was fired upon. Chesnut assured him he would be. It was only polite. It was then that Anderson made his other very controversial remark. In a conversational tone, almost in passing, Anderson said, "If you do not batter us to pieces, we shall be starved out in a few days."[39]

Anderson has often been criticized for this comment. He is accused of giving critical intelligence to the enemy. Sometimes this statement is offered as proof of Anderson's disloyalty. This is unfair. Anderson was actually rather sly here. Anderson was buying time. Every moment the guns were not firing was an opportunity for some other eventuality: a political solution perhaps, or the fleet pushing through to his rescue. As a career army officer, he understood that this piece of offhand information would be reported to Beauregard and passed to the governor— maybe even to the Confederate president. It would be discussed, and perhaps a new plan of action would be developed. All of this would take time and would occur while the guns were silent.

General Beauregard passed this news by telegraph to the Confederate secretary of war. An hour later, Beauregard had the secretary's response. If Anderson would "state the time at which he will evacuate and agree in the meantime he will not use his guns against us," Beauregard was authorized to disregard his earlier orders to destroy the fort.[40]

Nine hours after their first trip, the three Confederate officers returned to Fort Sumter just after midnight on April 12. There was a fourth officer on this trip, Virginia congressman Roger Pryor. He changed his mind and decided to remain in the boat when they reached Fort Sumter—probably the proper decision, considering he was a sitting congressman for a state that was still very much in the Union.

Chisholm, Chesnut, and Lee were once again escorted into the guardroom by the fort's main gate, where they presented Anderson with the new letter from Beauregard. Anderson left the three Confederates so that he could once again confer with his officers, the majority of whom had to be woken from much-needed sleep.

Anderson and his officers discussed the offer, their situation, their duty, and their orders for nearly three hours. Captain Lee would later write that he felt Anderson was intentionally delaying them.[41] Perhaps Lee was correct; Anderson and his officers had no reason to rush, but they also had a very difficult decision to make. It was the most important one of their lives, if not the life of their country.

Anderson asked the garrison doctor, Samuel Crawford, how long the garrison could remain in fighting condition with their current supplies. Five days was his answer, the last three being with no rations. Anderson's orders from Secretary Cameron were picked apart, looking for an answer. It was unhelpful. They were clearly not expected to make an Alamo-style last stand, nor were they expected to starve to death by their guns. They were to "hold out, if possible, till the arrival of the expedition."[42] The decision was reached around three in the morning that if they held out until noon on April 15, they had done their duty.

Anderson wrote out the official reply. He would accept their offer to aid his evacuation of Fort Sumter at noon on April 15. He would not fire on Confederate forces unless they fired on Fort Sumter or "the flag it bears."[43] These last words were key. If Anderson had agreed to the terms presented, he would have been unable to support Fox's expedition with Fort Sumter's guns. This would have been almost the same as a complete surrender.

Beauregard's aids were authorized to make a decision. They rejected Anderson's terms. That the fort would aid the relief expedition if it arrived was a deal-breaker. Chesnut wrote Anderson a formal, official reply. Confederate guns would open in one hour. Anderson escorted the three officers to their boat. He shook their hands and offered them the nineteenth-century soldier's farewell. "If we never meet in this world again, God grant that we may meet in the next."[44] Meanwhile, Anderson's officers woke the men, informing them that war was about to commence and that the soldiers were to stay where they were until further orders.

The soldiers, those not on watch, were sleeping in the casemates, the gun emplacements on the lower tier. That was by far the safest place in the fort to be. Per Anderson's orders, Fort Sumter would not return fire until daylight. With the limited supply of ammunition, firing into the darkness would do little good. The first few hours would be extremely one-sided, with no question of who began hostilities.

The four Confederates were rowed the more than two thousand yards to Fort Johnson on James Island. There, in command of the mortar battery, was Captain George S. James. He was given the order to fire the signal to the forty-seven other pieces of artillery surrounding Fort Sumter that war had begun. James offered to Roger Pryor the honor of firing the first shot of the Southern War of Independence. The captain was a great admirer of this outspoken supporter of secession. Pryor considered but refused.[45] Whether his status as a representative of a state still in the Union may have been crossing a line he was not yet willing to cross, or as Lee would later suggest, the weight of what was to come finally settled on him is not known.

At precisely four-thirty, Captain James pulled the rope that caused the friction primer to ignite the powder, whose explosion sent the ten-inch mortar shell streaking across the sky to burst over Fort Sumter. In only a moment, all the guns forming an almost complete ring around the fort began firing as quickly as they could reload.

At six on the morning of April 12, reveille was sounded inside Fort Sumter. It was doubtful that anyone was asleep. Roll call was done inside since explosive shells were making the parade ground rather unsafe. After a quick, unsatisfying breakfast of salt pork and water, their only fare for the last week, the soldiers were given their orders. The garrison was split into three details, the first under Doubleday, followed by Davis, and then Crawford. It was highly unusual to give this kind of command to a surgeon, but Crawford would prove himself worthy of this trust in the years to come.

Anderson ordered his men to be careful and to remain in the casemates where they would be safe. This order had been greeted with disappointment by many of the officers and men. The fort's most powerful guns, with the lon-gest range, were off-limits. The garrison would be fighting with one hand tied behind its back.[46] Anderson had a few reasons for this order. There were 128 men in the fort. Anderson could not take casualties and continue to hold out. He was also a humanitarian who wanted to limit death. There was also the forlorn hope that even after Fort Sumter had been fired upon, a peaceful solu-tion might still be possible. Even that slim hope would disappear if men died at Fort Sumter.

Although there is some debate about who fired the first shot of the war on the Confederate side, there is no question on the Union side. That honor went to Abner Doubleday, and he cherished it. Unlike Anderson, Doubleday entered the conflict with no moral qualms. To Doubleday, "The contest was inevitable and was not of our seeking. The United States was called upon not only to defend its sovereignty but its right to exist as a nation". Just before seven, Doubleday fired the historic shot. It bounced harmlessly off the iron armor of the floating battery.[47]

Over the previous several hours, concern had been growing among the Southern soldiers and the growing crowds of civilians along the waterfront and rooftops that Fort Sumter would not return fire. The soldiers feared this would sully their victory, and the civilians were concerned that this would spoil the show. Doubleday's shot breathed new life into the opposition.[48]

For the next thirty-four hours, the two sides pounded each other with artillery. After Doubleday's first shot, Anderson's three divisions also fired as quickly as they could reload. Each big gun took six men to load and haul back into place after the recoil hurled it to the back of the casement. This limited the number of guns the small garrison could work.

The garrison also began with only seven hundred cartridges. Artillery car-tridges were simply linen bags filled with gunpowder. The bag was rammed down the barrel, followed by the projectile. Fort Sumter had plenty of gun-powder and an ample supply of shot and shell. It was the bags that were the problem. Prior to the opening of the battle, the men had been busily engaged in sewing cartridges. These were made from sheets, extra clothes, or anything that could be scrounged. Throughout the battle, men sewed. Never more than six of them, however. The other thing they were desperately short of was sewing needles.

By the middle of the day, Anderson was forced to reduce the number of guns being worked so that they would not run out of cartridges. Two guns fired toward Morris Island. Its battery on the northernmost point, Cummings Point, was the closest to Fort Sumter. Two guns fired toward the garrison's old home of Fort Moultrie. Although significant damage was done to the interior of the old fort, the guns and their crews remained untouched. The Union gunners later learned that the Confederates were blocking the gun ports with cotton bales between shots, a highly effective strategy to protect the crews from shrapnel. The last two guns fired at the western end of Sullivan's Island, at the floating battery. They did nothing but put a few dents in the outer shell of the iron monster.

A few other targets were fired at sporadically. The Confederates had placed old ships in the main channel to set on fire if Fox's expedition attempted to run the gauntlet at night. The garrison took a few shots at those old hulks but stopped when it became obvious that they were unoccupied. Doubleday took a couple of shots at secessionists on Sullivan's Island who came a little too close or seemed to be enjoying the display a little too much. A hotel that had been flying the Palmetto flag proudly for the last several months received a cannonball from Doubleday's men, even though the flag had been lowered as soon as the shooting had started.

After months of frustrating inaction, the physical exertions of firing the guns lifted the spirits of the men and officers. However, as it was becoming evident that they were doing only minor damage to the enemy, there was growing frustration that they had been ordered not to use the upper-tier guns or the makeshift mortars in the courtyard. If these guns could be worked, it might be a very different fight. The big Columbiads and howitzers not only would be able to reach Charleston but would have been very effective in battering Fort Moultrie and the floating battery. Those top-tier guns were also the only ones capable of firing explosive shells.

This frustration was too much for some men to handle. Private John Carmody secretly climbed the stairs to the barbette tier. The big guns were loaded and aimed in roughly the right direction. One by one, Carmody fired each gun on the Fort Moultrie side before returning to his post. He probably would have continued to disobey his orders had there been any physical way for him to reload. Two sergeants secretly fired the giant Columbiad aimed at Cummings Point. The first shot came so close to putting a Confederate battery out of commission that they attempted a second shot. They were able to reload but could not push the giant gun back into place. They fired it anyway. The recoil overturned it and knocked over the neighboring gun. These shots were generally ineffective, but they did cause the Confederates to redirect the fire to where there were no longer men.[49]

Confederate shots and shells did only minor damage to the fort's twelve-foot-thick walls. However, the West Point–trained Beauregard knew his business, and his batteries were masterfully placed. The Confederate guns were able to fire plunging shots. Coming in at a high angle, they exploded on or above the ramparts and courtyard. Those areas became a no-man's-land. Had

Anderson not given the order to stay off the ramparts, the battle would have been much costlier.

Fort Sumter was designed to fight against a fleet of wooden ships. Had the British fleet that attacked Fort McHenry during the War of 1812 been reassembled to attack Fort Sumter fifty years later, they would not have stood a chance. Those old ships would not have been able to get close enough to fire over the walls. As such, there was not much concern about making the interior of the fort bomb-proof, which would prove to be Fort Sumter's downfall.

The Confederates were firing hot shot, iron balls heated until they glowed red. These caused a great deal of destruction among the wooden barracks and other buildings. Peter Hart, whom Mrs. Anderson had brought from New York, justified the faith she had put in him by bravely leading the men who fought these fires as Confederate shells still fell.

At around one o'clock, three ships appeared outside the bar. It was obvious to everyone that, unlike the *Star of the West*, these were warships. What they were going to do was anyone's guess. Anderson gave the order to decrease the rate of fire. Each gun would now only fire once every ten minutes. If Fox's fleet was going to fight their way into the harbor, Anderson wanted to make sure he had enough ammunition to support them.[50]

The arrival of the ships was no surprise to Beauregard. Not only had he been informed of their departure from New York, but small craft had been watching the approaches to Charleston since the *Star of the West* incident. However, the sight of the American flag cheered the garrison of Fort Sumter. With fresh supplies and more men, they believed they could hold out indefinitely. If they could work all of the fort's guns, they could give as good as they had received for the last eight hours. This, however, was a forlorn hope. Although the commander of the *Pawnee* wanted to fight his way into the harbor in broad daylight and share the fate of the garrison, he was stopped by Fox, who was still vainly waiting for the rest of his fleet to arrive.[51]

Commander Stephen C. Rowan of the *Pawnee* was the first of many examples of the power that the events of Fort Sumter would have on the American public. The night before, Rowan had refused to enter the harbor. He would only strictly follow his written orders, which, due to the confusion over the two expeditions, meant he was under the command of an officer not then present. Now, as he watched US soldiers being fired upon, he was ready to enter the fight with the probable outcome that his ship would be battered to pieces. The night before, the crew of the *Harriet Lane,* a revenue cutter, had been on the point of mutiny when they learned what was expected of them. After the Confederates began firing on Fort Sumter, the same crew began pressuring their officers to accept any risk in order to relieve Fort Sumter.[52]

Confederate forces firing on Fort Sumter. Courtesy, Library of Congress, LC-DIG-ppmsca-35361.

Fox was still hopeful that he could successfully carry out his mission. He just needed four more ships to arrive. One was the *Powhatan,* which, unknown to Fox, was already in the Gulf of Mexico along with the sailors and small boats he needed, at least three days away. The other three were the tugboats that were key to his plan. Of the three, two had been delayed by storms and would never arrive. The owners of the third tugboat had lost their nerve and backed out of the project at the last minute. Fox and Rowan came up with a counterplan while they waited. Stumbling into the wrong place at the wrong time was a couple of ice ships. Carrying ice to Southern ports was a lucrative business in the days before icemakers. The benefit these ships had for Fox was that these two particular ships were small enough to cross the bar, and because they were filled with ice, they would continue to float no matter how many holes were shot through them. How seriously this plan was considered is not known. Rain and poor visibility kept them from taking action. Fox remained hopeful that his missing ships would arrive.[53]

Anderson and his men welcomed darkness and the storm. The rain extinguished the barracks' fires they had been fighting for most of the day. They also believed that the stormy weather and poor visibility that it brought would make it easier for the relief expedition to sneak in undetected. This was another example of the disconnect between soldiers and sailors that marred the Fort Sumter situation from the beginning. No ship's officer in darkness would enter a harbor they did not know. That was more dangerous than the Confederate batteries.

Anderson ordered his guns to stop firing. Shooting into the darkness was an unnecessary waste of his precious supply of ammunition. Although he tried to rest as many men as possible, he also kept a close and careful watch. When Fox made his move, Fort Sumter's garrison would have to act quickly to get men and supplies inside the fort and get the ships moving again before the Confederates could target them. They also had to be watchful for a Confederate storming party. The dark night would offer a good opportunity for Beauregard to try to overrun Fort Sumter.

The primary concern would be if armed men from small boats landed on the wharf at night; could Anderson and his men tell if they were friendly or hostile? Setting off the explosives the garrison had planted under the wharf to stop an assault would be disastrous if it was US soldiers landing. It would be equally bad if they reacted slowly to a Confederate attack.[54]

Beauregard slowed his rate of fire to a mortar shell every fifteen minutes. After the day's long fight, the night was relatively quiet. Everyone watched and waited. At any moment, the night could bring the need for fast, decisive action and the potential for slaughter. Fox scanned the horizon for any signs of the ships that would allow him to finally carry out his mission. Beauregard, his gunners, and the people of Charleston watched for Fox to try and make his run. Anderson and his men watched hopefully for Fox and nervously for a Confederate assault.

When the sun rose, nothing had changed. The storm had cleared, but to the great frustration of Fox, no ships had arrived, and to the even greater frustration of the Fort Sumter garrison, the three ships still sat where they had been the day before, watching, but it seemed little else. Beauregard was pleased with the inactivity but knew he might not have another day before the navy tried to fight their way through. His batteries began firing with as much speed as possible at daylight on the morning of April 13.

After another unsatisfying breakfast of salt pork, Fort Sumter's soldiers returned to their guns. They concentrated their fire on Fort Moultrie. It was the target they felt they were having the most success against. At around eight, Fort Sumter's barracks caught on fire again. Peter Hart, once again, led a group of men in putting out the fire. The smoke caught the attention of Fort Moultrie's gunners, who concentrated on the barracks with hotshot. It was not long before the buildings were aflame once more. The soldier tried to save the barracks as the enemy fire continued to pour in. Anderson realized the barracks could not be saved and that it was too dangerous to try. He ordered his men back into the relative safety of the casemates. Although they had been designed to be fireproof, the barracks had become a raging inferno.[55]

Anderson, who throughout the battle had kept his military bearing, calmly informed the men that the powder magazine was in danger of exploding. There were almost three hundred barrels of gunpowder inside, enough to level the fort. Per Anderson's orders, enough men remained at the guns to fire a shot every five minutes. The rest tried to clear pieces of the burning barracks away from the door, but this proved impossible. Anderson ordered the magazine emptied. Barrel after barrel was rolled out and stored in the casemates. They were covered in wet blankets to protect them from fire. Only about fifty were moved before the fire, and incoming Confederate shots made rolling barrels of explosives across the courtyard much too dangerous of a task. Anderson ordered the big metal doors shut, and a few brave men dug a shallow trench to prevent loose powder trails leading into the magazine from exploding. It was not long before a cannonball struck the door, making it impossible to open. They would have to fight with only what was in the casemates.

As the fire spread, even some of that powder had to be thrown out so that the heat would not cause them to explode. Because it was low tide, the barrels landed on solid ground instead of floating away. Confederate gunners witnessed this and began targeting the barrels. One extremely accurate shot set off one. The explosion came through the embrasure, dismounting one of the cannons.

The firing was also causing the hand grenades the garrison had made and stored at strategic points to explode, adding to the danger and misery of those inside the fort. When the wind shifted, heavy black smoke would pour into the casemates, making breathing nearly impossible. Men lay on the ground with wet cloths over their mouths and noses. Others got much closer to the embrasures than was prudent in their quest for breathable air.

In those impossible conditions, the gun crews kept to their work. Confederate soldiers and civilians watching from shore saw Fort Sumter fully ablaze. They expected surrender at any moment. The flag continued to fly. The garrison could only occasionally return fire. When one of the guns boomed, the Southerners cheered. This unbelievable resistance in the face of hellish conditions won the respect of the soldiers and civilians watching. They also jeered at the navy sitting idly and powerless outside the harbor.[56]

At around one in the afternoon, a shot tore off the top of the flagpole. With the ropes cut, the American flag floated to the ground. Lieutenant Norman Hall rushed into the flames to save the flag. He returned dirty and singed, with the flag ripped and burned on the edges. Along with Peter Hart, Lieutenant Snyder, and Captain Seymour, Hall made his way to the parapet and, with a makeshift pole, raised the flag. The garrison cheered as the men risked their lives on the open parapet in this patriotic act. The drawing of Hart nailing the flag into place was printed in newspapers nationwide.

On Cumming's Point, the former Texas senator and current Confederate colonel Louis Wigfall saw the flag go down but did not see the heroic raising. Without orders, Wigfall, along with a private and two slaves to row the boat, crossed over to Fort Sumter. They were not seen, and Wigfall landed safely. It was good that he brought Private Young with him because as Wigfall stepped out of the boat, the two slaves tried to row away. Confederate gunners were still targeting the fort. A rowboat floating by the fort was not a safe place to be. Young held them at gunpoint until Wigfall returned.

With the gate burning and off its hinges, Wigfall had to climb through a window, much to the surprise of Private John Thompson, the first to see him. Wigfall was waving a white flag at the end of his sword. When Lieutenant Davis arrived, Wigfall shouted over the roar, "Your flag is down, you are on fire, and you are not firing your guns. General Beauregard desires to stop this." Davis corrected him. The flag was flying, and they were still firing, not much, but the occasional forty-two-pounder was still being fired at Fort Moultrie. Wigfall continued. "Let us stop this firing. Will you hoist this?" Meaning his white flag. Davis refused. It was Wigfall's flag; he could fly it. Wigfall squeezed past the gun and waved the flag out the embrasure. The gunners at Fort Moultrie did not notice and continued firing. The American flag flying on the parapet was what mattered. As long as it was flying, the battle continued.[57]

When Major Anderson arrived, Wigfall introduced himself and repeated his plea. Anderson understood that it was over. Relief was not coming. "I have already stated the terms to General Beauregard. Instead of noon on the 15th, I will go now." These terms were accepted, and the US flag came down and was replaced by a white sheet. Wigfall returned to Morris Island, confident he had secured his place in history. The problem was that Wigfall, unbeknownst to Anderson, had no authority to offer or accept terms. This became embarrassingly clear on the arrival of the three official representatives of the Confederate general.

Anderson met Steven D. Lee, Roger Pryor, and William Porcher Miles on the wharf, with the burning fort behind him. Once Anderson learned that Wigfall did not represent General Beauregard, the major told his guests, "There is a misunderstanding on my part, and I will at once run up my flag and open fire." Anderson was frustrated. Throughout this ordeal, Anderson had followed strict military etiquette. Even in the blazing heat, he wore his full uniform. Now Wigfall, the amateur, had clumsily introduced himself into the situation, making a mockery of the protocol. Beauregard's three aides convinced Anderson to discuss the issue before he took down the white flag. The four men retired to the closest casemate that was still habitable, the one converted to Dr. Crawford's quarters.

Lee set to work writing down the terms Anderson would accept and those offered by Wigfall. Because of the heat and the stress, Pryor took a drink from one of Crawford's bottles, assuming it was whiskey. He was quickly rewarded for his bad manners. It was not whiskey. He had downed a fatal dose of iodide of potassium. Crawford was called. He took a panicked Pryor out to the parade ground and induced vomiting, thus saving the Virginian's life. Doubleday would later write, "Some of us questioned the doctor's right to interpose in a case of this kind. It was argued that if any rebel leader chose to come over to Fort Sumter and poison himself, the Medical Department had no business to interfere with such a laudable intention." Crawford offered a tongue-in-cheek defense for his actions. "He, himself, was held responsible for the medicine in the hospital, and therefore he could not permit Pryor to carry any of it away."[58]

Before the trio left, another representative of Beauregard arrived. Major D. R. Jones had a message from the general. Beauregard offered the same terms from two days earlier. Anderson accepted. The Battle of Fort Sumter was over. None of Anderson's men had been killed. This was an amazing fact considering the last two days' events. Over three thousand iron balls and explosive shells had been fired at the fort.

The terms that Anderson demanded were that he and his men would not be prisoners and that he would lower his flag with all honors. They could barely scrap together enough cartridges to fire the hundred-gun salute as the flag was lowered. The exhausted men were formed up on the parade ground for the ceremony. Anderson was almost overcome with emotion as the flag was lowered. He could have been the only man watching the ceremony who understood that the flag was being lowered on more than this beat-up fort. Regardless of what the next four years would bring, the country as it had existed would never be again.

Tragedy struck as the gunners loaded the fiftieth shot. A cartridge went off prematurely in the hot cannon, immediately killing the nearest man, Private Daniel Hough. Five others were wounded. Hough was the first death in the American Civil War.

The streets of Charleston took on a festive attitude; bands played, and soldiers paraded. Mary Boykin Chesnut recorded in her diary that it was "the very liveliest crowd I think I ever saw." She added several lines later, "We have burned our ships—we are obliged to go on now."[59] This allusion to Alexander the Great's invasion of Persia was very fitting. War had come. There was no going back.[60]

CHAPTER 13

GENERAL ANDERSON'S CIVIL WAR

On Sunday morning, April 14, 1861, the two battered companies of the First Artillery boarded the small sailing ship *Isabel*. Three men were left behind. Private Daniel Hough was buried under the parade ground. Two other victims of the exploding gun were transferred to a Charleston hospital.

Anderson carried the singed and battered flag that had flown during the battle. This US flag would not be a prize of war, nor would Anderson's sword that hung by his side. The *Isabel* missed the outgoing tide, and Anderson and his men had to spend another night in Charleston Harbor. They had to witness the Palmetto flag raised over the fort. They also watched a Charleston fire company spend the entire night trying to extinguish the raging fire. It was still burning as they left the harbor. They also had to spend the night listening to Charleston's wild celebration.

On Monday morning, the *Isabele* sailed past Morris Island to the open Atlantic. The Confederate forces on that island lined the beach and saluted the men who had bravely taken everything they had thrown at them over the last three days. Once outside the harbor, the garrison boarded the *Baltic* for the voyage to New York. The men ate better than they had for weeks, if not months. The *Baltic* was built for civilian passengers, so the accommodations were much better than the men were used to, not that it mattered to the exhausted soldiers.

Fox and Anderson could commiserate over their failures. Fox did not relieve Fort Sumter, and Anderson did not maintain the peace. The reasons for each man's failure were beyond their control.

The stress and physical toll of the previous five months showed on Anderson as the ship steamed northward. He did not have the strength to write the final report of his assignment. A sympathetic Fox played secretary to the defeated old soldier. Anderson dictated:

Having defended Fort Sumter for thirty-four hours, until the quarters were entirely burned, the main gates destroyed by fire, the gorge walls seriously impaired, the magazine surrounded by flames, and its door closed from the effects of the heat, four barrels and three cartridges of powder only being available, and no provisions remaining but pork, I accepted terms of evacuation offered by General Beauregard, being the same offered by him on the 11th instant, prior to the commencement of hostilities, and marched out of the fort on Sunday afternoon, the 14th instant, with colors flying and drums beating, bringing away company and private property, and saluting my flag with fifty guns.[1]

Anderson would have imagined each word read aloud in a court-martial. He did not yet know how his superiors would view his actions. The press, with only partial facts, was divided on their judgment. The *New York Courier*, in a much-reprinted story, saw Anderson as a traitor, no better than the officers like General Twiggs, who handed over their command without a shot fired. James Watson Webb, the editor of the *Courier*, from the comfort of his desk, believed that since the wall had not yet been breached, the defense of Fort Sumter "was but a sham" and "that Anderson arranged with Beauregard for the surrender of Sumter before it was assaulted." He added that the actions of Benedict Arnold "are almost rendered respectable, when compared with the more damning infamy which from present appearances must forever attach to that of Robert Anderson."[2] If Anderson had access to that paper, his mood would have been blacker. However, most newspapers across the North were filled with praise for "the brilliant and patriotic conduct of Major Anderson."[3]

It was a beautiful, clear afternoon when the *Baltic* steamed into New York Harbor. Anderson and his men were given a welcome customarily reserved for conquering heroes. Shore batteries in the harbor fired salutes. The ships in the harbor rang their bells, sounded their whistles, and waved their flags. The *Baltic* raised the US flag that had flown over Fort Sumter in response.

As the sailors tied the *Baltic* to the pier, the men and officers of the First Artillery stood on the quarterdeck in full uniform. Tens of thousands of New Yorkers crowded the streets for a glance of the returning heroes. Anderson, wearing his overcoat, stood on top of the wheelhouse and saluted the cheering crowd. One reporter described him as "careworn and fatigued, and apparently feeble gentleman, whose very appearance give the lie to any doubt of his courage or patriotism."[4]

When he disembarked, he was mobbed by the press. "Too exhausted and too much overcome by his emotions to speak," he directed them to his officers, saying he would endorse anything they said. They crowded Captain Doubleday. Not only was he the next in seniority and a New Yorker, but thanks to his brother, Doubleday's letters critical of Anderson had appeared in the newspapers. When asked about the letters and charges of disloyalty against Anderson, Doubleday exploded. Any claim of treason was an "infamous lie." They had fought as hard as possible, and how dare the press publish his personal letters "warped from their original meaning, in order to form a basis for a charge against an officer who has done his duty bravely and well."[5]

Doubleday brought up an interesting point about the Battle of Fort Sumter. South Carolina claimed there were no Southern casualties, a claim that historians have generally accepted. However, Doubleday asks, why would Beauregard offer a truce to "stop the bloodshed" if there were no bloodshed? Some Northern newspapers wrote that South Carolina's zero deaths were propaganda. One New York newspaper reported that they had eyewitness accounts of 49 killed and at least 130 wounded.[6]

Friends of Anderson whisked him away in a carriage to the Brevoort House, the hotel where his wife and children had spent the last six months. He was cheered by the crowd in the street and lobby as he went upstairs to reunite with his family. Although he occasionally would appear on the balcony to show himself to the gathered cheering crowd, including local elementary school students who marched by in the hundreds, he mostly remained in the privacy of his apartment for the next couple of days.

Letters of praise and congratulations flowed into the Brevoort House, including an official one from Secretary of War Simon Cameron, thanking him for his service. He also received odd letters—from cranks suggesting easy ways to defeat the South and one curious letter from a Savannah newspaper editor asking Anderson to fact-check his paper's coverage of the battle.[7]

Anderson's self-imposed exile did not last long. He was the most popular man in the city, and the people wanted to see him. He received dinner invitations from leading members of society, tickets to concerts, memberships to civic and literary organizations, and invitations to raise the flag at schools across the city among countless other groups. Large Union meetings were held where speakers gave patriotic speeches and urged men to volunteer. Although not an orator, Anderson was honored at many of these gatherings. His presence brought men through the door while others gave the recruiting speeches. He received many gifts, including an engraved sword from Tiffany's. A local importer sent him a beaver hat, a gift he surely would have appreciated during the cold Charleston winter. The famous American artist William Henry Powell invited Anderson to his studio to pay his respects and to show him his latest work, *Battle of Lake Erie*, soon to be displayed in the nation's capital. Powell was a friend of Anderson's brothers, Charles and Larz. Of course, on the first Sunday he was in New York, Major and Mrs. Anderson attended services at Trinity Church.[8]

Robert Anderson, in
the Matthew Brady
photograph taken
shortly after the
fall of Fort Sumter.
Courtesy of the
Library of Congress,
LC-DIG-cwpbh-01210.

His image was much in demand. Matthew Brady began his mission of
photographing the Civil War with an invitation to Major Anderson to visit
his studio. The portrait artist Joseph Ames painted Anderson, the proceeds of
which would go to charity.

Anderson also received requests for his expertise. Numerous groups, like
the New York Jewish Ladies Sewing Circle, wanted his advice on what they
could do to help soldiers. He received a telegram from P. C. Sherman, chair-
man of the Committee of Home Defence in Pittsburgh. Now that the Virginia
Legislature had voted to secede, "Western Pennsylvania and western Virginia
are in serious peril." Assuming Anderson could have any command he wanted,
the committee wanted him to seek the federal command of the area. Anderson
thanked them for the honor but telegraphed that he was "not now well enough
to perform any duty."[9]

The next request Anderson could not refuse. Direct from the hand of the
president, they were not technically orders but an invitation to the White
House. In a warm letter, Lincoln thanked Anderson for his "services and

fidelity." He also suggested he would "explain some things on my part, which you may not have understood."[10] Lincoln would write a similar letter to Fox, informing him that the failure of his mission was not Fox's fault. Not only was Lincoln doing justice to the two men, he still needed their service.

On learning Anderson needed to go to the capital, William Aspinwall, owner of the Pacific Mail Steamship Company, offered to carry Anderson to Washington by steamship and personal launch. Anderson took the more direct route by train through Annapolis. Soldiers along the way cheered for the war's first hero. Rumors followed him. He was obviously coming to the capital for orders. That he arrived in Washington on a train carrying a half million dollars in gold from Maryland banks to the US Treasury fueled the press interest in his movement and the rumors that he was involved in some sort of secret mission.[11]

While in the capital, a huge crowd and a brass band showed up outside Anderson's hotel. In the tradition of the day, they demanded a speech. He appeared on the balcony and gave them a short one.

"Fellow citizens: I thank you for this general outburst of enthusiasm, but you must expect a speech. My business is not to speak; my business is to act."[12]

On May 7, Anderson met with Lincoln in the White House. Unfortunately, we do not know what was said in this meeting. Lincoln had promised to explain some things about the events in Charleston. We can assume he kept his word. Lost to history is whether either man remembered the last time they met and discussed their shared experience in the Black Hawk War, or if Anderson told Lincoln that the last time he had been in the White House, the president whose portrait hung in Lincoln's second-floor East Wing office sat behind the desk. We know Lincoln respected and trusted Anderson after this meeting, if not before, because he gave him a critical and sensitive mission. We can also assume, like so many others, that Anderson was won over by Lincoln because he accepted the assignment even though, as he had told so many people, he was not physically ready for duty. The *Baltimore Sun* reported that just by looking at him, it was obvious that his "health is broken."[13]

As soon as Congress could approve it, Anderson would be a brigadier general. This would have been an extreme daydream forty years ago when Anderson left Louisville for West Point. This was no reward for years of loyal service. Lincoln had a job for Anderson, and it would be more complex and stressful than his assignment to Charleston. He was going back home as commander of the Department of Kentucky.

Initially, the appointment was kept secret. That he was traveling to Kentucky could not be kept from the public. Anderson was too much in the spotlight. Without official word, the newspapers printed speculation as fact. Many reported that a regiment of loyal Kentuckians had been formed, and Anderson was their new commander. Some even wrote that the Kentucky regiment would soon be on its way to recapture Fort Sumter. This story was widely believed enough that people began referring to Anderson as colonel, the rank he would need to command a regiment. Other newspapers reported Anderson was going to Kentucky on his own account, either to use his personal influence to win Kentucky for the Union cause or just to stay with family until his health recovered.[14]

From the firing on Fort Sumter to Anderson's meeting with Lincoln and acceptance of the Kentucky command, events had moved quickly in the rest of the country. Lincoln met with his cabinet and senior military leaders to decide what action to take. He drafted the famous proclamation that called for seventy-five thousand men from the state militias for three months and ordered "treasonable combinations to disperse within twenty days." He also called for a new session of Congress to convene on July 4. Lincoln has often been ridiculed for his naivety in his call for so few men, considering the Union Army would reach almost a million by 1865. Lincoln did all that the law allowed. In this sense, Buchanan had been right; Congress would have to act. However, the call for militia let it be known that he intended to fight to hold together the Union. The nation wanted bold action. They first saw it in Anderson and now in Lincoln's call for militia.

Even before they received the official telegram requesting troops, governors of Northern states began raising men. The North was swept with patriotic furor brought about by the firing on the US flag. Northern Democrats competed with Republicans to see who could most support the cause. Had Anderson hauled down his flag or been the aggressor, this outpouring of support Lincoln was enjoying would have been unlikely.

When Beauregard gave the order to fire on Fort Sumter, seven states made up the Confederacy. The great question was what the other four slaveholding states would do now that battle lines were being drawn. Governor John Letcher of Virginia responded to Lincoln's call in an unwelcome but not unexpected way. He accused Lincoln of inaugurating civil war. To the leadership of Virginia, Arkansas, North Carolina, and Tennessee, Lincoln's militia mobilization was the first act of war, not the bombardment of Fort Sumter. By June, those states had joined the Confederacy. The border states of Maryland, Kentucky, and Missouri were more complicated situations.

Anderson's new position as commander of the Department of Kentucky was even more complex and politically sensitive than Charleston had been. This justified the secrecy surrounding his posting. Maryland was dealt with more directly. Federal troops under the command of General Benjamin Butler marched into that state. Secessionist politicians were arrested and held without trial. In Missouri, Lincoln put John C. Frémont in command. The former

Republican presidential candidate proved a poor choice. Although remaining in the Union, Missouri remained a problem for the Northern cause.

Kentucky called for more discrete handling. If done correctly, Kentucky could be saved for the Union without resorting to military force. Both Lincoln and Jefferson Davis were born in Kentucky. Breckenridge, the southern Democratic presidential candidate, was a favorite son of Kentucky. It was a slave-holding state but with strong economic ties to the Midwest. Kentucky was balanced in its loyalties but overwhelmingly wanted to avoid war. The state took the unique position of declaring neutrality. Among Kentucky's political leadership were men who wanted the state to join the Confederacy. Men like Breckenridge and John Hunt Morgan would fight for the cause. There were also men like the Blairs who wanted Kentucky to help destroy the secessionists. Both sides believed that regardless of their sympathies, the people of Kentucky wanted peace and would take up arms against the side they viewed as trying to force the state into the war.[15]

Unionists dominated the state legislature, but the governor was a Confederate sympathizer. Since Governor Beriah Magoffin was in command of the state's armed forces, Unionists feared he would take control of the state. They needed to raise and arm a force strong enough to counter the state forces without being viewed as the aggressor. One of the strongest voices for this course of action was longtime Kentucky politician and former Whig Garrett Davis. He wrote to Secretary of War Simon Cameron and President Lincoln to request that the United States raise and arm a force of twenty thousand men to protect Kentucky. Garrett wanted Anderson as its commander. He believed the people would not object to the Kentucky-born hero of Fort Sumter commanding a force of Kentuckians with the mission of protecting Kentucky. The situation required a brave, loyal Union man who could show restraint and good sense, all qualities Anderson had proven at Fort Sumter.

Anderson made his headquarters in Cincinnati. As Anderson rode the train to Ohio, he became more comfortable giving speeches. The common theme in his recruitment speech was the brutality of the Confederates. He stressed how they continued to fire on Fort Sumter as it burned. Southern newspapers angrily reported the contents of his speeches, pointing out, perhaps accurately, that he could have struck his colors at any time.[16]

The Department of Kentucky, soon renamed the Department of the Cumberland, was initially set up outside the state, specifically in Larz Anderson's living room. Anderson organized two training camps: Camp Clay on the outskirts of Cincinnati and Camp Joe Holt in Indiana just across the river from Louisville. By the start of June, the first companies of Kentucky troops began arriving at Camp Clay.

Anderson received his official promotion to brigadier general in June 1861. Although the timing of the promotion would cause him seniority issues as there were a tremendous amount of brigadier promotions at the same time, including several of his subordinates, he was confident that the pay would allow him and Eliza "to educate our children and live comfortably."[17] Along with his promotion, he was granted two weeks off to regain his health. She was still in New York, but he wrote his wife he should not travel that far away from his command. He suggested the family reunite at Cresson, Pennsylvania, a railroad junction town that would become the summer home of many Pennsylvania and New York elite. Family friends, the Douglases, lent their farm to Mrs. Anderson. General Anderson asked his wife not to accept complimentary train tickets for her and the children.[18]

Neither the reunion nor the time off happened. He would not leave Kentucky as long as there was work to do. Not only was he still walking a political tightrope by recruiting men, but he also had to supply and equip them. This involved not only making requests from the War Department but also dealing with private manufacturers of everything from guns and powder to shoes and blankets. Honors and autograph requests still flooded his office. He received letters from acquaintances and total strangers requesting positions for sons and nephews. Even Truman Seymour's father wrote Anderson to suggest his son was not getting promoted fast enough. His health continued to decline as he worked to exhaustion. He even got to the point where he was dictating to his sister his letters to Eliza.[19]

In June, Kentucky held statewide elections. The newly formed Democratic Union Party defeated the newly formed States' Rights Party. Even though most voters saw a Democratic Union Party victory as the best chance for continued neutrality, Lincoln saw it as support for the Union war effort and began taking a harder stance toward Kentucky secessionists. On August 6, Lincoln ordered the formation of a base inside the state. Camp Dick Robinson, named after the owner of the farm where the camp was located, quickly became the home of five infantry and a cavalry regiment. Except for two regiments of Tennessee Unionists, they were all Kentucky men. Pro-Confederate forces began to organize inside the state, and Union and Confederate troops began massing on the borders. Tension grew, and Kentucky's ability to remain neutral grew less likely every moment.

In late July, Anderson was granted some relief from his massive workload. He was allowed to name four brigadier generals to assist him. He requested George Thomas, Don Carlos Buell, Ambrose Burnside, and William T. Sherman. All had served in the Third Artillery, fought in the Second Seminole War, and, except Sherman, served in Mexico. All were fresh from the disaster of the Battle of First Manassas and were pleased and surprised to be promoted. Buell and Burnside chose to remain with the Army of the Potomac. Sherman learned of his promotion when Anderson asked him to a meeting at the Willard Hotel in Washington. Several prominent Kentucky and Tennessee politicians, including Tennessee senator Andrew Johnson, were at the meeting. Anderson and Sherman met with Lincoln several times, including at least once at the Willard. Lincoln doubted the wisdom of appointing the Virginian Thomas to such an important position, but Anderson and Sherman strongly endorsed Thomas and his loyalty.[20] Anderson bringing Sherman and Thomas to the western theater would have a massive effect on the outcome of the war.

In August, Anderson was summoned to the nation's capital. He had hoped that he could arrive without much fanfare. He was wrong. A brass band was at the station, and the men of the Twentieth Indiana Infantry wanted a speech. The general gave them his usual "the time to talk had passed, it was time to act" speech. He had a friendly and informal meeting with the president. Lincoln was concerned about Anderson's health and asked about his family. Anderson also had a private meeting with Winfield Scott. The old general would be retiring within the month. He also met with Andrew Johnson and US representative Horace Maynard from Tennessee. They wanted to officially add East Tennessee to Anderson's department.[21]

On August 30, General Frémont issued a declaration of martial law for Missouri, which included the abolition of slavery. Many Kentucky Unionists, regardless of their feelings about slavery, were afraid that Frémont's actions would drive Kentucky into the Confederacy. Anderson was among them. He quickly telegraphed Lincoln that the proclamation was "producing most disastrous results in this state" and "if not immediately disavowed and annulled, Kentucky will be lost to the Union."[22] Anderson was not the only one to offer Lincoln this advice, and the commander in chief agreed that the time was not yet right for an emancipation proclamation.

Kentucky neutrality was probably an impossibility from the start. As it became obvious that the nation was facing a protracted war with the future at stake, it also became apparent that a state as strategically crucial as Kentucky could not be ignored. Although the Confederates argued that Camp Dick Robinson and small Union incursions had already broken the truce, it was the South that pushed the state from its dream of sitting out the war. General Ulysses Grant moved his small army into Belmont, Missouri, across the Mississippi River from Columbus. General Leonidus Polk of the Confederate Army believed Grant intended to seize Columbus and sent part of his army to get there first. Confederate secretary of war Leroy Pope Walker ordered Polk to withdraw and continue to respect Kentucky neutrality, but he was overridden by President Davis, who believed that the Confederacy "cannot permit the indeterminate quantities, the political elements, to control our action in cases of military necessity."[23] Over the next several days, federal and Confederate armies crossed the border into Kentucky.

Although the governor and pro-Southern state legislators argued that Lincoln was as guilty or more guilty of violations of neutrality, the pro-Union-dominated legislature overwhelmingly passed a series of laws ending neutrality and siding with the Union. The first and most difficult part of Anderson's mission was complete.

Just prior to the legislature's action, Anderson moved his headquarters to his hometown of Louisville. Confederate forces were at Columbus. They had secured the Cumberland and Tennessee Rivers with Forts Henry and Donnelson and held the Cumberland Gap. The Confederate position that worried Anderson the most was Simon Bolivar Buckner's army at Bowling Green. Anderson sent Sherman south along the railroad with as many troops as they could scrape together to prevent Buckner's force from moving on Louisville.

By mid-September 1861, the stress and fatigue of the command proved too much for the man who had never recovered from Fort Sumter. Anderson wrote the War Department asking to be relieved of command and suggesting his old friend Sherman as his replacement. He summoned Sherman to Louisville. On October 5, he told Sherman "he could not stand the mental torture of his command any longer, and that he must go away, or it would kill him."[24] Sherman was sympathetic; he did not want the command either. The stress of the command would have such an effect on Sherman that the secretary of war and the press would label him insane and unfit for duty. Anderson's request was granted, Sherman was given a command that he did not want, and Anderson was summoned to Washington. Hoping that the hero of Fort Sumter would recover his health, the War Department told Anderson to simply wait for orders. He returned to New York City with his family. It would be over a year and a half before those orders arrived.

General Anderson remained a celebrity during his time in New York. He still made public appearances, gave speeches, and helped recruitment efforts when he could. More than once, he traveled to Carlisle Barracks to give newly trained regiments a motivating send-off.

In May 1863, a deputy US marshal visited Mrs. Anderson with questions about any communications she had had with friends and family in Confederate service. She had three brothers in the Confederate Army or state forces that she worried about a great deal. Union officers who served with Anderson wrote Eliza anytime they had solid information. When General Sherman captured Savannah, he wrote Mrs. Anderson that two of her brothers were now prisoners. The youngest brother, Sherman, visited and gave a "terrible scold-ing" for joining forces "with those who aime the shot at the noble gentleman and loving husband to his own sister."[25] Of course, anyone who had been part of the antebellum army had friends on the other side. Not only was she ques-tioned, she was also followed when she left home. General Anderson wrote Lin-coln with more anger than he had ever shown about this "abuse" of his wife.[26] The president was obviously upset by the treatment the Andersons received. Within a day, Anderson received a telegraph with an apology and an explana-tion. There was a General Anderson on the Confederate side whose wife lived in New York, and law enforcement had confused the two.[27]

Anderson had to deal with financial issues as well. He exchanged a series of letters with the War and Treasury Departments about the exact date of his promotion to brigadier general and whether the army should pay his expenses while he waited for orders. He also had southern investments complicated by the war. General Sherman would destroy Anderson's investment in Georgia and Florida railroads. Mrs. Anderson was owed more than ten thousand dollars for the slaves she inherited from her father. Her brother sold them on credit, and with interest accruing, the new owner owed more than the original price. Judge John C. Cocks of New Orleans was the debtor, and he decided that since Anderson was fighting a war to end slavery, thus making his property worthless, he did not have to pay.[28]

Nothing could be done for Anderson's railroad problem, an issue many investors in southern infrastructure would face in the postwar years. The prob-lem of his debtor was solved when Commodore David Farragut and the US Navy captured New Orleans. General Benjamin Butler, the military governor of the city, was a lawyer and politician before the Civil War. He had served on the West Point Board of Visitors in 1860 and would have known Anderson. Butler had the judge's property seized for the nonpayment of debt and disloyal activities. Butler then rented the property for the use of the US government, with an appropriate payment sent to its loyal owner, General Anderson.[29]

The question of Anderson's salary and expenses while he awaited orders was more complicated. In 1862, Congress passed a series of laws dealing with pay and expenses of army officers. These were meant to prevent abuses of expense claims and of officers collecting pay while not on duty. While unintended, these laws affected Anderson, who had been collecting pay and claiming expenses while waiting for orders. Lincoln himself went to the War Department in an attempt to find a solution. Lincoln wrote Anderson with a simple and Lincol-nesque solution. Give Anderson orders. In a discussion with General Henry Halleck, Anderson was given command of Fort Adams in Newport, Rhode Island. It was a quiet post that "will require substantially no labor." Not only was the pay situation resolved, but it was hoped that the pleasant climate and stress-free environment would be an ideal place for him to recover.[30]

Anderson's health did not recover. Tropical disease, stress, and years of privations had wrecked his fifty-eight-year-old body. In September 1863, he appeared in front of a military retirement board, chaired by General Irvin McDowell, in Wilmington, Delaware. Anderson testified about his military service and the Fort Sumter crisis, and army surgeon Major Charles McCormick testified about his health. The board retired Anderson from active service. It ruled that "Brigadier General Robert Anderson, US Army, is incapacitated for active service and that his incapacity results from long and faithful service and sickness and exposure" and "from wounds and injuries received in the line of duty."[31]

Anderson returned to New York and was appointed to the staff of General John Dix, commander of the Department of the East.[32] Not a great deal was expected of him; it was an advisory role. At almost the exact same time, he was brevetted major general and placed on the list of retired officers. He retired only one rank below Winfield Scott.

From the same apartment where his wife, teenage daughters, and young son followed the events of Fort Sumter, Anderson followed the rest of the Civil War. He still received honors and autograph requests. P. T. Barnum asked to borrow the Fort Sumter garrison flag to display. His fellow officers kept him informed beyond what he could read in the newspapers. Anderson and Truman Seymour kept up an active correspondence during the war. When Seymour's death was reported after the Battle of Olustee in Florida, Anderson was one of the first people he informed otherwise. Seymour would later confess to Anderson that he had been "a little bitter" that Anderson had not put the officers from Fort Sumter forward for brevet promotions. He later learned from the garrison's doctor, now General Crawford, that Anderson had indeed put them all forward for honors, but an overwhelmed War Department had not acted.[33]

Anderson followed the careers of former subordinates of the Third Artillery. He took pride in the successes of Sherman and Thomas. They were two of the top generals of the war. Of his officers at Fort Sumter, five reached the rank of general. Anderson also closely followed the Sixty-Second New York Volunteers. Raised during the heady days after the battle of Fort Sumter, the unit took the name Anderson's Zouaves. They were part of the Army of the Potomac and fought in every one of that army's major battles, from the siege of Yorktown to Appomattox. In early 1865, as the regiment's numbers shrank, they were liable to be consolidated with another undersized unit. Anderson wrote the governor on behalf of himself and the people of New York City, asking that the regiment have the honor of serving in the entire war under the original designation. The governor forwarded the letter to General Grant. Whether the letter had an effect or the war ended before reorganization hit the Sixty-Second is anyone's guess, but Anderson's Zuoaves were still in existence when the Army of Northern Virginia laid down its arms.[34]

The war was all but over as 1865 began. There were still Confederate armies in the field and even Confederate naval vessels on the high seas, but it would have taken a miracle to produce a Southern victory. It was Anderson's fellow Third Artilleryman, subordinate in the Seminole War and the stressful days of Kentucky, who was one of the major reasons for Confederate defeat. General William T. Sherman led the army that captured Atlanta and assured Lincoln's reelection in 1864. Sherman then, with a force of about ninety thousand men, marched nearly unopposed across Georgia to capture the port city of Savanah. With naval transport unavailable to carry Sherman and his army to Virginia to join General Grant in his campaign against Lee, Sherman marched north to join the final battle. As Sherman moved through South Carolina, it was obvious to General Beauregard, back in South Carolina after a less-than-stellar Civil War career, that Charleston was untenable. The Confederate Army evacuated the city on February 15, and three days later the Union Army that had been besieging the city for two years took possession.

With the cradle of secession back in the Union, President Lincoln and his secretary of war rightly decided that the anniversary of the start of the conflict should be marked by once again raising the American flag over Fort Sumter. Not just an American flag, but the flag that had flown over the fort during the battle and had been in Anderson's possession ever since it was lowered. All agreed that General Anderson should have the honor of raising the flag once again over Fort Sumter. Assistant Adjutant General Edward Townsend was given the duty of organizing the ceremony. Anderson once again received orders to report to Charleston. No request by Anderson for guests would be refused. After four years of hard war, many Americans wanted to be present at this ceremony. Anderson's mail was filled with requests from old friends and acquaintances seeking an invitation. The man most responsible for the recapture of Charleston, Sherman, wrote Anderson that he would "be there in thought but not in person." He signed the letter affectionately, "Your lieutenant." Besides his immediate family, Anderson only requested two guests, his old aide Sergeant Peter Hart and General Truman Seymour. Hart was present for the ceremony, but Seymour, because of what he claimed was his "usual luck, the invitation was not received until after the anniversary had been celebrated."[35]

In the late afternoon of April 13, 1865, the *Oceanus* edged her way into Charleston Harbor. Aboard the steam ocean liner were 180 passengers who had left New York three days before. They had paid one hundred dollars to see the American flag raised once more over Fort Sumter. The deck of the *Oceanus* was crowded with men and women straining through opera glasses to see the sights they had been reading about in the newspapers for so long. The band played patriotic songs, and the passengers cheered as they passed Fort Wagner, where the brave Colonel Robert Gould Shaw fell in command of the now-famous Fifty-Fourth Massachusetts. As they passed the warships sitting in the harbor, the news of Robert E. Lee's surrender was shouted across to the sailors. The fate of the Army of Northern Virginia had just been learned on the morning the ship had left New York. This welcome information was greeted with waving flags and joyous noises of all kinds.[36]

As they passed the battered walls of Fort Sumter, all fell silent. Stretched in the evening breeze was "the Banner of the Republic, never again to be displaced by the hand of a traitor."[37] This was what they had come to see.

On the morning of Friday, April 14, the passengers of the *Oceanus* toured the streets of Charleston. War had not been kind to the cradle of secession. The mansions along the Battery, Charleston's fashionable district, having suffered from Union shells and a fire unrelated to the war, had been abandoned, and most were now occupied by former slaves. A favorite destination of these tourists was the grave of John C. Calhoun, that fiery South Carolina politician who had become a symbol of Southern nationalism.[38] Forty-five years earlier, a fifteen-year-old Robert Anderson had written Secretary of War Calhoun accepting a position in the corps of cadets at West Point.[39]

At ten o'clock, small transports took the visitors across the harbor to Fort Sumter. The small fleet carried honored guests, soldiers, freedmen, and curious Yankees like those aboard the *Oceanus*. Every craft in the harbor was decorated with flags and banners. Bands played, and cannons fired in celebration. Inside the partially destroyed remains of the fort was a small speakers' platform facing the new flagstaff. Rising fifteen feet over the platform were four columns connected by thin arches decorated with the national colors. Surrounding the flagstaff and speakers' platform were bleachers. There were not enough seats for the more than three thousand people streaming into the fort, and many stood on the ramparts and piles of rubble to see the ceremony.[40]

The festivities began with composer William B. Bradbury, famous for the hymn "Jesus Loves Me." He led the crowd in singing "Victory at Last," a song he composed for the occasion, and "Rally 'round the Flag" from the foot of the flagstaff. Cheers broke out as the guests of honor began arriving and taking their places on the speakers' platform.[41]

The Reverend Matthias Harris, the garrison's chaplain four years earlier, had the honor of saying the opening prayer. It was brief, and he asked for God's blessing for the nation. This was followed by the reading of several selections from the book of Psalms by the relatively famous Reverend Dr. Richard Salter

Storrs Jr. of the Congregational Church of Brooklyn. The psalms chosen all dealt with God delivering victory to the worthy.[42]

General Townsend read Anderson's 1861 dispatch announcing the fall of Fort Sumter. As soon as Townsend had finished the statement, Peter Hart stepped forward with a canvas army mail bag and removed the exact flag that had flown over Fort Sumter four years earlier. This honor was richly deserved.[43]

The crowd cheered wildly as the flag was fastened to the halyards by three sailors who were veterans of the Union Navy's attack on Confederate-held Fort Sumter. A wreath of evergreens and roses was attached just above the flag. This was the cue for Major General Robert Anderson to step forward. According to one witness, "Joy and sadness struggled upon his manly face."[44] Victory had come; the same American flag would fly over Fort Sumter that had flown four years earlier. The country he loved was whole again. However, it was a different country that this flag would wave over, just as it was a different Fort Sumter after four years of brutal war.

Never a speechmaker, Anderson delivered only a few words.

> I am here, my friends, my fellow citizens, and fellow soldiers, to perform an act of duty to my country, and which all of you will appreciate and feel. Had I observed the wishes of my heart, it should have been done in silence: but in accordance with the request of the Honorable Secretary of War, I make a few remarks, as by his order, after four long, long years of war, I restore to its proper place this flag which floated here during peace, before the first act of this cruel Rebellion. I thank God that I have lived to see this day and to be here to perform this, perhaps the last act of my life of duty to my country.[45]

He then indeed performed his last official duty for his country. Anderson had served the United States in war and peace. Since his graduation from West Point forty-five years earlier, he had fought Natives, been wounded seriously in the war with Mexico, passed the time in lonely frontier posts, worked to modernize and professionalize the army, and helped prevent war with the British along the Canadian border. Anderson's life is the story of the antebellum army. The fifty-nine-year-old Anderson drew on the rope that lifted that "old smoke-stained, shot-pierced flag" into "its native air."[46]

The crowd went wild. They cried, laughed, and sang. When the flag was secure in place, the six remaining guns of Fort Sumter fired their salute. The Union fleet in the harbor answered with a hundred-gun salute, as did the guns of every fortification.[47]

When the echo died away, the Reverend Henry Ward Beecher moved to the speakers' podium. The long-haired, energetic abolitionist was a striking contrast to the older Anderson. Although Beecher's speech was veiled in terms

A photograph of the flag-raising ceremony over Fort Sumter. The ceremony was held to celebrate the end of the Civil War. Courtesy of the Library of Congress, LC-DIG-ppmsca-35223.

of reconciliation, it would have been difficult for the crowd not to have seen it for what it was: a victory speech. Anderson placed as much blame on the speaker and men like him for the war as he did on the South Carolina fire-eaters. Beecher, the radical abolitionist, had supported "free-staters" in "bleeding Kansas" to the point that rifles smuggled into the state in crates marked "Bibles" were known as "Beecher bibles." Anderson had done all that he could have done in 1861 to avoid war and fulfill his oath and duty as a US Army officer, while radicals on both sides made war inevitable.

The ceremony ended as it began, with a long prayer. Those in attendance mulled around the fort, picking up souvenirs and shaking hands with the VIPs in attendance. The night's festivities concluded with a formal dinner held at the Charleston Hotel by General Quincey Gilmore, who had commanded the Union siege of Charleston. It was not lost on any of the honored guests that exactly four years early, the same room had seen a party held by South Carolina's governor celebrating the fall of Fort Sumter. William Lloyd Garrison gave a speech before dinner. Anderson politely refused to give a speech. He only offered a toast to the president's health.[48] Before the last guest left the dinner, Lincoln had been felled by an assassin's bullet. It was the final tragedy of the war. When news reached Charleston, the joyous crowds became as melancholy as Anderson had been.

CHAPTER 14

HIS DUTY DONE

After the flag-raising at Fort Sumter, Anderson and his family returned to their New York apartment. His oldest daughter was twenty, and their youngest, Robert Anderson Jr., was only seven. The oldest daughter remained home to aid her infirmed parents while the other two returned to boarding school.

For the most part, Anderson stayed quietly at home, avoiding the contentious politics of Reconstruction. As always, he kept a close eye on his finances. He was able to recoup most of what the government owed him for expenses and royalties for his text on artillery tactics. He had much less luck with his southern investments. His brothers-in-law signed over all the land and assets they had inherited from their father to their sister, hoping Anderson's status as a national hero would protect them. In this, they were unsuccessful. General Clinch's property had been consumed by General Sherman's Field Order 15. The Clinch family land was given to veterans of the Twenty-First United States Colored Troops. All Anderson's reputation earned the Clinches was a personal "no" and an apology from General Oliver Otis Howard, the head of the Bureau of Refugees, Freedmen, and Abandoned Lands.[1]

The Andersons were still much sought after for public events. On the nation's first birthday after the end of the war, Anderson was invited to Boston. He and Admiral David Farragut were the guests of honor at the city's celebration. Anderson and his family had the honor of staying at Paul Revere's house.[2] They were the favorites of New York society. Eliza Anderson received a letter from Mary Roosevelt asking her to try to convince General Anderson, Mrs. Roosevelt's "hero," to spend the weekend at their Oyster Bay home. This opens the interesting possibility that having already met six future, former, or current presidents, Anderson may have met another at Oyster Bay. The seven-year-old Theodore Roosevelt would likely have been introduced to the hero of Fort Sumter when the general visited his aunt's home. It is also a strong possibility

Robert Anderson, his wife Eliza Anderson, and son Robert Anderson Jr. This photograph was taken shortly after Anderson's return to New York following the fall of Fort Sumter. *The Photographic History of the Civil War in Ten Volumes,* vol. 1: *The Opening Battles* (New York: The Review of Reviews Co., 1911).

that Theodore Roosevelt would have been asked to entertain the seven-year-old Robert Anderson Jr.[3]

In February 1869, Anderson ended his service with the US Army. Although officially on the retired list, he had enjoyed limited duty since 1863, basically as an adviser to the Eastern Department headquartered in New York. The only time his services had been called for during this time was the ceremony at Fort Sumter.

During this period of semiretirement, Anderson worried about the future of his beloved West Point. Would an institution that had provided so many men to the Confederacy survive in the hyperpolitical age of Reconstruction? Anderson wrote his old friend Sylvanus Thayer with the suggestion of forming an Association of Graduates. The organization's mission would be "to perfect and perpetuate this truly national institution."[4]

The first meeting took place at the office of the president of the College of the City of New York. Dr. Horace Webster was an Academy graduate and the association's first president. Neither Anderson nor Thayer attended. Both men were too ill. Without their guidance, the association became a purely social organization, not one to take part in the management of the Academy. The association held its first annual meeting in 1869, bringing together graduates from both North and South. Anderson was never able to attend one of these reunions, nor did he live long enough to see how his initial idea helped heal the wounds of the Civil War.

It was only a few days after the association's first meeting that Anderson and his family boarded a steamship for Europe. The family toured the German states and Switzerland before settling in France. The family moved into a small house in the country outside of Nice on the Mediterranean coast. He hoped the mild climate would help him recover his health. Whenever he made a rare public appearance, he donned the plain blue uniform he had worn so much of his life. The locals referred to him simply as "le general."

While living quietly in France, Anderson once again found himself at the center of controversy in America's newspapers, although he probably never realized it. A rumor spread that Anderson was destitute in Switzerland. The rumors might have had honest origins. A tourist may have mistaken Anderson's illness and simple lifestyle for poverty. Northern newspapers presented this as a national tragedy, while Southern ones reported it as fitting. When the press reported his death, many papers pointed out that Anderson was on a general's pay; money was not a problem.[5]

Brevet Major General Robert Anderson passed away on October 26, 1871. Years of illness, stress, and injury in the service of his nation finally caught up with him. He was sixty-six years old. The French government paid Anderson the honor of transporting his remains home on the French warship *Guerrière*. At none of the ceremonies honoring Anderson were guns fired in salute. Organizers must have assumed he had heard enough during his lifetime.

His family returned to New York City. Robert Anderson Jr. was studying law at Columbia when he died of natural causes in 1879. The three daughters lived with their mother until her death in 1905. The oldest daughter, Eliza, married a wealthy New York businessman only a year younger than her mother. She used his wealth and her social connections to preserve and defend her father's reputation. In the end, she was unsuccessful in what had been her mother's mission as well. Anderson's memory faded after her death. Besides his stone at the West Point cemetery and a marker at Fort Sumter, there is no monument to Robert Anderson.

Robert Anderson served his nation for more than forty years. As a cadet, he shook hands with John Adams. As an officer, he met Andrew Jackson and Abraham Lincoln in their White House office. He served under ten of the first sixteen presidents of the United States. He fought in four of his nation's wars and was key in preventing a fifth. Through his time as a West Point instructor as an officer, and his work producing artillery manuals, Anderson trained most of the men who led Civil War armies. He is most remembered for his six months at Forts Moultrie and Sumter. Major Anderson is often portrayed as a man caught up in the swirl of grand events. While this is undoubtedly true, he was much more than a leaf caught in the wind. His inaction at times and bold action at others helped rally the people of the North to the Union cause and ultimate victory.

Notes

Chapter 1

1. E. L. Anderson, *Soldier and Pioneer: A Biographical Sketch of Lt.-Col. Richard C. Anderson of the Continental Army* (New York: G. P. Putnam's Sons, 1879), 1–13, 20–25.
2. John R. Alden, *A History of the American Revolution* (1969; repr. New York: Da Capo, 1989), 410–12.
3. Anderson, *Soldier and Pioneer*, 25–27.
4. Anderson, 41.
5. Bruce Grant, *American Forts, Yesterday and Today* (New York: E. P. Dutton, 1965), 107–8; Anderson, *Soldier and Pioneer*, 41.
6. Anderson, 41.
7. Gordon S. Wood, *The American Revolution: A History* (New York: Random House, 2003), 117.
8. Ben Cassedy, *A History of Louisville, From Its Earliest Settlement till the Year 1852* (Louisville, KY: Hull and Brother, 1852), 116.
9. Cassedy, 108–15; K. Jack Baur, *Zachary Taylor: Soldier, Planter, Statesman of the Old Southwest* (Baton Rouge: Louisiana State University Press, 1985), 2–3.
10. Anderson, *Soldier and Pioneer*, 53–54; Charles Anderson, "The Story of Soldier's Retreat" (unpublished manuscript, Filson Historical Society, Louisville, KY, 4–10).
11. Anderson, "Story of Soldier's Retreat," 4–10.
12. Anderson, "Story of Soldier's Retreat," 54–55; and Richard Clough Anderson Jr., *The Diary and Journal of Richard Clough Anderson, Jr., 1814–1826* (Durham, NC: Duke University Press, 1964), 107.
13. Baur, *Zachary Taylor*, 2–3.
14. Anderson, "Story of Soldier's Retreat," 4, 8.
15. Anderson, 22.
16. Daniel Walker Howe, *What Hath God Wrought? The Transformation of America, 1815–1848* (New York: Oxford University Press), 166–68; Anderson, "Story of Soldier's Retreat," 8.
17. Everett Dick, *The Dixie Frontier, A Social History* (1948; repr. Norman: University of Oklahoma Press, 1993), 128–29.
18. Alfred Tischendorf and E. Taylor Parks, introduction to Anderson, *Diary and Journal*, xvii.

19. Anderson, *Story of Soldier's Retreat,* 95.
20. Anderson, 16, 45, 57, 58.
21. Anderson, 40.
22. Anderson, 8.
23. Anderson, 28, 48; Receipt 1820, Robert Anderson Papers, Volume 1, Library of Congress Manuscript Division.
24. Robert Anderson to Richard C. Anderson, Jr., April 18, 1819, quoted in Anderson, *The Story of Soldier's Retreat,* 58–59.
25. Anderson, *The Story of Soldier's Retreat,* 51.
26. Leroy J. Halsey, *Memoir of the Life and Character of Rev. Lewis Warner Green, D.D., with a Selection from His Sermons* (New York: Charles Scribner and Co., 1871), 6–7.
27. Robert Anderson to Richard C. Anderson, Jr., April 18, 1819.
28. Robert Anderson to Richard C. Anderson, Jr., April 18, 1819.
29. Halsey, *Memoir of the Life and Character of Rev. Lewis Warner Green,* 6–7.
30. Robert Anderson to His Sister, 1827, Robert Anderson Papers, Volume I, Library of Congress Manuscript Division.
31. Richard Clough Anderson to John C. Calhoun, July 13, 1820, Anderson Papers, United States Military Academy Library.
32. Robert Anderson to John C. Calhoun, March 1, 1821, Anderson Papers, United States Military Academy Library.
33. John Driscoll, *All That Is Glorious around Us: Paintings from the Hudson River School* (Ithaca, NY: Cornell University Press, 1997), 8, 50.
34. Robert Anderson to His Sister, 1821, Robert Anderson Papers, Volume I, Library of Congress Manuscript Division.
35. Albert Church, *Personal Reminiscences of the Military Academy from 1824 to 1831: A Paper Read to the U.S. Military Service Institute, West Point, March 28, 1878* (West Point: USMA Press, 1878), 5; Douglas Southall Freeman, *R. E. Lee: A Biography* (New York: Charles Scribner's Sons, 1934), 48.
36. Stephen E. Ambrose, *Duty, Honor, Country: A History of West Point* (1966; repr. Baltimore, MD: Johns Hopkins University Press, 1999), 7–13.
37. Theodore J. Crackel, *West Point, A Bicentennial History* (Lawrence: University Press of Kansas, 2002), 50; Samuel J. Watson, "Developing 'Republican Machines': West Point and the Struggle to Render the Officer Corps Safe for America," in Robert M. S. McDonald, ed., *Thomas Jefferson's Military Academy: Founding West Point* (Charlottesville: University Press of Virginia, 2004), 154–81.
38. Crackel, *West Point,* 84; Ambrose, *Duty, Honor, Country,* 24–29.
39. Ambrose, 63–64.
40. Crackel, *West Point,* 92–93; Ambrose, *Duty, Honor, Country,* 56–59, 77–78.
41. Ambrose, 67–80.
42. Personal note, Anderson Papers, United States Military Academy Library.
43. Ronald Anderson and Anne Koval, *James McNeill Whistler: Beyond the Myth* (New York: Carroll & Graf, 1994), 30.
44. Ambrose, *Duty, Honor, Country.* 77.
45. Timothy D. Johnson. *Winfield Scott: The Quest for Military Glory* (Lawrence: University of Kansas Press, 1998), 82–83.
46. John C. Calhoun's Reduction of the Army Report, December 12, 1820, quoted in Johnson, *Winfield Scott,* 81.

47. Freeman, *Lee*, 48–49.
48. "John C. Calhoun to Robert Anderson, 1820," Robert Anderson Papers, Volume I, Library of Congress Manuscript Division; Ambrose, *Duty, Honor, Country*, 82–83.
49. Douglas Southall Freeman quoted in Edward S. Wallace, *General William Jenkins Worth, Monterey's Forgotten Hero* (Dallas: SMU Press, 1953), 30.
50. William Clarence Burrage, *The Visit of the West Point Cadets to Boston 1821*, 12 vols. (Boston: The Bostonian Society Publications, 1910), 6:53–54.
51. Burrage, 6:55–56, 62.
52. John Adams, "My Young Fellow Citizens," delivered at Braintree, Massachusetts, 1821, West Point Archives.
53. John K. Findlay, speech at West Point reunion, 1881, quoted in Burrage, *Visit of the West Point Cadets to Boston 1821*, 6:61.
54. Burrage, *The Visit of The West Point Cadets to Boston 1821*, 6:62.
55. Robert Anderson to Maria W. Latham, 1821, Robert Anderson Papers, Volume I, Library of Congress Manuscript Division.
56. Freeman, *Lee*, 53.
57. Lee Kennett, *Sherman, A Soldier's Life* (New York: HarperCollins, 2001), 15; "Cadet Life before the Mexican War," *US Military Academy Library Bulletin* no. 1, 12–13, quoted in Freeman Cleaves, *The Rock of Chickamauga: The Life of General George H. Thomas* (Norman: University of Oklahoma Press, 1948), 11.
58. J. H. Colton, *A Guide Book to West Point and Vicinity: Containing Historical and Statistical Sketches of the United States Military Academy, and of Other Objects of Interest* (New York: J. H. Colton, 1844), 12; Freeman, *Lee*, 56–57.
59. John H. B. Latrobe, *West Point Reminiscences from September, 1818, to March, 1882* (East Saginaw, MI: Evening News, Printers and Binders, 1887), 19–20; Colton, *A Guide Book to West Point and Vicinity*, 42; George W. Cullum, *Register of Officers and Graduates of the United States Military Academy*, 8 vols. (West Point, NY: US Military Academy, 1879), 1:211.
60. Freeman, *Lee*, 52–53.
61. West Point diploma, July 4, 1825, Robert Anderson Papers, Volume I, Library of Congress, Manuscript Division.

Chapter 2

1. Richard Clough Anderson Jr., *The Diary and Journal of Richard Clough Anderson Jr., 1814–1826* (Durham, NC: Duke University Press, 1964), xvii–xviii.
2. Anderson, xviii.
3. "Treaty for the Suppression of the Slave Trade, Negotiated by Mr. Anderson, Our Minister at Bogota, with the Colombian Republic," *Aurora and Franklin Gazette* (Philadelphia), March 14, 1825.
4. "The Citizens of Louisville, in Kentucky, Offered to Their Fellow-Citizen Richard C. Anderson," *Louisville Public Advertiser*, July 30, 1825; "In Announcing the Return to the United States of Mr. ANDERSON, Our Minister to Colombia, the Federal Gazette Makes the Following Observations, the Justice of Which All Who Have Previously Known Mr. A Will Readily Believe In," *Daily National Intelligencer*, May 21, 1825; Wilkins B. Winn, "The Issue of Religious Liberty in the United States Commercial Treaty with Colombia, 1824," *The Americas* 26, no. 3 (January 1970): 291–301.

5. "Mr. Richard C. Anderson, Minister Plenipotentiary at Bogota," February 25, 1825, *Aurora and Franklin Gazette* (Philadelphia).

6. Andrew R. L. Cayton, "The Debate over the Panama Congress and the Origins of the Second American Party System," *The Historian* 47, no. 2 (February 1985): 219–38.

7. Cayton.

8. Ralph Sanders, "Congressional Reaction in the United States to the Panama Congress of 1826," *The Americas* 11, no. 2 (October 1954): 143.

9. Samuel Flag Bemis, *John Quincy Adams and the Foundations of American Foreign Policy* (New York: Alfred A. Knopf, 1965), 557–58.

10. Anderson, *Diary and Journal*, xvii.

11. Anderson, *Diary and Journal*, 208–10.

12. Anderson, *Soldier and Pioneer*, 55; Anderson, *Diary and Journal*, 211.

13. Robert Anderson to Marie Latham, October 8, 1825, Anderson Papers, Filson Center.

14. Anderson, *Diary and Journal*, 217.

15. Anderson, 220; Robert Anderson to His Cousin, November 18, 1825, Robert Anderson Papers, Volume I, Library of Congress Manuscript Division.

16. Anderson to Maria W. Latham, March 6, 1826, Robert Anderson Papers, Volume I, Library of Congress Manuscript Division.

17. Anderson to recipient unknown (copy), 1826, Robert Anderson Papers, Volume I Library of Congress Manuscript Division.

18. Anderson, *Diary and Journal*, 221; Anderson to recipient unknown (copy), 1826.

19. Anderson, *Diary and Journal*, 221; Anderson to recipient unknown (copy), 1826.

20. Anderson to recipient unknown (copy), 1826.

21. Anderson, *Diary and Journal*, 221; Anderson to recipient unknown (copy), 1826.

22. Anderson, *Diary and Journal*, 224.

23. Robert Louis Gilmore and John Parker Harrison, "Juan Bernardo Elbers and the Introduction of Steam Navigation on the Magdalena River," *The Hispanic American Historical Review* 28, no. 3 (August 1948): 338–40.

24. Anderson, *Diary and Journal*, 226.

25. Gilmore and Harrison, "Juan Bernardo Elbers," 335.

26. Anderson, *Diary and Journal*, 222–35.

27. Anderson, *Diary and Journal*, 230.

28. Anderson, *Diary and Journal*, 233.

29. Anderson, *Diary and Journal*, 233–35.

30. Anderson, *Diary and Journal*, 236.

31. Josiah Conder, *The Modern Traveler: A Popular Description, Geographical, Historical and Topographical of the Various Countries of the Globe*, vol. 8 (Boston: Wells & Lilly, 1830), 293–308.

32. Anderson, *Diary and Journal*, 241, 245; Daniel Walker Howe, *What Hath God Wrought: The Transformation of America, 1815–1848* (New York: Oxford University Press, 2007), 258.

33. John Quincy Adams quoted in David Head, "A Different Kind of Maritime Predation: South American Privateering from Baltimore, 1816–1820," *International Journal of Naval History* 7, no. 12 (August 2008): 12; Anderson, *Diary and Journal*, 236; Head, "Different Kind of Maritime Predation," 12, 19. Although Anderson could

give him no assurances, he would return to Baltimore and would not be prosecuted. The case of James Chaytor would be used by Great Britain during the negotiations that led to the Treaty of Washington when the United States was seeking damages for the actions of ships built in Great Britain during the American Civil War. Great Britain, *The Case of Great Britain as Laid before the Tribunal of Arbitration, Convened at Geneva under the Provisions of the Treaty between the United States of America and Her Majesty the Queen of Great Britain, Concluded at Washington, May 8, 1871*, 3 vols. (Washington, DC: Government Printing Office, 1872), 3:190.

34. R. C. Anderson Jr. to R. C. Anderson, February 9, 1826, Anderson Papers, Filson Society.

35. Anderson, *Diary and Journal*, 241, 246; Anderson, *The Story of Soldier's Retreat*, 63.

36. Anderson, *Diary and Journal*, 249, 251, 254, 259.

37. "The Senate have confirmed the nominations of Richard C. Anderson, of Kentucky, and John Sergeant, of Pennsylvania, as Commissioners on the part of the United States, to attend the deliberations of the Congress of the South American Republics, at the Isthmus of Panama," *Providence Patriot*, March 22, 1826; Anderson, *Diary and Journal*, 263.

38. Anderson, *Diary and Journal*, 264–65.

39. Anderson, *Diary and Journal*, 268.

40. Anderson, *Diary and Journal*, 268.

41. Richard M. Swiderski, *Colonel in America: Mercurial Panacea, War, Song and Ghosts* (Boca Raton, FL: Brown Walker Press, 2009), xiii; Anderson, *Diary and Journal*, 270.

42. Anderson, *Diary and Journal*, 270.

43. J. M. MacPherson to Henry Clay, July 26, 1826, quoted in Anderson, *Diary and Journal*, 271–72.

44. Bemis, *John Quincy Adams*, 558–59.

45. "Col. Richard C. Anderson," *Daily National Journal* (Washington, DC), November 11, 1826; Robert Anderson to Maria Anderson, September 22, 1826, Anderson Family Papers, Filson Historical Society.

Chapter 3

1. Janice E. McKenney, *The Organizational History of Field Artillery, 1775–2003* (Washington DC: US Army Center of Military History, 2007), 32–34.

2. Robert B. Roberts, *Encyclopedia of Historic Forts: The Military, Pioneer, and Trading Posts of the United States* (New York: Macmillan, 1988), 816–17; J. E. Kaufmann and H. W. Kaufmann, *Fortress American: The Forts That Defended America, 1600 to the Present* (Cambridge, MA: Da Capo Press, 2004), 216.

3. McKenney, *The Organizational History of Field Artillery*, 54.

4. Robert Anderson to Maria W. Latham, September 22, 1826, Anderson Family Papers, Filson Historical Society.

5. E. D. Keyes, *Fifty Years' Observation of Men and Events, Civil and Military* (New York: Charles Scribner's Sons, 1884), 368.

6. Robert Anderson to Maria W. Latham, 1827, Robert Anderson Papers, Volume I, Library of Congress Manuscript Division.

7. Robert Anderson to Maria W. Latham, May 28, 1827, Anderson Family Papers, Filson Historical Society; Anderson to Latham, 1827.

8. J. Thomas Russell, "Edgar Allan Poe, The Army Years," *United States Military Academy Bulletin* no. 10 (1972): 5–6.
9. "Advice to a Young Officer by a French Officer," translated by Robert Anderson. Robert Anderson Papers, Volume I, Library of Congress Manuscript Division; Russell, "Edgar Allan Poe."
10. George Gordon Greenough, Address Delivered at the USMA, at the Exercises Incident to the Centenary of Major General Robert Anderson, US Army, June 14, 1905, US Army History Center Archives, Carlisle, PA.
11. "Brig Crawford," *Louisiana Advertiser*, July 13, 1827.
12. "The Pirates," *Daily National Intelligencer* (Washington, DC), July 24, 1827.
13. "The Providence Insurance office, in which the brig Crawford and her cargo were insured, has manifested a just sense of the services of Mr. Dobson, the mate, by presenting him five hundred dollars," *Daily National Journal* (Washington, DC), August 11, 1827.
14. Greenough, Address delivered at the USMA.
15. Oliver Lyman Spaulding, *The United States Army, In War and Peace* (New York: G. P. Putnam's Sons, 1937), 148–49.
16. Rembert W. Patrick, *Aristocrat in Uniform, General Duncan Clinch* (Gainesville: University Press of Florida, 1963), 48–49.
17. Baton Rouge was not part of the Louisiana Purchase. In 1810, American residents of Baton Rouge seized the town from the Spanish and declared the Republic of West Florida, the original Lone Star Republic. Within a month, the republic asked to join the United States.
18. Lars Anderson to Robert Anderson, November 11, 1828, Robert Anderson Papers, Volume I, Library of Congress Manuscript Division.
19. Robert Anderson to Maria W. Latham, May 7, 1828, Anderson Family Papers, Filson Historical Society.
20. Robert Anderson to Maria W. Latham, December 8, 1832, Anderson Family Papers, Filson Historical Society.
21. Robert Anderson to Maria W. Latham, March 10, 1833, Anderson Family Papers, Filson Historical Society.
22. Eliza Clinch interview, "Daughter of a Soldier," unidentified newspaper clipping, Duncan Clinch Papers, University of Florida, Special Collection.
23. Anderson to Latham, May 7, 1828.
24. Lars Anderson to Robert Anderson, November 11, 1828., Robert Anderson Papers, Volume I, Library of Congress Manuscript Division.
25. C. F. Smith to Robert Anderson, December 18, 1830, Robert Anderson Papers, Volume I, Library of Congress Manuscript Division.
26. Receipt, September 30, 1831, Robert Anderson Papers, Volume I, Library of Congress Manuscript Division.

Chapter 4

1. Robert Anderson to Larz Anderson, August 5, 1832, Robert Anderson Papers, Volume I, Library of Congress.
2. Patrick J. Jung, *The Black Hawk War of 1832* (Norman: University of Oklahoma Press, 2007), 18–20.

3. John W. Hall, *Uncommon Defense: Indian Allies in the Black Hawk War* (Cambridge, MA: Harvard University Press, 2009), 113; Roger L. Nichols, *General Henry Atkinson: A Western Military Career* (Norman: University of Oklahoma Press, 1965), 154.

4. "Robert Anderson to E. B Washburne, May 10, 1870," *Journal of the Illinois State Historical Society* 10 (1908–1984), no. 3 (October 1917): 422–28.

5. Nichols, *General Henry Atkinson*; "Anderson to Washburne."

6. Emerson W. Gould, *Fifty Years on the Mississippi; or, Gould's History of River Navigation: Containing a History of Steam as a Propelling Power on Ocean, Lakes and Rivers* (St. Louis: Nixon-Jones Printing Company, 1889), 142–48.

7. Nichols, *General Henry Atkinson*.

8. Mahan to Robert Anderson, July 18, 1832, Robert Anderson Papers, Volume I, Library of Congress.

9. William T. Hagan, "General Henry Atkinson and the Militia," *Military Affairs* 23, no. 4 (Winter 1959–1960): 194–97.

10. Julius E. Olson, "Lincoln in Wisconsin," *The Wisconsin Magazine of History* 4, no. 1 (September 1920): 44–54.

11. John Reynolds, *My Own Times, Embracing the History of My Life* (Chicago: Illinois Press, 1855), 325–31.

12. Jessie McHarry, "John Reynolds," *Journal of the Illinois State Historical Society* 6 (1908–1984), no. 1 (April 1913): 42–43.

13. Lee Sandlin, *Wicked River The Mississippi* (New York: Pantheon, 2010), 114–16.

14. Joseph I. Lambert, "The Black Hawk War: A Military Analysis," *Journal of the Illinois State Historical Society* 32 (1908–1984), no. 4 (December 1939): 457.

15. Dodge to Atkinson, July 22, 1832, quoted in Jung, *Black Hawk War*, 219–20.

16. Robert Anderson to Larz Anderson, August 5, 1832, Robert Anderson Papers, Volume I, Library of Congress.

17. Edward Deering Mansfield, *Illustrated Life of General Winfield Scott: Commander-in-Chief of the Army in Mexico*, illus. D. H. Strother (New York: A. S. Barnes & Co., 1847).

18. Robert Anderson to Larz Anderson, August 5, 1832.

19. Robert Anderson to E. B. Washburne, May 10, 1870.

20. William Clark to Winfield Scott, August 5, 1832, Filson Historical Collection.

21. "The Subscribed Germans," February 11, 1834, Robert Anderson Papers, Volume I, Library of Congress.

Chapter 5

1. Robert Anderson to Maria Latham, March 10, 1833. Filson Collection.

2. Office of the Commanding General, Sustenance, to Captain Symington, May 1833, Anderson Papers, Volume I, Library of Congress.

3. Robert Anderson to Allen Latham, March 22, 1834, Filson Collection.

4. William B. Skelton, *An American Profession of Arms: The Army Officer Corps, 1784–1861* (Lawrence: University Press of Kansas, 1992), 296–97.

5. Robert Anderson to Sarah Anderson, September 7, 1834, Filson Collection; Robert Anderson to Maria Latham, May 23, 1834, Anderson Papers, Volume II, Library of Congress.

6. Zebina James Duncan Kinsley to Anderson, July 10, 1835; Samuel Cooper "Order 52," August 28, 1835; Robert Anderson to Sarah Anderson, November 21, 1835, all in Anderson Papers, Volume I, Library of Congress.

7. Robert Anderson to Bradford Alden, February 12, 1842, quoted in Samuel J. Watson, *Peacekeepers and Conquerors: The Army Officers Corps on the American Frontier, 1821–1846* (Lawrence: University Press of Kansas, 2013), 228.

8. "Special Order 90. Adjutant General's Office to Anderson," November 7, 1837, Anderson Papers, Volume II, Library of Congress; John K. Mahon, *History of the Second Seminole War, 1835–1842* (Gainesville: University Press of Florida, 1985).

9. Kenneth W. Porter, *The Black Seminoles: History of a Freedom-Seeking People* (Gainesville: University Press of Florida, 1996), 124–26.

10. Joshua R. Giddings, *The Exiles of Florida* (1858; repr. Gainesville: University Press of Florida, 1965), 78–95.

11. Mahon, *History of the Second Seminole War*, 100–107.

12. Robert Buchanan to Robert Anderson, March 22, 1838, Anderson Papers, Volume II, Library of Congress; Robert Anderson to Sarah Anderson, February 5, 1837, Anderson Papers, Volume II, Library of Congress.

13. Joe Knetsch, "Strategy, Operations, and Tactics in the Second Seminole War, 1835–1842," in William S. Belko, ed., *America's Hundred Years' War* (Gainesville: University Press of Florida, 2011), 142; Chester L. Kieffer, *Maligned General: The Biography of Thomas Sidney Jesup* (San Rafael, CA: Presidio Press, 1979), 155–59.

14. Adjutant General's Office to Robert Anderson, Special Order 90, November 7, 1837. Anderson Papers, Volume II, Library of Congress.

15. Anderson Datebook, January 5–6, 1838, Anderson Papers, Volume II, Library of Congress, Box 3.

16. Mahon, *History of the Second Seminole War*, 227–31; Anderson Datebook, January 16, 1838, Anderson Papers, Volume II, Library of Congress

17. George Rollie Adams, *General William S. Harney, Prince of Dragoons* (Lincoln: University of Nebraska Press, 2001), 65–66; John and Mary Lou Missall, *The Seminole Struggle: A History of America's Longest Indian War* (Palm Beach, FL: Pineapple Press, 2020), 200–201; Kenneth J. Hughes, *A Chronological History of Fort Jupiter and U.S. Military Operations in the Loxahatchee Region, 1838–1858* (Fort Lauderdale: Florida Coast Research and Publishing, 1992), 17–18.

18. Hughes, 17–18.

19. Conrad E. Harvey, "An Army without Doctrine: The Evolution of US Army Tactics in the Absence of Doctrine, 1779 to 1847," MA thesis, US Army War College, 2007, 68–70.

20. Mahon, *History of the Second Seminole War*, 234; Missall, *Seminole Struggle*, 200–201.

21. Anderson Datebook, February 1838, Anderson Papers, Volume II, Library of Congress.

22. Mahon, *History of the Second Seminole War*, 237.

23. J. R. Poinsett to Jessup, March 1, 1838, quoted in John T. Sprague, *The Origin, Progress, and Conclusion of the Florida War* (New York: D. Appleton & Company, 1848), 200–201; Mahon, *History of the Second Seminole War*, 237.

24. George E. Buker, *Swamp Sailors: Riverine Warfare in the Everglades, 1835–1842* (Gainesville: University Press of Florida, 1975), 66.

25. Anderson Datebook, March 23, 1838, Anderson Papers, Volume II, Library of Congress.
26. Anderson Datebook, April 1838, Anderson, Volume II, Library of Congress.
27. James Bankhead to Thomas Jessup, March 29, 1838, copy, Robert Anderson Papers, Volume II, Library of Congress; Adams, *General William S. Harney*, 67–68.
28. Hugo L. Black III, "Richard Fitzpatricks's South Florida, 1822–1840," *Tequesta: Journal of the Historical Association of Southern Florida* (1981): 35–36; Anderson Datebook, May 1838, Anderson Papers, Volume II.
29. Adams, *General William S. Harney*, 67–68; Anderson Datebook, August 1838, Anderson Papers, Volume II, Library of Congress.

Chapter 6

1. Anderson Date Book, May 12, 1838, Anderson Papers, Volume II, Box 3, Library of Congress.
2. Printed address of Major General Winfield Scott to the Cherokee, May 10, 1838, John Ross Papers, Thomas Gilcrease Institute of American History and Art.
3. Scott to the Cherokee.
4. Robert Anderson to Sarah Anderson, August 28, 1838, Anderson Papers, Filson collection.
5. Robert Anderson to Sarah Anderson, August 28, 1838.
6. Headquarters Eastern Division, Cherokee Agency, Special Order 64, July 8, 1838, Adjutant General's Office, Washington DC; Special Order 53, August 15, 1838, Anderson Papers, Volume II, Library of Congress; Indecipherable to Anderson, September 4, 1838, Anderson Papers, Volume II, Library of Congress; H. D. Hetz to Anderson, October 10, 1838, Anderson Papers, Volume II, Library of Congress; Samuel J. Watson, *Peacekeepers and Conquerors: The Army Officers Corps on the American Frontier, 1821–1846* (Lawrence: University Press of Kansas, 2013), 166.
7. "Canadian Impudence," *Buffalo Commercial Advertiser*, January 5, 1839.
8. Watson, 303–4.
9. Major L. Wilson, *The Presidency of Martin Van Buren* (Lawrence: University of Kansas Press, 1984), 162–63.
10. Robert Anderson, "Journal 1841," Anderson Papers, Volume II, Library of Congress, 1–2.
11. E. D. Keyes, *Fifty Years' Observation of Men and Events, Civil and Military* (New York: Charles Scribner's Sons, 1884), 48–51.
12. Anderson, "Journal 1841," 6.
13. Keyes, *Fifty Years' Observation of Men and Events*, 48–51.
14. Anderson, "Journal 1841," 8.
15. Anderson, "Journal 1841," 8.
16. Bounont Newhall, *The Daguerreotype in America* (New York: Dover Publications, 1976), 32.
17. Anderson, "Journal 1841," 12.
18. Anderson, "Journal 1841," 12; Watson, *Peacekeepers and Conquerors*, 304–5.
19. Anderson, "Journal 1841," 15.
20. Robert Anderson to Sarah Anderson, August 17, 1840, Filson Papers.
21. "The Story of Her Interesting Life," *Chicago Daily News*, newspaper clipping, date unknown, Clinch Family Papers. University of Florida Special Collections.

22. Duncan Clinch to Robert Anderson, May 25, 1843, Anderson Papers, Volume IV, Library of Congress; Anderson to Sister, May 1843, Filson Center.

23. Matthew Pinsker, "The Soldiers' Home: A Long Road to Sanctuary," *Washington History: Historical Society of Washington, DC* 18, no. 1/2 (2006): 4–19.

Chapter 7

1. Edgar Allen Poe, "The Gold-Bug," in *The Works of Edgar Allan Poe in One Volume* (New York: P. F. Collier & Son, 1927), 53; Walter J. Frazer, *Charleston! Charleston!: The History of a Southern City* (Columbia: University of South Carolina Press, 1989), 1.

2. David Detzer, *Allegiance: Fort Sumter, Charleston, and the Beginning of the Civil War* (New York: Harcourt, 2002), 31; Secretary of the Treasury, Moultrieville to Robert Anderson, July 5, 1845, Anderson Papers, Library of Congress.

3. Anderson to General Jones, December 7, 1846, Robert Anderson Papers, Library of Congress, Box 3.

4. George Ballentine, *The Autobiography of an English Soldier in the United States Army, Comprising Observations and Adventures in the States and Mexico* (New York: Stringer and Townsend, 1853), 124.

5. Ballentine, 124.

6. Robert Anderson to Eliza Bayard Anderson, January 3, 1847, January 25, 1847, in *An Artillery Officer in the Mexican War 1846–47, Letters of Robert Anderson, Captain 3rd Artillery, U.S.A.* (1911; repr. New York: Books for Libraries Press, 1971), 8–11.

7. Robert Anderson to Eliza Bayard Anderson, January 25, 1847, 13.

8. Robert Anderson to Eliza Bayard Anderson, January 25, 1847, 12, 13.

9. Ballentine, *Autobiography of an English Soldier in the United States Army*, 137–40; George C. Furber, *The Twelve Months Volunteer, or, Journal of a Private in the Tennessee Regiment of Cavalry, in the Campaign, in Mexico, 1846–7* (Cincinnati: U. P. James, 1857), 394–401.

10. Robert Anderson to Eliza Bayard Anderson, January 25, 1847, 15; Furber, *Twelve Months Volunteer*, 394–408.

11. Jack Bauer, *The Mexican War, 1846–1848* (Lincoln: University of Nebraska Press, 1993), 75; Robert Anderson to Eliza Bayard Anderson, January 27, 1847, 16.

12. Robert Anderson to Eliza Bayard Anderson, January 27, 1847, 16, and Furber, *Twelve Months Volunteer*, 409.

13. Robert Anderson to Eliza Bayard Anderson, January 31, 1847, in *Artillery Officer in the Mexican War*, 24.

14. Robert Anderson to Eliza Bayard Anderson, January 28–29, 1847, in *Artillery Officer in the Mexican War*, 18, 19.

15. Furber, *Twelve Months Volunteer*, 416; Ballentine, *Autobiography of an English Soldier*, 141.

16. Robert Anderson to Eliza Bayard Anderson, January 28, 1847, in *Artillery Officer in the Mexican War*, 18; Furber, *Twelve Months Volunteer*, 404–5.

17. Robert Anderson to Eliza Bayard Anderson, February 17–18, 1847, in *Artillery Officer in the Mexican War*, 47–48.

18. Timothy D. Johnson, *A Gallant Little Army: The Mexico City Campaign* (Lawrence: University Press of Kansas, 2007).

19. Robert Anderson to Eliza Bayard Anderson, February 20–21, 1847, in *Artillery Officer in the Mexican War*, 51.

20. "Island of Lobos," *Raymond Daily Gazette* (Mississippi), March 12, 1847; and Timothy D. Johnson, *Winfield Scott: The Quest for Military Glory* (Lawrence: University Press of Kansas, 1988), 171.

21. Robert Anderson to Eliza Bayard Anderson, February 21 and 24, 1847, in *Artillery Officer in the Mexican War*, 54–56.

22. Robert Anderson to Eliza Bayard Anderson, February 24, 1847, in *Artillery Officer in the Mexican War*, 55.

23. Robert Anderson to Eliza Bayard Anderson, February 24, 1847, 56.

24. Robert Anderson to Eliza Bayard Anderson, February 24, 1847, 56, and Robert Anderson to Eliza Anderson, letter from Robert Anderson Papers, United States Military Academy Library.

25. Robert Anderson to Eliza Bayard Anderson, February 25, 1847, in *Artillery Officer in the Mexican War*, 58.

26. Robert Anderson to Eliza Bayard Anderson, March 6, 1847, in *Artillery Officer in the Mexican War*, 68.

27. Robert Anderson to Eliza Bayard Anderson, March 6, 1847.

28. Jack Baur, *Surfboats and Horse Marines: U.S. Naval Operations in the Mexican War, 1846–48* (Annapolis, MD: United States Naval Institute, 1969), 83.

29. Baur, 83–84.

30. Robert Anderson to Eliza Bayard Anderson, March 8, 1847, in *Artillery Officer in the Mexican War*, 71.

31. Winfield Scott, *Memoirs of Lieut.-General Scott, LL.D. Written by Himself* (New York: Sheldon & Company, 1861), 418.

32. William G. Temple, "Landing at Vera Cruz," in George Winston Smith and Charles Judah, eds., *Chronicles of the Gringos: The U.S. Army in the Mexican War, 1846–1848, Accounts of Eyewitnesses & Combatants* (Albuquerque: University of New Mexico Press, 1968), 179–81; John Corey Henshaw, *Recollections of the War with Mexico*, ed. Gary F. Kurtz (Columbia: University of Missouri Press, 2008), 113–14.

33. Ballentine, *Autobiography of an English Soldier*, 146.

34. George B. McClellan, *The Mexican War Diary of George B. McClellan* (Princeton, NJ: Princeton University Press, 1917), 83.

35. Johnson, *Winfield Scott*, 176.

36. Furber, *12 Months Volunteer*, 505.

37. Baur, *Surfboats and Horse Marines*, 86; Robert Anderson to Eliza Bayard Anderson, March 12/13, 1847, in *Artillery Officer in the Mexican War*, 72–73, 77.

38. Robert Anderson to Eliza Bayard Anderson, March 19–20, 1847, in *Artillery Officer in the Mexican War*, 85–89; McClellan, *Mexican War Diary*, 62–63.

39. Anderson never identifies McClellan by name, referring to him instead as the "young engineer." Only through McClellan's journal do we know it was him. He described leading Anderson's work party but does not mention his late-night wanderings. Anderson would have known McClellan. In his writing Anderson rarely refers to an officer by anything but his name. Anderson did not, even in a private letter to his wife, want to discredit another officer—although in the descriptions of the terrain in the letters and journals of other men, this seems like a forgivable

error, especially since there was no damage done except probably to McClellan's pride. Robert Anderson to Eliza Bayard Anderson, March 19–20, 1847, in *Artillery Officer in the Mexican War*, 85–85; McClellan, *Mexican War Diary*, 62–63.

40. Robert Anderson to Eliza Bayard Anderson, March 19–20, 1847, in *Artillery Officer in the Mexican War*, 85–85; McClellan, *Mexican War Diary*, 62–63.

41. Robert Anderson to Eliza Bayard Anderson, March 19–20, 1847, in *Artillery Officer in the Mexican War*, 85–85; McClellan, *Mexican War Diary*, 62–63.

42. Baur, *Surfboats and Horse Marines*, 88.

43. Robert Anderson to Eliza Bayard Anderson, March 23, 1847, in *An Artillery Officer in the Mexican War*, 91, 93.

44. McClellan, *Mexican War Diary*, 70; Robert Anderson to Eliza Bayard Anderson, March 30, 1847, in *Artillery Officer in the Mexican War*, 104.

45. Robert Anderson to Eliza Bayard Anderson, March 23, 1847, in *Artillery Officer in the Mexican War*, 91–92.

46. Johnson, *Gallant Little Army*.

47. Robert Anderson to Eliza Bayard Anderson, March 23, 1847, in *Artillery Officer in the Mexican War*, 91–92.

48. Robert Anderson to Eliza Bayard Anderson, March 23, 1847.

49. Robert Anderson to Eliza Bayard Anderson, April 12, 1847, in *Artillery Officer in the Mexican War*, 131.

50. Jalapa was officially renamed Xalapa by President Benito Juarez in an attempt to return Native place names to Mexico.

51. "Letters from Mexico," *Boston Advertiser;* reprinted in Smith and Judah, *Chronicles of the Gringos,* 217.

52. Robert Anderson to Eliza Bayard Anderson, April 26, 1847, in *Artillery Officer in the Mexican War*, 143.

53. Robert Anderson to Eliza Bayard Anderson, April 26, 1847, 148–49.

54. Robert Anderson to Eliza Bayard Anderson, April 26, 1847, 148–49.

55. Robert Anderson to Eliza Bayard Anderson, June 21, 1847, in *Artillery Officer in the Mexican War*, 220–21.

56. Johnson, *Gallant Little Army*, 147–50.

57. Robert Anderson to Eliza Bayard Anderson, August 9, 1847, in *Artillery Officer in the Mexican War*, 280, 282.

58. Robert Anderson to Eliza Bayard Anderson, August 13, 1847, in *Artillery Officer in the Mexican War*, 286.

59. Johnson, *Gallant Little Army*, 154–55.

60. Smith and Judah, *Chronicles of the Gringos*, 235, 237.

61. Robert Anderson to Eliza Bayard Anderson, August 24, 1847, in *Artillery Officer in the Mexican War*, 293.

62. Johnson, *Gallant Little Army*, 159.

63. Robert Anderson to Eliza Bayard Anderson, August 24, 1847, 294.

64. Lyon quoted in Johnson, *Gallant Little Army*, 185.

65. Robert Anderson to Eliza Bayard Anderson, August 27, 1847, in *Artillery Officer in the Mexican War*, 298.

66. Francis S. Belton to his wife and son, Palacio Nacional de Mexico, September 26, 1847, copy located in Center for Greater Southwestern Studies, University of Texas, Arlington Library Special Collections.

67. Robert Anderson to Eliza Bayard Anderson, August 24, 1847, 295.
68. Robert Anderson to Eliza Bayard Anderson, August 24, 1847, 296.
69. Edward M. Coffman, *The Old Army: A Portrait of the American Army in Peacetime, 1784–1898* (New York: Oxford University Press, 1986), 57–58; "Brevet Major McClintock," *Daily Atlas* (Boston). July 20, 1843; Francis Bernard Heitman, *Historical Register and Dictionary of the US Army from September 29, 1789 to March 2, 1903* (Washington, DC: Government Printing Office, 1903), 657.
70. Robert Anderson to Eliza Bayard Anderson, August 24, 1847, 295; Belton to his wife and son, September 26, 1847.
71. Johnson, *Gallant Little Army*.
72. Robert Anderson to Eliza Bayard Anderson, September 2, 1847, in *Artillery Officer in the Mexican War*, 306.
73. Robert Anderson to Eliza Bayard Anderson, September 2, 1847.
74. Johnson, *Gallant Little Army*, 201–2.
75. John D. Eisenhower, *Agent of Destiny: The Life and Times of General Winfield Scott* (New York: Free Press, 1997), 289–90, 294.
76. Robert Anderson to Eliza Bayard Anderson, September 22, 1847, in *Artillery Officer in the Mexican War*, 312–13.
77. Robert Anderson to Eliza Bayard Anderson, October 9, 1847, in *Artillery Officer in the Mexican War*, 324.
78. Robert Anderson to Eliza Bayard Anderson, October 9, 1847, 327.

Chapter 8

1. "House of Representatives," *Daily Constitutionalist and Republic* (Savannah), December 4, 1849.
2. Robert Anderson to Lafayette Montgomery Flourney, November 9, 1853, Filson Papers; Judge Hall to Robert Anderson, August 22, 1858, Anderson Papers, Volume IV, Box 9, Library of Congress.
3. Eba Anderson Lawton, *History of the Soldiers' Home, Washington, D.C.* (New York: G. P. Putnam's Sons, 1914), 7–18.
4. Lawton, 18.
5. Lawton, 7–18; Robert Anderson to Jefferson Davis, Anderson Papers, Volume VII, Library of Congress.
6. Robert Anderson to Eliza Anderson, September 1, 1860, West Point Archives.
7. "Duncan L. Clinch Anderson," December 8, 1855, *New York Post*.
8. Special Order 210, Samuel Cooper, November 7, 1859; Samuel Cooper to Robert Anderson, November 2, 1859, Anderson Papers, Library of Congress, Volume VII.
9. Special Order 242, Samuel Cooper, December 1859, Anderson Papers, Volume VIII, Box 9, Library of Congress.
10. Crackle, *West Point*, 128–29.
11. Ambrose, *Duty, Honor, Country*.
12. Robert Anderson to Eliza Anderson, July 19, 1860, West Point Collection.
13. Robert Anderson to Eliza Anderson, August 12, 1860, West Point Collection.

Chapter 9

1. Philip Shriver Klein, *President James Buchanan: A Biography* (University Park: Pennsylvania State University Press, 1962), 361.

2. Klein, 361; David Detzer, *Allegiance: Fort Sumter, Charleston, and the Beginning of the Civil War* (New York: Harcourt, 2001), 68–69.

3. John B. Floyd quoted in "The Floyd Banquet," *New York Herald*, January 17, 1861.

4. Winfield Scott, *Memoirs of Lieut.-General Scott, LL.D. Written by Himself* (New York: Sheldon & Company, 1861), 610–11.

5. Timothy D. Johnson, *Winfield Scott: The Quest for Military Glory* (Lawrence: University of Kansas Press, 1998).

6. "Southern Victories," *The Mercury* (Charleston, SC), October 20, 1860.

7. "The Commercial Policy of the South," *The Intelligencer* (Washington, DC), November 1, 1860.

8. Steven A. Channing, *Crisis of Fear: Secession in South Carolina* (New York: W. W. Norton, 1970), 22; Elizabeth R. Varon, *Disunion! The Coming of the American Civil War, 1789–1859* (Chapel Hill: University of North Carolina Press, 2008), 45–46.

9. "The New Commandant," *The Mercury*, November 17, 1860.

10. Abner Doubleday, *Reminiscences of Forts Sumter and Moultrie in 1860–61* (New York: Harper Brothers, 1876), 41–42.

11. Ord to Anderson, November 26, 1860, Anderson Papers, Volume VIII, Library of Congress.

12. Wesley Moody, *The Battle of Fort Sumter: The First Shots of the American Civil War,* Critical Moments in American History (New York: Routledge, 2016), 55–60.

13. Anderson to Colonel Samuel Cooper, December 1, 1860; *War of the Rebellion: A Compilation of the Official Records of the Union and Confederate Armies*, Series 1, Volume 1 (Washington, DC: Government Printing Office, 1880–1901), 81.

14. "Instructions for Running Guard," November 25, 1860, Anderson Papers, Volume VIII, Library of Congress.

15. Samuel Cooper to Anderson, December 4, 1860, Anderson Papers, Volume VIII, Library of Congress.

16. Doubleday, *Reminiscences of Forts Sumter and Moultrie in 1860–61*, 43–44.

17. "The Forts at Charleston," *Buffalo (NY) Commercial*, December 7, 1860.

18. Anderson to George P. [Shrie?] , December 12, 1860, Anderson Papers, Volume VIII, Library of Congress.

19. W. A. Swanberg, *First Blood: The Story of Fort Sumter* (New York: Charles Scribner's Sons, 1957), 46.

20. December 12, 1860, Anderson Papers, Library of Congress.

21. Don Carlos Buell to Robert Anderson, December 11, 1861; *The War of the Rebellion*, Series 1, Volume 1, 88–89.

22. George W. Cullum, "Robert Anderson," *Third Annual Reunion, 1872*, West Point, 1872, 30, quoted in Detzer, *Allegiance*; Doubleday, *Reminiscences of Forts Sumter and Moultrie in 1860–61*, 58.

23. "Interstate Celebration," *Charleston Mercury*, December 7, 1860.

24. Larz Anderson to Robert Anderson, December 6, 1860, Anderson Papers, Volume VIII, Library of Congress.

25. Anderson Papers, Volume VIII, Library of Congress.

26. Quoted in J. G. Randall, *The Civil War and Reconstruction* (Boston: D. C. Heath and Company, 1953), 183–85.

27. Doubleday, *Reminiscences of Forts Sumter and Moultrie in 1860–61*, 56.

28. Anderson to George P. [Shrie?], December 12, 1860.

29. Eba Anderson Lawton, *Major Robert Anderson and Fort Sumter, 1861* (New York: Knickerbocker Press, 1911), 9.

30. Edward L. Anderson, "A Defense of Major Robert Anderson," *Harpers Weekly*, June 10, 1876.

31. E. L. Anderson, *Soldier and Pioneer: A Biographical Sketch of Lt.-Col. Richard C. Anderson of the Continental Army* (New York: G. P. Putnam's Sons, 1879), 1–13, 20.

32. Swanberg, *First Blood*, 95–96.

33. Doubleday, *Reminiscences of Forts Sumter and Moultrie in 1860–61*, 60.

34. Swanberg, *First Blood*, 94–101; Detzer, *Allegiance*, 112–15.

35. Doubleday, *Reminiscences of Forts Sumter and Moultrie in 1860–61*, 59–64.

36. Doubleday, 65–66.

37. Anderson quoted in Roy Meredith, *Storm over Sumter: The Opening Engagement of the Civil War* (New York: Simon and Schuster, 1957), 61.

38. Anderson quoted in Meredith, *Storm over Sumter*, 61.

39. Swanberg, *First Blood*, 101

Chapter 10

1. Roy Meredith, *Storm over Sumter: The Opening Engagement of the Civil War* (New York: Simon and Schuster, 1957), 61; David Detzer, *Allegiance: Fort Sumter, Charleston, and the Beginning of the Civil War* (New York: Harcourt, 2002), 126–27.

2. W. A. Swanberg, *First Blood: The Story of Fort Sumter* (New York: Charles Scribner's Sons, 1957), 103–5.

3. Philip Shriver Klein, *President James Buchanan, A Biography* (University Park: Pennsylvania State University Press, 1962), 371.

4. Abner Doubleday, *Reminiscences of Forts Sumter and Moultrie in 1860–61* (New York: Harper Brothers, 1876), 80.

5. Samuel Wyllie Crawford, *The Genesis of the Civil War: The Story of Sumter, 1860–1861* (New York: Charles L. Webster & Company, 1887), 112.

6. Swanberg, *First Blood*, 134

7. Report of John G. Foster, *War of the Rebellion*, Volume 1, 4–5.

8. James Chester, "Inside Fort Sumter," *Battles and Leaders*, 55; Robert Underwood Johnson and Clarence Clough Buel, eds., *Battles and Leaders of the Civil War: Being for the Most Part Contributions by Union and Confederate Officers* (New York: Century Co., 1887).

9. Chester, 56–57.

10. Quoted in Doubleday, *Reminiscences*, 73.

11. Swanberg, *First Blood*, 61–63.

12. Klein, *President James Buchanan*, 378.

13. Swanberg, *First Blood*, 111–12.

14. John B. Floyd to Anderson, December 27, 1860, War of the Rebellion, Series 1, Volume 1, 3.

15. Bruce Catton, *The Coming Fury* (New York: Doubleday, 1961), 173.

16. Catton, 173.

17. Anderson to Floyd, *War of the Rebellion*, Series 1, Volume 1, 3.

18. Larz to Anderson, December 23, 1860, Anderson Papers, Volume VIII, Library of Congress.

19. Buell quoted in Swanberg, *First Blood*, 113.

20. Stanton quoted in Swanberg, *First Blood*, 114.
21. Buchanan quoted in Swanberg, *First Blood*, 114.
22. "Melee at Washington," *Chicago Tribune*, December 29, 1860.
23. "Major Anderson's Master Stroke," *Daily Cleveland Leader*, December 31, 1860; "From Washington D.C.," *Cincinnati Commercial Appeal*, December 28, 1860; "The Charleston Forts," *Philadelphia Inquirer*, December 28, 1860.
24. "Important from Charleston," *Delaware Gazette*, December 28, 1860; "The President Wavering," *New York Daily Tribune*, December 29, 1860.
25. "The Progress of Events," *Abbeville Press*, South Carolina, January 4, 1861.
26. "Washington DC," *Daily Nashville Patriot*, December 31, 1860.
27. Swanberg, *First Blood*, 117.

Chapter 11

1. L. R. Hurbert to Robert Anderson, December 31, 1860, Anderson Papers, Library of Congress, Manuscript Division.
2. A. G. Radley to Robert Anderson, December 31, 1860, Anderson Papers, Library of Congress, Manuscript Division.
3. Adam W. Spies to Robert Anderson, December 28, 1860, Anderson Papers, Library of Congress, Manuscript Division.
4. Alfred Beckley to Robert Anderson, December 28, 1860, Anderson Papers, Library of Congress, Manuscript Division.
5. "War Commenced on the US Government by South Carolina," *The Recorder*, December 31, 1860. {{QY: City of publication?}}
6. "The New Year," *Baltimore Sun*, January 1, 1861.
7. Anderson notes, January 1, 1861, Anderson Papers, Library of Congress, Manuscript Division.
8. W. A. Swanberg, *First Blood: The Story of Fort Sumter* (New York: Charles Scribner's Sons, 1957), 140.
9. Eliza Anderson to Robert Anderson, undated, Anderson Papers, Library of Congress, Manuscript Division.
10. "Peter Hart Saves the Flag," *New York Star*, May 1880.
11. Swanberg, *First Blood*, 137.
12. "By Yesterday's Evening Mail," January 8, 1861, *Anderson Daily Intelligencer* (South Carolina).
13. Chester, *Battles and Leaders,* I, 61. Robert Underwood Johnson and Clarence Clough Buel, eds., *Battles and Leaders of the Civil War: Being for the Most Part Contributions by Union and Confederate Officers* (New York: Century Co., 1887).
14. Samuel Wyllie Crawford, *The Genesis of the Civil War: The Story of Sumter, 1860–1861* (New York: Charles L. Webster & Company, 1887), 175.
15. Swanberg, *First Blood*, 156–58.
16. David Detzer, *Allegiance: Fort Sumter, Charleston, and the Beginning of the Civil War* (New York: Harcourt, 2002), 168.
17. William C. Davis, *Look Away! A History of the Confederate States of America* (New York: Free Press, 2002).
18. Jefferson Davis, *The Rise and Fall of the Confederate Government* (New York: D. Appleton & Co., 1881), 250–51.

19. Richard N. Current, *Lincoln and the First Shot* (Urbana-Champaign: University of Illinois Press, 1963), 121–22.
20. Charles Anderson to Robert Anderson, March 20, 1861, Anderson Papers, Volume XI, Library of Congress.
21. Davis, *Rise and Fall of the Confederate Government*, 185.
22. Anderson quoted in Roy Meredith, *Storm over Sumter: The Opening Engagement of the Civil War* (New York: Simon and Schuster, 1957), 80.
23. Crawford, *Genesis of the Civil War*, 134.
24. "Major Anderson's Letter to Mr. Beechers," *New York Times,* February 27, 1861.
25. David Herbert Donald, *Lincoln* (New York: Simon & Schuster, 1995), 285.

Chapter 12

1. Robert Anderson to Cooper, January 25, 1861, Anderson Papers, Volume IX, Library of Congress.
2. W. A. Swanberg, *First Blood: The Story of Fort Sumter* (New York: Charles Scribner's Sons, 1957), 207–8; Eliza Anderson to Robert Anderson, March 8, 1861, Anderson Papers, Library of Congress, Manuscript Division.
3. Robert Anderson to Cooper, January 27, 1861, Anderson Papers, Volume IX, Library of Congress.
4. Albert Woldman, *Lincoln and the Russians: The Story of the Russian-American Diplomatic Relations during the Civil War* (Cleveland: World, 1952), 53–54.
5. Swanberg, *First Blood*, 222–23.
6. David Detzer, *Allegiance: Fort Sumter, Charleston, and the Beginning of the Civil War* (New York: Harcourt, 2002), 217–19.
7. Winfield Scott to Gustavus Fox, January 30, 1861; Gustavus Fox, *Confidential Correspondence of Gustavus Vasa Fox,* ed. Robert Means Thompson (New York: The Naval Historical Society, 1920), 3.
8. Fox to wife, February 7, 1861; Fox, *Confidential Correspondence of Fox,* 6–7.
9. Fox, 8–9.
10. Abner Doubleday, *Reminiscences of Forts Sumter and Moultrie in 1860–61* (New York: Harper Brothers, 1876), 130.
11. Seward quoted in Donald, *Lincoln,* 286.
12. Jefferson Davis, *The Rise and Fall of the Confederate Government* (New York: D. Appleton & Co., 1881), 212.
13. Bruce Catton, *The Coming Fury* (New York: Doubleday, 1961), 293–94.
14. Seward quoted in Swanberg, *First Blood,* 227.
15. Swanberg, 227.
16. For example, Donald, *Lincoln* 292, and Catton, *Coming Fury,* 288–89.
17. Davis, *Rise and Fall of the Confederate Government,* 250–51.
18. Samuel Wyllie Crawford, *The Genesis of the Civil War: The Story of Sumter, 1860–1861* (New York: Charles L. Webster & Company, 1887), 203.
19. Swanberg, *First Blood,* 248.
20. Robert Anderson to Lorenzo Thomas, March 22, 1861, *War of the Rebellion,* Series I, Volume 1, 211.
21. Richard N. Current, *Lincoln and the First Shot* (Urbana-Champaign: University of Illinois Press, 1963), 89.

22. Anderson to Scott, April 1, 1861, Anderson Papers, Volume XII, Library of Congress, Manuscript Division.

23. Scott to Anderson, March 29, 1861, Anderson Papers, Volume XI, Library of Congress.

24. Anderson to Scott, April 1, 1861, Anderson Papers, Volume XII, Library of Congress.

25. Swanberg, *First Blood*, 252.

26. Fox to Montgomery Blair, March 31, 1861, in Fox, *Confidential Correspondence of Fox*, 13.

27. Swanberg, *First Blood*, 223–24; Donald, *Lincoln*, 300.

28. Swanberg, *First Blood*, 279–80.

29. Crawford, *Genesis of the Civil War*, 187–89.

30. *Abraham Lincoln: Speeches and Writings 1859–1865*, ed. Don E. Fehrenbacher (New York: Library of America, 1989), 244.

31. Lincoln, quoted in Donald, *Lincoln*, 290.

32. Lincoln, quoted in Donald, *Lincoln*, 290.

33. Swanberg, *First Blood*, 286.

34. Leroy Walker to P. G. T. Beauregard, April 10, 1861, *War of the Rebellion*, Series I, Volume 1, 297.

35. Swanberg, *First Blood*, 205, 288, 294.

36. Crawford, *Genesis of the Civil War*, 423.

37. Stephen D. Lee, "The First Step in the War," in Robert Underwood Johnson and Clarence Clough Buel, eds., *Battles and Leaders of the Civil War: Being for the Most Part Contributions by Union and Confederate Officers*, 4 vols. (New York: Century Co. 1887), 1:75.

38. Doubleday, *Reminisces of Forts Sumter and Moultrie*, 141.

39. Walker to Beauregard, April 11, 1861, War of the Rebellion, Series I, Volume 1, 301.

40. Lee, *Battles and Leaders of the Civil War*, 1:75.

41. Lee, *Battles and Leaders of the Civil War*, 1:75.

42. Cameron to Anderson, April 4, 1861, in *The War of the Rebellion*, Series I, Volume 1, 14, 235.

43. Anderson quoted in Lee, *Battles and Leaders*, I, 76.

44. Lee, I, 76.

45. Doubleday, *Reminisces of Forts Sumter and Moultrie*, 140.

46. Doubleday, 145–46.

47. Swanberg, *First Blood*, 301.

48. Chester, *Battles and Leaders*, I, 69–70.

49. Roy Meredith, *Storm over Sumter: The Opening Engagement of the Civil War* (New York: Simon and Schuster, 1957), 174–75.

50. Fox to Montgomery Blair, April 17, 1861, in Fox, *Confidential Correspondence of Fox*, 33–36.

51. B. S. Osborne, *A Sailor of Fortune* (New York: McClure, Phillips & Co., 1906), 119–20.

52. Fox to Montgomery Blair, April 17, 1861, in Fox, *Confidential Correspondence of Fox*, 33–36.

53. Chester, *Battles and Leaders*, 70–71.

54. Chester, 71–72.

55. Swanberg, *First Blood*, 314–15.
56. Doubleday, *Reminisces of Fort Sumter and Moultrie*, 163–64.
57. Lee, *Battles and Leaders*, I, 79.
58. Doubleday, *Reminisces of Fort Sumter and Moultrie*, 169–70.
59. Mary Boykin Chesnut, April 15, 1861, in *Mary Chesnut's Civil War*, 50.
60. Moody, *Battle of Fort Sumter*, 134.

Chapter 13

1. "Robert Anderson to Simon Cameron," April 18, 1861, quoted in W. J. Tenney. *Military and Naval History of the Rebellion in the United States* (New York: D. Appleton & Co., 1866), 26.
2. "Treason," *New York Daily Courier*, April 14, 1861.
3. "Distressing News from Charleston," *New York Journal of Commerce*, April 18, 1861.
4. "Major Anderson," *New York Times*, April 19, 1861; "Arrival of Major Anderson," *New York Herald*, April 19, 1861.
5. "Arrival of Major Anderson."
6. "The Killed at Fort Moultrie," *Newark Advocate* (New Jersey), April 17, 1861.
7. "Editor Savannah Daily Republican to Anderson," April 19, 1861, Anderson Papers, Library of Congress, Manuscript Division.
8. "Powell to Anderson," April 20, 1865, Anderson Papers, Volume XII, Library of Congress.
9. P. C. Sherman to Anderson, April 27, 1861, Anderson Papers, Volume XII, Library of Congress.
10. Lincoln to Anderson, May 1, 1861, *Abraham Lincoln: Complete Works*, ed. John G. Nicolay and John Hay (New York: Century Co., 1920), 2:40.
11. "Major Anderson Left Washington," *Smyrna Times* (Delaware), May 9, 1861.
12. "Anderson's Movements," *National Republican* (Washington, DC), May 9, 1861.
13. "Anderson," *Baltimore Sun*, May 7, 1861.
14. "A Rumor about Major Anderson," *Grand Haven News* (Michigan), May 1, 1861.
15. James W. Fink, *Divided Loyalties: Kentucky's Struggle for Armed Neutrality in the Civil War* (El Dorado Hills, CA: Savas Beatie, 2012).
16. "Major Anderson, Late of Fort Sumter," *Semi-Weekly Standard* (Raleigh, NC), May 4, 1861.
17. Robert Anderson to Eliza Anderson, June 28, 1861, Anderson Papers, Volume XIII, Library of Congress.
18. Robert Anderson to Eliza Anderson, June 28, 1861.
19. Robert Anderson to Eliza Anderson, June 6, 1861, Anderson Papers, Volume XIII, Library of Congress; Seymour to Anderson, July 5, 1861, Anderson Papers, Volume XIII, Library of Congress.
20. William Tecumseh Sherman, *Memoirs of General William T. Sherman* (New York: D. Appleton & Co., 1889), 192–93; Lee Kennett, *Sherman, A Soldier's Life* (New York: HarperCollins, 2001), 128.
21. Anderson to Eliza, June 6, 1861, Anderson Papers, Volume XIII, Library of Congress.
22. Anderson to Lincoln, September 13, 1861, Filson Collection.
23. Jefferson Davis to Leonidus Polk, September 15, 1861, *War of the Rebellion*, Series 1, Volume 4, 188.

24. Sherman, *Memoirs of General William T. Sherman,* 199.

25. Sherman quoted in Wesley Moody, *Demon of the Lost Cause: Sherman and Civil War History* (Columbia: University of Missouri Press, 2011), 33.

26. Anderson to Lincoln, May 25, 1863, Anderson Papers, Volume XVI, Library of Congress.

27. Cambridge Livingston to Anderson, May 25, 1861, Anderson Papers, Volume XIII, Library of Congress.

28. "Card to Major Anderson," May 16, 1861, *New Orleans Delta;* reprinted in *Milwaukee Morning Sentinel,* May 29, 1861.

29. Winfield Scott to Charles Peabody, January 29, 1863, Anderson Papers, Volume XV, Library of Congress.

30. Special Orders 370, War Department, Anderson Papers, Volume XV, Library of Congress; Lincoln to Anderson, August 15, 1863, *The War of the Rebellion,* VI, 386.

31. Board Transcript, Volume 3, Box 96, Military Order of the Loyal Legion of the United States Commandery of the State of Massachusetts Civil War Collection, Hollis Archive, Houghton Library, Harvard University.

32. Special Order 480, Anderson Papers, Volume XVI, Library of Congress.

33. P. T. Barnum to Anderson, undated, Anderson Papers, Library of Congress, Manuscript Division; and Seymour to Anderson, May 22, 1865, Anderson Papers, Library of Congress, Manuscript Division.

34. Anderson to Reuben Fenton, March 8, 1865, US Grant Presidential Library, Series 3, Box 26, Folder 266 (New York).

35. Seymor to Anderson, May 22, 1865, Anderson Papers, Volume XVI, Library of Congress.

36. J. Clement French and Edward Cary, *The Trip of the Steamer Oceanus to Fort Sumter and Charleston, SC* (Brooklyn: Union Steam Printing House, 1865), 4, 22–30.

37. French and Cary, 25.

38. French and Cary, 34, 38, 39, 42; "A Trip to Fort Sumter," *The Liberator,* May 5, 1865.

39. Robert Anderson to John C. Calhoun, March 1, 1820, Archives, United States Military Academy, West Point, NY.

40. "Raising the Flag on Fort Sumter," *Vermont Chronicle,* April 22, 1865; French and Cary, *Trip of the Steamer Oceanus,* 46.

41. French and Cary, 47; William Arnold Spicer, *The Flag Replaced on Sumter: A Personal Narrative* (Providence, RI: Providence Press Company, 1885), 42.

42. French and Cary, *Trip of the Steamer Oceanus,* 48.

43. French and Cary, 50; "Local Military Movements," *New York Times,* May 5, 1861.

44. French and Cary, 50.

45. Robert Anderson quoted in French and Cary, 51.

46. French and Cary, 52.

47. French and Cary, 53.

48. Swanberg, *First Blood,* 338–39.

Chapter 14

1. Oliver Otis Howard to Robert Anderson, September 17, 1865, Anderson Papers, Volume XVI, Library of Congress.

2. Frederick W. Lincoln to Robert Anderson, June 15, 1865, Anderson Papers, Volume XVI, Library of Congress.

3. Mary Roosevelt to Eliza Anderson, September 19, 1865, Anderson Papers, Volume XVI, Library of Congress.
4. Robert Anderson, quoted in David A. Pinder, "The Association of Graduates of the U.S. Military Academy, 1869–1902: The Healing Years" (unpublished thesis, USMA Tactical Officer Education Program, 1993), 2.
5. General Robert Anderson, October 28, 1871, *Cincinnati Enquirer*.

Bibliography

Archives

Anderson Family Papers, Filson Historical Society, Louisville, Kentucky.

Colonel Francis S. Belton Mexican War Letters, 1847–1854. Center for Greater Southwestern Studies, University of Texas, Arlington Library Special Collections.

Duncan Clinch Papers, The University of Florida, Special Collection.

US Grant Presidential Library, Mississippi State University.

John Ross Papers, Thomas Gilcrease Institute of American History and Art, Tulsa, Oklahoma.

Military Order of the Loyal Legion of the United States Commandery of the State of Massachusetts Civil War Collection, Hollis Archive, Houghton Library, Harvard University.

Robert Anderson Papers, Library of Congress, Manuscript Division.

Robert Anderson Papers, United States Military Academy Library.

US Army History Center Archives, Carlisle, Pennsylvania.

Unpublished Manuscripts and Published Primary Sources

Anderson, Charles. "The Story of Soldiers Retreat." Manuscript. Filson Historical Society, Louisville, Kentucky.

Anderson, Richard Clough, Jr. *The Diary and Journal of Richard Clough Anderson, Jr., 1814–1826.* Durham, NC: Duke University Press, 1964.

Anderson, Robert. *An Artillery Officer in the Mexican War, 1846–47: Letters of Robert Anderson, Captain 3rd Artillery. U.S.A.* 1911; reprint: New York: Books for Libraries Press, 1971.

"Anderson, Robert, to E. B. Washburne, May 10, 1870." *Journal of the Illinois State Historical Society* 10 (1908–1984), no. 3 (October 1917): 422–28.

Ballentine, George. *The Autobiography of an English Soldier in the United States Army, Comprising Observations and Adventures in the States and Mexico.* New York: Stringer and Townsend, 1853.

Chesnut, Mary Boykin. *Mary Chesnut's Civil War.* Edited by C. Vann Woodward. New Haven, CT: Yale University Press. 1981.

Church, Albert. "Personal Reminiscences of the Military Academy from 1824 to 1831: A Paper Read to the U.S. Military Service Institute, West Point, March 28, 1878." West Point, NY: USMA Press, 1878.

226

Crawford, Samuel Wyllie. *The Genesis of the Civil War, The Story of Sumter, 1860–1861.* New York: Charles L. Webster & Company, 1887.

Davis, Jefferson. *The Rise and Fall of the Confederate Government.* New York: D. Appleton & Co., 1881.

Doubleday, Abner. *Reminiscences of Forts Sumter and Moultrie in 1860–61.* New York: Harper Brothers, 1876.

Fox, Gustavus Vasa. *Confidential Correspondence of Gustavus Vasa Fox.* Edited by Robert Means Thompson. New York: The Naval Historical Society, 1920.

French, J. Clement, and Edward Cary, *The Trip of the Steamer Oceanus to Fort Sumter and Charleston, SC.* Brooklyn: The Union Steam Printing House, 1865.

Furber, George C. *The Twelve Months Volunteer, or, Journal of a Private in the Tennessee Regiment of Cavalry, in the Campaign, in Mexico, 1846–7.* Cincinnati: U. P. James, 1857.

Great Britain. *The Case of Great Britain as Laid before the Tribunal of Arbitration, Convened at Geneva under the Provisions of the Treaty between the United States of America and Her Majesty the Queen of Great Britain, Concluded at Washington, May 8, 1871.* Washington, DC: Government Printing Office, 1872), vol. 3.

Henshaw, John Corey, and Gary F. Kuruz, eds. *Recollections of the War with Mexico.* Columbia: University of Missouri Press, 2008.

Johnson, Robert Underwood, and Clarence Clough Buel, eds. *Battles and Leaders of the Civil War: Being for the Most Part Contributions by Union and Confederate Officers.* New York: Century Co., 1887.

Keyes, E. D. *Fifty Years' Observation of Men and Events, Civil and Military.* New York: Charles Scribner's Sons, 1884.

Latrobe, John H. B. *West Point Reminiscences from September 1818 to March 1882.* East Saginaw, MI: Evening News, Printers and Binders, 1887.

Lincoln, Abraham. *Abraham Lincoln: Complete Works,* ed. John G. Nicolay and John Hay, ed. New York: The Century Co., 1920.

———. *Abraham Lincoln: Speeches and Writings, 1859–1865,* ed. Don Fehrenbacher. New York: Library of America, 1989.

McClellan, George B. *The Mexican War Diary of George B. McClellan.* Princeton, NJ: Princeton University Press, 1917.

Osborne, B. S. *A Sailor of Fortune.* New York: McClure, Phillips & Co., 1906.

Reynolds, John. *My Own Times, Embracing the History of My Life.* Chicago: Illinois Press, 1855.

Scott, Winfield. *Memoirs of Lieut.-General Scott, LL.D. Written by Himself.* New York: Sheldon & Company, 1861.

Sherman, William Tecumseh. *Memoirs of General William T. Sherman.* New York: D. Appleton & Co., 1889.

Smith, George Winston, and Charles Judah, eds. *Chronicles of the Gringos: The U.S. Army in the Mexican War, 1846–1848, Accounts of Eyewitnesses & Combatants.* Albuquerque: University of New Mexico Press, 1968.

Spicer, William Arnold. *The Flag Replaced on Sumter: A Personal Narrative.* Providence, RI: Providence Press Company, 1885.

United States Department of War. *The War of the Rebellion: A Compilation of the Official Records of the Union and Confederate Armies.* Washington, DC: Government Printing Office, 1880–1901.

Periodicals

Abbeville Press (SC)
Anderson Daily Intelligencer (SC)
Aurora and Franklin Gazette (PA)
Baltimore Sun
Boston Advertiser
Buffalo Commercial
Charleston Mercury
Chicago Tribune
Cincinnati Commercial Appeal
Cincinnati Enquirer
Daily Atlas
Daily Cleveland Leader
Daily Constitutionalist and Republic (Savannah, GA)
Daily Nashville Patriot
Daily National Intelligencer (Washington, DC)
Daily National Journal (Washington, DC)
Delaware Gazette
Grand Haven News (MI)
Harper's Weekly
Intelligencer (Washington, DC)
Liberator (Boston)
Louisiana Advertiser (New Orleans)
Louisville Public Advertiser
The Mercury (Charleston, SC)
Milwaukee Morning Sentinel
National Republican (Washington, DC)
Newark Advocate (NJ)
New Orleans Delta
New York Daily Courier
New York Daily Tribune
New York Herald
New York Journal of Commerce
New York Post
New York Star
New York Times
Philadelphia Inquirer
Providence Patriot
Raymond Daily Gazette (MS)
Recorder (Hillsborough, NC)
Semi-Weekly Standard (Raleigh, NC)
Smyrna Times (Delaware)
Vermont Chronicle (Bellows Falls)

Books and Articles

Adams, George Rollie. *General William S. Harney, Prince of Dragoons*. Lincoln: University of Nebraska Press, 2001.

Alden, John R. *A History of the American Revolution*. 1969; reprint: New York: Da Capo, 1989.

Ambrose, Stephen E. *Duty, Honor, Country; A History of West Point*. 1966; reprint: Johns Hopkins University Press, 1999

Anderson, E. L. *Soldier and Pioneer: A Biographical Sketch of Lt.-Col. Richard C. Anderson of the Continental Army*. New York: G. P. Putnam's Sons, 1879.

Anderson, Ronald, and Anne Koval. *James McNeill Whistler: Beyond the Myth*. New York: Carroll & Graf, 1994.

Baur, Jack. *Surfboats and Horse Marines: U.S. Naval Operations in the Mexican War, 1846–48*. Annapolis, MD: US Naval Institute, 1969.

Bauer, Jack. *The Mexican War, 1846–1848*. Lincoln: University of Nebraska Press, 1993.

Baur, K. Jack. *Zachary Taylor: Soldier, Planter, Statesman of the Old Southwest*. Baton Rouge: Louisiana State University Press, 1985.

Bemis, Samuel Flag. *John Quincy Adams and the Foundations of American Foreign Policy*. New York: Alfred A. Knopf, 1965.

Black, Hugo L, III. "Richard Fitzpatrick's South Florida, 1822–1840." *Tequesta, Journal of the Historical Association of Southern Florida*, Part I." (1981): 47–71.

Buker, George E. *Swamp Sailors: Riverine Warfare in the Everglades, 1835–1842*. Gainesville: University Press of Florida, 1975.

Burrage, William Clarence. "The Visit of the West Point Cadets to Boston 1821." In vol. 6 of 12 vols. Boston: Bostonian Society Publications, 1910.

Cassedy, Ben. *A History of Louisville, From its Earliest Settlement till the Year 1852* Louisville, KY: Hull and Brother, 1852.

Catton, Bruce. *The Coming Fury*. New York: Doubleday, 1961.

Cayton, Andrew R. L. "The Debate over the Panama Congress and the Origins of the Second American Party System." *The Historian* 47, no. 2 (February 1985): 219–38.

Channing, Steven A. *Crisis of Fear: Secession in South Carolina*. New York: W. W. Norton Company, 1970.

Cleaves, Freeman. *The Rock of Chickamauga: The Life of General George H. Thomas*. Norman: University of Oklahoma Press, 1948.

Coffman, Edward M. *The Old Army: A Portrait of the American Army in Peacetime, 1784–1898*. New York: Oxford University Press, 1986.

Colton. J. H. *A Guide Book to West Point and Vicinity, Containing Historical and Statistical Sketches of the United States Military Academy, and of Other Objects of Interest*. New York: J. H. Colton, 1844.

Conder, Josiah. *The Modern Traveler: A Popular Description, Geographical, Historical and Topographical of the Various Countries of the Globe*. Volume 8. Boston: Wells & Lilly, 1830.

Crackel, Theodore J. *West Point, A Bicentennial History*. Lawrence: University Press of Kansas, 2002.

Cullum, George W. *Biographical Register of the Officers and Graduates of the U.S. Military Academy, from 1802 to 1867. Rev. Ed., with a Supplement Continuing the Register of Graduates to January 1, 1879*. New York: J. Miller, 1879.

Current, Richard N. *Lincoln and the First Shot*. Urbana-Champaign: University of Illinois Press, 1963.

Davis, William C. *Look Away! A History of the Confederate States of America*. New York: Free Press, 2002.

Detzer, David. *Allegiance: Fort Sumter, Charleston, and the Beginning of the Civil War.* New York: Harcourt, 2002.

Dick, Everett. *The Dixie Frontier: A Social History.* 1948; reprint: Norman: University of Oklahoma Press, 1993.

Donald, David Herbert. *Lincoln.* New York: Simon & Schuster, 1995.

Driscoll, John. *All That Is Glorious around Us: Paintings from the Hudson River School.* Ithaca, NY: Cornell University Press, 1997.

Eisenhower, John D. *Agent of Destiny: The Life and Times of General Winfield Scott.* New York: Free Press, 1997.

Frazer, Walter J. *Charleston! Charleston!: The History of a Southern City.* Columbia: University of South Carolina Press, 1989.

Fink. James W. *Divided Loyalties: Kentucky's Struggle for Armed Neutrality in the Civil War.* El Dorado Hills, CA: Savas Beatie, 2012.

Freeman, Douglas Southall. *R. E. Lee: A Biography.* New York: Charles Scribner's Sons, 1934.

Giddings, Joshua R. *The Exiles of Florida.* 1858; reprint: Gainesville: University of Florida Press, 1965).

Gilmore, Robert Louis, and John Parker Harrison. "Juan Bernardo Elbers and the Introduction of Steam Navigation on the Magdalena River." *The Hispanic American Historical Review* 28, no. 3 (August 1948): 335–45.

Gould, Emerson W. *Fifty Years on the Mississippi; or, Gould's History of River Navigation: Containing a History of Steam as a Propelling Power on Ocean, Lakes and Rivers.* St. Louis: Nixon-Jones, 1889.

Grant, Bruce. *American Forts, Yesterday and Today.* New York: E. P. Dutton & Co., 1965.

Greenough, George Gordon. "Address Delivered at the USMA, at the Exercises Incident to the Centenary of Major General Robert Anderson, U.S. Army, June 14, 1905." US Army History Center Archives, Carlisle, PA.

Hagan, William T. "General Henry Atkinson and the Militia." *Military Affairs* 23, no. 4 (Winter 1959–1960): 194–97.

Hall, John W. *Uncommon Defense: Indian Allies in the Black Hawk War.* Cambridge, MA: Harvard University Press, 2009.

Halsey, Leroy J. *Memoir of the Life and Character of Rev. Lewis Warner Green, D.D., with a Selection from His Sermons.* New York: Charles Scribner and Co., 1871.

Harvey, Conrad E. "An Army without Doctrine: The Evolution of US Army Tactics in the Absence of Doctrine, 1775 to 1847." MA thesis, US Army War College, 2007.

Head, David. "A Different Kind of Maritime Predation: South American Privateering from Baltimore, 1816–1820." *International Journal of Naval History* 7, no. 2 (August 2008): 1–38.

Heitman, Francis Bernard. *Historical Register and Dictionary of the US Army from September 29, 1789 to March 2, 1903.* Washington, DC: Government Printing Office, 1903.

Howe, Daniel Walker. *What Hath God Wrought: The Transformation of America, 1815–1848.* New York: Oxford University Press, 2007.

Hughes, Kenneth J. *A Chronological History of Fort Jupiter and U.S. Military Operations in the Loxahatchee Region, 1838–1858.* Fort Lauderdale: Florida Coast Research and Publishing, 1992.

Johnson, Timothy D. *A Gallant Little Army: The Mexico City Campaign.* Lawrence: University Press of Kansas, 2007.

———. *Winfield Scott: The Quest for Military Glory.* Lawrence: University of Kansas Press, 1998.

Jung, Patrick J. *The Black Hawk War of 1832.* Norman: University of Oklahoma Press, 2007.

Kaufmann, J. E., and H. W. Kaufmann. *Fortress America: The Forts That Defended America, 1600 to the Present.* Cambridge, MA: Da Capo Press, 2004.

Kennett, Lee. *Sherman, A Soldier's Life.* New York: HarperCollins, 2001.

Kieffer, Chester L. *Maligned General: The Biography of Thomas Sidney Jesup.* San Rafael, CA: Presidio Press, 1979.

Klein, Philip Shriver. *President James Buchanan, A Biography.* University Park: Pennsylvania State University Press, 1962.

Knetsch, Joe. "Strategy, Operations, and Tactics in the Second Seminole War, 1835–1842." In *America's Hundred Years' War*, ed. Wiliam S. Belko, 128–54. Gainesville: University Press of Florida, 2011.

Lambert, Joseph I. "The Black Hawk War: A Military Analysis," *Journal of the Illinois State Historical Society* 32 (1908–1984), no. 4 (December 1939): . 442–73.

Lawton, Eba Anderson. *History of the Soldier's Home, Washington D.C.* New York: G. P. Putnam's Sons, 1914.

———. *Major Robert Anderson and Fort Sumter, 1861.* New York: Knickerbocker Press, 1911.

Mahon, John K. *History of the Second Seminole War, 1835–1842.* Gainesville: University Press of Florida, 1985.

Mansfield, Edward Deering. *Illustrated Life of General Winfield Scott: Commander-in-Chief of the Army in Mexico; Illustrated by D. H. Strother.* New York: A. S. Barnes & Co., 1847.

McDonald, Robert M. S., ed. *Thomas Jefferson's Military Academy: Founding West Point.* Charlottesville: University Press of Virginia, 2004.

McHarry, Jessie. "John Reynolds." *Journal of the Illinois State Historical Society* 6 (1908–1984), no. 1 (April 1913): 8–57.

McKenney, Janice E. *The Organizational History of Field Artillery, 1775–2003.* Washington DC Center of Military History, US Army, 2007.

Meredith, Roy. *Storm over Sumter: The Opening Engagement of the Civil War.* New York: Simon and Schuster, 1957.

Missall, John, and Mary Lou Missall. *The Seminole Struggle: A History of America's Longest Indian War.* Palm Beach, FL: Pineapple Press, 2020.

Moody, Wesley. *The Battle of Fort Sumter: The First Shots of the American Civil War.* Critical Moments in American History. New York: Routledge, 2016.

———. *Demon of the Lost Cause: Sherman and Civil War History.* Columbia: University of Missouri Press, 2011.

Newhall, Bounont. *The Daguerreotype in America.* New York: Dover Publications, 1976.

Nichols, Roger L. *General Henry Atkinson, A Western Military Career.* Norman: University of Oklahoma Press, 1965.

Olson, Julius E. "Lincoln in Wisconsin." *The Wisconsin Magazine of History* 4, no. 1 (September 1920): 44–54.

Patrick, Rembert W. *Aristocrat in Uniform: General Duncan Clinch*. Gainesville: University Press of Florida, 1963.

Pinder, David A. "The Association of Graduates of the U.S. Military Academy, 1869–1902: The Healing Years." Unpublished thesis, USMA Tactical Officer Education Program, 1993.

Pinsker, Matthew. "The Soldiers' Home: A Long Road to Sanctuary." *Washington History: Historical Society of Washington, D.C.* 18, no. 1/2 (2006): 4–19

Poe, Edgar Allan, *The Works of Edgar Allan Poe in One Volume*. New York: P. F. Collier & Son, 1927. Porter, Kenneth W. *The Black Seminoles: History of a Freedom-Seeking People*. Gainesville: University Press of Florida, 1996.

Randall, J. G. *The Civil War and Reconstruction*. Boston: D. C. Heath and Company, 1953.

Roberts, Robert B. *Encyclopedia of Historic Forts: The Military, Pioneer, and Trading Posts of the United States*. New York: Macmillan, 1988.

Russell, J. Thomas. "Edgar Allan Poe, The Army Years." *United States Military Academy Bulletin* no. 10 (West Point. NY: USMA, 1972), 5–6.

Sanders, Ralph. "Congressional Reaction in the United States to the Panama Congress of 1826." *The Americas* 11, no. 2 (October 1954) : 141–54.

Sandlin, Lee. *Wicked River: The Mississippi*. New York: Pantheon, 2010.

Skelton, William B. *An American Profession of Arms: The Army Officer Corps, 1784–1861*. Lawrence: University Press of Kansas, 1992.

Spaulding, Oliver Lyman. *The United States Army, in War and Peace*. New York: G. P. Putnam and Son, 1937.

Sprague, John T. *The Origin, Progress, and Conclusion of the Florida War*. New York: D. Appleton & Company, 1848.

Swanberg, W. A. *First Blood: The Story of Fort Sumter*. New York: Charles Scribner's Sons, 1957.

Swiderski, Richard M. *Colomel in America: Mercurial Panacea, War, Song and Ghosts*. Boca Raton, FL: Brown Walker Press, 2009.

Tenney. W. J. *Military and Naval History of the Rebellion in the United States*. New York: D. Appleton & Co., 1866.

Varon, Elizabeth R. *Disunion! The Coming of the American Civil War, 1789–1859*. Chapel Hill: University of North Carolina Press, 2008.

Wallace, Edward S. *General William Jenkins Worth: Monterey's Forgotten Hero*. Dallas: Southern Methodist University Press, 1953.

Watson, Samuel J. *Peacekeepers and Conquerors: The Army Officers Corps on the American Frontier, 1821–1846*. Lawrence: University Press of Kansas, 2013.

Wilson, Major L. *The Presidency of Martin Van Buren*. Lawrence: University of Kansas Press, 1984.

Winn, Wilkins B. "The Issue of Religious Liberty in the United States Commercial Treaty with Colombia, 1824 " *The Americas* 26, no. 3 (January 1970): 291–301.

Woldman, Albert. *Lincoln and the Russians: The Story of the Russian-American Diplomatic Relations during the Civil War*. Cleveland: World, 1952.

Wood, Gordon S. *The American Revolution: A History*. New York: Random House, 2003.

INDEX

The manufacturer's authorized representative in the EU for product safety is Mare Nostrum Group B.V., Mauritskade 21D, 1091 GC Amsterdam, The Netherlands email: gpsr@mare-nostrum.co.uk

www.ingramcontent.com/pod-product-compliance
Lightning Source LLC
Chambersburg PA
CBHW020444100426
42812CB00036B/3439/J